BEND THE
CURVE

BEND THE CURVE

Accelerate Your Startup's Success

ANDREW RAZEGHI

FG PRESS | BOULDER, COLORADO

CREATIVE DIRECTOR | Kevin Barrett Kane

EDITOR | David Heal

Printed and bound in the United States of America

ISBN 978-1941018231

FG PRESS, *Publishers*
Boulder, Colorado
fgpress.com

For the talented & the scrappy

TABLE OF CONTENTS

IX | AUTHOR NOTE

XI | FOREWORD

1 | INTRODUCTION

6 | CHAPTER 1
Beginner's Mind

22 | CHAPTER 2
Extreme Bootstrapping

36 | CHAPTER 3
Creating and Hiring for Culture

46 | CHAPTER 4
The Art of Doing Things Differently

57 | CHAPTER 5
The Unit Economics of Your Dream

67 | CHAPTER 6
Getting Customers to Care

79 | CHAPTER 7
Brand What You Stand For

88 | CHAPTER 8
Building a Useful Financial Model

102 | CHAPTER 9
Legal Issues for Entrepreneurs

115 | CHAPTER 10
Optimizing Customer Acquisition

122 | CHAPTER 11
The Game of Search (SEO)

133 | CHAPTER 12
The Science of Going Viral

144 | CHAPTER 13
Unlucky 13

146 | CHAPTER 14
Are You a Venture Business?

164 | CHAPTER 15
Angel Investors Vs. Venture Capitalists

174 | CHAPTER 16
Raising Capital

190 | CHAPTER 17
Introduction to Term Sheets

201 | CHAPTER 18
Founder and Team Compensation

209 | CHAPTER 19
Board of Directors

225 | CHAPTER 20
Investor Communication

234 | CHAPTER 21
Getting Distribution

244 | CHAPTER 22
Entrepreneurial Selling

257 | AFTERWORD

259 | ACKNOWLEDGMENTS

265 | FEATURED MENTORS

283 | ABOUT THE AUTHOR

AUTHOR NOTE

IT'S SUPPOSED TO LOOK LIKE a hockey stick: up and to the right. Growth curves of runaway hits are even more dramatic—akin to *field* hockey sticks—quick start, short dip, followed by an immediate near-vertical climb in a northeasterly direction. It's a beautiful thing. The problem with growth curves is that they're like footprints in the sand. You can only see them in hindsight. To make matters more difficult, innovation is a non-linear business. Success does not come in the form of a straight line. As Woody Allen suggests, "If you want to make God laugh, tell him about your plans."

The reality is that growth curves look more like yo-yo diets—a squiggly line at the start turns south, levels off, suddenly spikes upward (press release), shoots further north (early adopters), stalls (new competitor), plummets (better competitor), doubles back on itself (product iteration), slides sideways (catching up), and occasionally finds its way back *up and to the right*. More often than not, however, the curve ends abruptly, leaving behind nothing but skid marks and the faint traces of opportunity lost. Innovation is messy.

As mentors and investors, our job is to help founders improve the trajectory of their success and, in some cases, to ensure that success is even an option. Our primary job is to help them bend the curve: *up and to the right*. At Techstars, we do this by providing seed capital, just-in-time education, networking, and access to people who've built successful companies from the ground up. What you'll find in this book are not ideas about what is *supposed to work* but rather practical rules of thumb about what *has been proven to work* from people who have the evidence to back it up.

My role in writing this book is to share their wisdom. The narrative voice you'll meet in the book is mine. In some chapters, you'll hear more from me than from others. In other chapters, you'll barely hear from me at all. I hope this book gives you a sense of not only what it takes to build, manage, and scale a successful venture, but I also hope it gives you a sense of what we are about at Techstars: what we believe, how we think, and what we stand for as members of the venture community. Most of all, I hope it inspires you to start. As founder of SV Angel and Techstars mentor Ron Conway suggests, "*Anytime* is a good time to start a company!" If you have already started and you are now looking to scale, I hope this book helps you bend the curve—up and to the right.

FOREWORD

IN MAY OF 1999, I sat in a windowless conference room (the landlord had called it a closet, but he lacked my entrepreneurial vision) in our SparkNotes office on Mass Ave. in Cambridge, naively poring over a term sheet from an angel syndicate in New York. On the phone I had our attorney, a senior partner from a leading law firm dedicated to "emerging companies." Despite having the best counsel money could buy, I unknowingly gave our investors twice as much equity in our company as I thought, because I had agreed to certain so-called "standard terms."

I could regale you with dozens—no, hundreds—of mistakes my partners and I (mostly me) made in the founding, building, selling, and selling again of our first company. We had supportive investors and expensive lawyers, but we lacked even a single experienced entrepreneur to mentor us through the high-level strategy or the low-level, get-the-details-right tactics that can make all the difference. I suspect countless other entrepreneurs shared this fate.

When we started SparkNotes, few, if any, entrepreneurs had figured out the five-year-old consumer web. People talk about technology costs as the primary reason why startups in the '90s raised so much more money than comparable start-ups do today. This overlooks a perhaps more salient dynamic: founders in the '90s spent hundreds of millions of their investors' dollars on their own on-the-job training. Like real-world pioneers who could not benefit from others' cartographic advances, we all got lost in the same wilderness, making the same mistakes over and over and over again.

Conservatively, I would say that at SparkNotes alone— just one teeny, tiny, essentially irrelevant company—we squandered over $50 million in equity value that we could have captured had the Sam Yagan of today—or better yet, today's Chuck Templeton, Steve Farsht, Jason Fried, Adam Koopersmith, David Cohen, Lon Chow, Brad Feld, or any of the other contributors to *Bend the Curve*—mentored me back in 1999.

Born in Chicago and raised in the cornfields south and west of the city, I left Chicago in 1995 to chase educational and entrepreneurial pursuits in Boston, New York, and Palo Alto. After spending twelve years in three of the most robust startup ecosystems, I returned to my too-hot-in-the-summer and too-cold-in-the-winter roots in 2007 for the same reason so many Chicago expats do: Chicago is the best city in the world.

As it turns out, the Chicago area has some pretty good startup cred. In 1985, the National Science Foundation chartered the National Center for Supercomputing Applications (NCSA) at the University of Illinois as one of four original supercomputer centers (along with Cornell, Princeton, and San Diego). In 1986, NCSA released NCSA Telnet (as open-source before that term even existed). In 1993, NCSA released

Marc Andreessen's Mosaic web browser before he founded Netscape. (Even "Mozilla" allegedly traces its etymological roots to "Mosaic killer.") Of course, Mosaic itself later provided the foundation for Internet Explorer. The more technical readers may also know NCSA HTTPd as the Apache HTTP Server. All of this happened right in Chicago's backyard.

While the NCSA's heyday may have ended in the '90s, Illinoisans have continued to impact the Internet you know and love. Max Levchin graduated from the University of Illinois, as Larry Ellison would have had he not dropped out. And from just one local high school, the Illinois Mathematics and Science Academy, hailed my classmates Russell Simmons, co-founder and CTO of Yelp, and Steve Chen, co-founder of YouTube. Like my personal list of lessons learned, Illinois' list of technology success stories could go on and on: Siebel Systems, Advanced Micro Devices, Lotus, etc.

These companies all have one trait in common: their founders left the Chicago area to start their companies elsewhere. That trend showed no signs of waning as of 2009, when, of the nineteen companies that comprised Techstars, no fewer than five hailed from Chicago. Let me repeat that: over 25% of the startups at the most elite accelerator in the world had left Chicago, probably with no plans to return. This affirmed to me that Chicago had the single most important ingredient of any entrepreneurial ecosystem: entrepreneurs.

And so despite—or perhaps because of—my newness to Chicago, rather than opine on solutions, I wanted to get my hands dirty in helping to build the Chicago startup ecosystem. That call to action manifested itself in my becoming the CEO of Excelerate Labs, where I was the least important co-founder of the precursor to Techstars Chicago. Long before I got involved, many others had noticed the brain drain. But as we all know, ideas are a dime a dozen; among we entrepreneurs, only action matters. And for their action in securing the funding ($330,000!) and the leadership (yours truly) for the first class of Excelerate Labs, two groups should get special recognition: The i2A Fund (backed by J.B. Pritzker and at the time run by Kapil Chaudhary) and Sandbox Industries (run then and now by Nick Rosa and this initiative, at the time, led by Kelli Rhee).

At Excelerate Labs, we had a simple vision: replicate as much of the Techstars playbook as possible, leveraging our homegrown talent to mentor the startups that would otherwise leave to set up shop on the coasts. Under the leadership of Nick Rosa, Adam Koopersmith, Troy Henikoff, and me, Excelerate Labs quickly became recognized among the top three accelerator programs in the world along with Y Combinator and Techstars. Three years after we started Excelerate Labs, we agreed to merge Excelerate Labs with Techstars becoming the Chicago-based Techstars program. You may wonder why we chose the Techstars model as opposed to that of any of the myriad other accelerators out there.

In today's capital markets, almost anyone can raise money for almost any idea. Techstars believes that something more important and more scarce than capital drives success in startups: *access to the most successful entrepreneurial minds.* Techstars believes that having the right seasoned, experienced entrepreneurs just a phone call or text message away can provide much more value to a founder than undifferentiated cash.

While the vast majority of the mentorship provided is bespoke to the company receiving it, we can generalize a non-trivial amount of it for consumption by entrepreneurs at large, even those with no Techstars affiliation. This book attempts to do just that.

Andrew Razeghi has tirelessly captured the brilliance and insights of over a dozen of our most sought-after mentors. As

I read this book the first time, the voices and ideas within it challenged my own long-held beliefs and added to my own stock of wisdom. As I read it a second time, I wished that I could apply to Techstars.

Perhaps controversially, I believe that the time I spend advising and mentoring entrepreneurs is as personally satisfying and socially important as many other (but surely not all) philanthropic activities. If you are a first-time entrepreneur, I hope you find the content here as useful—but more timely—than I do. If you've been around the block a few times (hopefully with less gray hair than I have) and you find yourself with the irresistible urge to write your own chapter, I hope you'll find one of the many Techstars programs near you and get involved.

I look forward to seeing many of you at Techstars Chicago!

Sam Yagan
Chief Executive Officer
The Match Group
Founding CEO
Excelerate Labs
Co-founder and General Partner
Corazon Capital

INTRODUCTION

"Make no little plans."

Daniel Burnham, architect of the City of Chicago

"I HAVE AN IDEA," you say, "an idea that could change the world." So you do what any aspiring entrepreneur would do. You quit your job, get a desk at a co-working space, convince a few friends and family members to fund your minimum viable product (MVP), and launch. The next thing you know you have customers. Fans, even. "This thing is really working," you think. "I knew I was right!" The media agrees with you—yet another heroic startup founder pursuing the dream. It's inspiring.

You're invited to speak at conferences, sit on panels, opine about life as an entrepreneur. The struggle always sells. T-shirts are printed. And then, something even more amazing happens: revenues. "Not only is my idea working," you think, "I'm going to be rich!" You start writing your *I told you so manifesto* soon to be sent to lost loves, your former boss, and that grade school teacher who said you'd never make it. It feels good. It feels *great!*

Customers pile on, as do investors. Your team expands, as does your vocabulary. Your conversations are now peppered with words like runways, raises, rounds, and exits. You're hiring and you've discovered an unexplainable newfound love of cycling. Never mind that you're not turning a profit. You're a growth company! You're not *supposed* to be profitable (yet). Burn is something to manage not something to avoid. That's why venture capital exists. Life is good. Until, it isn't.

Eighteen months after quitting your job, you find yourself alone, turning off servers, negotiating your way out of a long-term lease, dodging friends, family, and early investors who bet on you. Your business is cratering. Your dream has fast become a nightmare. Your tech has successfully been crunched.

"What happened?" you think. "What went wrong?" You seek solace in the fact that, in the startup world, failure is a badge of honor (or so you've been told). But it certainly doesn't feel like it. It stings. Badly. Case studies will surely be written. You have failed.

The fact is that there are more founders who fail than those who succeed. A lot more. The story of a once-promising young startup mothballing the dream is as common as, well, a once-promising young startup mothballing the dream. But why do they fail? Usually, lots of things go wrong all at once. But in the end, they just run out of money. And yet startup success is not just about managing cash. It's about managing expectations. If you fail to manage cash, you'll go broke. But if you fail to manage expectations, you will always disappoint.

Beware the hype. Success doesn't happen overnight. Certainly there are outliers—the multi-billion-dollar acquisitions that occur within 18 months of a company's birth. And these outliers make the news precisely because they are rare. The problem is that the outliers *always* make the headlines. In a 24-hour news cycle world, businesses built brick-by-brick over the course of a decade aren't as newsworthy. Contrary to the startup hype, it takes time to get it right. As writer and director Steven Spielberg suggests, "All good ideas start out as bad ideas. That's why it takes so long." Even successful entrepreneurs who have surpassed that critical inflection point in their growth wrestle with managing expectations. To quote ContextMedia founder & CEO Rishi Shah, "The trouble with high expectations is that you're always losing even when you're always winning." Among high-impact entrepreneurs like Shah, expectations never end. Manage expectations as deliberately as you manage cash.

Contrary to folklore, innovation is not only about speed. It's about velocity. Direction matters. Before you run as fast as you can, make sure you're headed somewhere worth going. Otherwise, you'll only end up going nowhere faster than anyone else. Linda Darragh, a colleague of mine and Executive Director of the Kellogg Innovation and Entrepreneurship Initiative (KIEI) at Northwestern University puts it best: "Patience," says Darragh, "seems to be the antithesis of the hard-charging, first-to-market mantras of modern-day entrepreneurship. Every early stage entrepreneur knows about lean startup methodology and the need to 'iterate' and 'pivot,' yet there is an overwhelming desire to start programming their minimum viable product (MVP) as soon as possible. Too often, early stage entrepreneurs have not done enough testing. Nor have they identified the customer's real problem. Even when they have, they often do not spent enough time refining the UI/UX. This rush to coding can lead to a significant waste of time and money, two precious commodities for entrepreneurs." Ev Williams, co-founder of Twitter, has made a similar observation in regard to customer-centricity and product development: "User experience is everything. It always has been, but it's undervalued and underinvested in. If you don't know user-centered design, study it. Hire people who know it. Obsess over it. Live and breathe it. Get your whole company on board."

It may sound like heresy when measured against the seductive bravado of "launch and learn," but be patient. Be deliberate. It takes time to change the world primarily because it takes time to change people. In the words of Coco Chanel: "Don't spend time beating on a wall hoping to transform it into a door." Willfulness is important but so too is reason.

The Age of Frictionless Entrepreneurship

We are entering the age of frictionless entrepreneurship. Creativity is the new competitive advantage. Makers abound. At no other time in history has the opportunity to commercialize creativity been as favorable as it is today. The friction between the innovator and the customer is melting away. Traditional barriers to entry are eroding—barriers including access to capital, means of production, distribution, marketing channels, and customers. We live in a world where you can dream it, design it, build it, promote it, distribute it, sell it, and get paid all from the comfort of your build-it-yourself IKEA sofa.

Consider this: Today, if you have an idea, you could design it yourself in Autodesk, manufacture it on a 3D printer, raise seed capital on Kickstarter to fund your minimum viable product (giving up zero equity in the process), raise additional capital on AngelList to fund marketing and sales, promote your product on Facebook and Twitter, sell it on Amazon and eBay, and get paid in Bitcoin! Then, after you've succeeded, you could take money off the table by selling stock in your private company via Nasdaq Private Market and subsequently retire inside the virtual world of SecondLife. *God bless frictionless capitalism!*

If you are among those who have made the decision to start a business or you've already started one and are looking to scale it, congratulations. Commitment is half the battle. Madam C.J. Walker (born in 1867 as Sarah Breedlove) put it best: "I am a woman who came from the cotton fields of the South. From there I was promoted to the washtub. From there I was promoted to the cook kitchen. And from there I promoted *myself* into the business of manufacturing hair goods and preparations...I have built my own factory on my own ground." Walker, a daughter of emancipated slaves, became one of the twentieth century's most successful entrepreneurs by doing what all entrepreneurs do at the beginning. She made the decision to start. As Walker put it, "I got my start by giving myself a start." Commitment is half the battle. The other half is work.

While there are very few guarantees in life, one guarantee I can offer you as the author of this book is that you can—and will—find conflicting advice across the chapters of this book just as you will find it outside of this book. Like all great entrepreneurs, your job is to determine what works for you. In the world of innovation, there is no single path forward. The only road that all entrepreneurs share is the road less traveled by. This is that road.

CHAPTER ONE

BEGINNER'S MIND

"In the beginner's mind there are many possibilities,
but in the expert's mind there are few."

Shunryu Suzuki, *Zen Mind, Beginner's Mind*

THE GUEST LIST MUST BE SUBMITTED by 12 noon the day before the event. Due to space constraints, attendees are advised to invite no more than 40 people to the ceremony. Children under 18 are allowed as long as someone could, if need be, remove a crying child. Phones must be turned off (or set to vibrate). Flash photography is not permitted. You are asked to not touch the studio walls, to keep your voice to a normal tone, and to remain behind the stanchions until directed otherwise by the event planners. And then, it's time. You take your place in front of the cameras. The room fills with music in driving crescendo. It's the soundtrack of anticipation. Those gathered around you break out in applause. The rhythm of your heart picks up a beat, pride swells from within your gut, erupting into a joyful smile on your face. And then, a countdown begins: '...*five, four, three, two, one!*' You hit a button, sign a card, and then you hear it: *clang-clang-clang-clang!* It's the sweet sound of success—the NASDAQ opening bell on the day your company goes public.

On May 21, 2009, Chuck Templeton, founder of the popular restaurant reservation system, OpenTable, celebrated yet another milestone for his company at the opening bell of NASDAQ. He even wore a suit (a rarity) and a tie (rarer still). The stock opened at $20 per share and closed at $32 per share (up 60%). "It was pretty cool," recalls Chuck. "To be up there and to see OPEN flashing all over the place was awesome. NASDAQ was also promoting a bunch of OPEN stuff on the big billboards in Times Square. To see this idea I started, in my bedroom on my little laptop computer, become an idea that attracted thousands of customers, millions of users, hundreds of employees, and an IPO—it was incredible."

Keep in mind, when Chuck started OpenTable back in 1998, most restaurants didn't have Wi-Fi. No one had Wi-Fi. Few had computers. And, if they did, they likely didn't have Internet connections. Not only did Chuck need to build a business, he needed to create the infrastructure on top of which he could create his business. To understand how difficult this was, consider this: In order to win one San Francisco restaurant's business, Chuck paid to install and run a physical Internet connection to the hostess stand. Given where the hostess stand was located—in the middle of the floor at the front of the restaurant (not near a wall)—this involved jackhammering the designer concrete floor, laying wire, and replacing the floor. It cost him several thousand dollars, but that account was an influential restaurant that many others followed. It mattered. And it worked. Today, OpenTable serves over 31,000 restaurant customers globally and helps over 12 million diners each month find restaurants. In 2014, 16 years after a Eureka moment inspired Chuck to start the online restaurant reservation service, Priceline acquired OpenTable for $2.6 billion (or $103 per share).

Technically, going public is a mechanism for raising capital. And ringing the bell is not a business goal per se. To quote
Facebook founder Mark Zuckerberg the day *he* rang the bell:
"Here's the thing. Our mission isn't to be a public company.
Our mission is to make the world more open and connected."
That said: the bell is symbolic. It's an entrepreneurial way-
point—public recognition of the struggle (and payoff) associated with building the dream. But more than public recognition, it's personal affirmation. In the case of OpenTable, after
a decade-long pursuit, the sound of the bell couldn't have
fallen on the ears of a more deserving entrepreneur, Chuck
Templeton.

Chicago has many single-named icons: Oprah, Jordan,
Ditka, 'Da Bears. (Okay, so 'Da Bears is two words, but it's
'Da Bears. We'll make an exception.) In the entrepreneurial
community, there's Chuck. His name fits his personality:
humble, soft spoken, generous, and genuinely curious about
making the world a better place. He is a self-described human-
ist, activist, and tireless advocate of impact entrepreneurs. And
he's a founder's founder. In addition to founding OpenTable,
Chuck is Founding Chairman at GrubHub, an advisor for
Braintree, and an investor in Cleversafe and a number of other
game changing businesses.

Chuck is a U.S. Army Ranger. To put that into perspective,
less than 1% of the entire U.S. Army is Ranger qualified. It's
an elite group. Moreover, during his time in military service
(1986–1989), Chuck was selected for Sniper School, an even
more elite group. There were three people in Chuck's class.
That's not a typo—there were only two other people besides
Chuck. Chuck has trained in the flats, in the mountains, and
in the desert. And that's just as a startup founder! In the army,
he spent time in the swamp as well. The man is focused.

Chuck's entrepreneurial journey began 11 years prior to

that glorious day ringing the bell on Wall Street. On July 2, 1998, Chuck recalls, "I was watching my wife attempt to make restaurant reservations using CitySearch, Microsoft's Sidewalk, and the Zagat Guide, which was not online yet. She spent three-and-a-half hours one Saturday morning trying to make restaurant reservations for the next Friday, Saturday, and Sunday nights. She left several messages, asked about menu items, etc. I thought, 'There had to be a better way.' I had a few friends that were starting companies in Silicon Valley and I thought that if they can do it, I could do it. I tried to get a job at like ten other Internet startups and no one would hire me. I didn't have enough Internet experience (in 1998!). I had a professor in my first attempt at an MBA that said the key to being successful in the Internet world was to make the way people were doing things in the real world exactly the same way in the virtual world. This would help to reduce the learning curve for customers to adopt anything new. And so that's what I did. We emulated exactly how restaurant hostesses took reservations. We didn't try to come up with some new way to do things. We just did the same things they normally did offline, online. For my market research, I hung out in a ton of restaurants, always near the hostess stands so I could listen to how they took calls. I wrote down exactly how they answered the phones when calls came in for reservations: *What did they say when they picked up the phone? What questions did they ask? In what order did they ask these questions?* And so on. We designed OpenTable to emulate these actions. We made it easy. And it worked."

Chuck is no longer active in the day-to-day management of OpenTable. He's moved on to tackle other challenges, specifically, social and environmental problems. In his current capacity as Chairman of Impact Engine, a startup incubator focused on companies with social or environmental impact, he spends his time coaching the next generation of world changers. He has re-purposed his success as a way to propel the success of others who are using disruptive business models to make the world a better place. He's a friend and a sage. And we're lucky to have him as a mentor at Techstars.

In this chapter, we'll talk about a few priceless *Chuck-isms*, namely:

- Don't worry. Be scrappy.
- Manage a white-hot vision with a sub-standard product.
- Get others vested in your success.
- Recruit for uncertainty & deal with doubt.
- Design for impact.
- Adopt a penchant for problem-solving & a bias towards action.

Don't Worry. Be Scrappy.

Dave McClure, founding partner of the seed fund 500 Startups, defines a startup as: "A company that is confused about: 1) What its product is; 2) Who its customers are; and 3) How to make money."

Startups, by definition, are learning organizations. They are built to learn. Part of learning is failing. But to quote Jeff Tweedy, front man of the band—and Chicago institution—Wilco, "I think somehow you need to get to a certain point in your life where the notion of failure is absurd." Designing your life to avoid mistakes is absurd because mistakes are the best teachers. Those who do everything they can to avoid screwing up learn only what *has been done*, not what *can be done*. That said: *you don't need to celebrate failure to celebrate learning.* Failure sucks if that's all you get out of it. It's a gift if you learn from it. Tweedy has also suggested, "I don't think you can be good in life without acknowledging the part of you that isn't good." People are only perfect in the photos of year-end holiday cards. Everywhere else on earth, we're imperfect. The challenge of course, in a startup, is that learning has a shelf life. Startups are constrained by capital. As a startup, you've got to learn a lot *really* fast. As serial entrepreneur and academic Steve Blank has suggested, "There is no such thing as a ten-year-old startup. There's a two-year-old startup attached to an eight-year-old failure." As a founder, you must learn to manage the ever-present tension between burn rate and learning. One of the great benefits of programs like Techstars is that our mentors have already made the classic mistakes in starting and scaling companies. You get to make and learn from *new* mistakes.

When you make new mistakes you are inherently trying to tackle problems in novel and creative ways. Sure, times change and what didn't work before may work at some point, but there are certain timeless truths about what works and what doesn't. Some of these truths are more philosophical; others are very practical methods and techniques used in the business of innovation. One such philosophical truth, according to Chuck, is to never lose your frugal mindset even after you've raised capital.

"To compensate for the extremely high risk associated with starting something," observes Chuck, "I've noticed that most successful entrepreneurs are super scrappy. They wrestle with every nickel before it goes at the door like it was their last—giving their company the longest runway possible to get the job done." In Chuck's case, he had raised $79 million over six financing rounds, including the initial public offering. Benchmark (Bill Gurley) and Impact Venture Partners (Adam Dell) were the biggest investors along with Zagat and several smaller investors. Raising money is hard, but trying not to spend it is even harder.

"When a company receives seed financing and, later on, venture financing," says Chuck, "there is a tendency to get really good at *spending* money." There is a risk of not *leveraging* or *conserving* money for when it can best be spent to grow the business. In Chuck's experience, "When founders are scrappy and conservative with their resources, they are able to give themselves as many *at bats* as possible. In order to hit a home run, you are going to need a lot of chances at it." Let there be no doubt that, in startups, luck is a factor. Luck is not the only factor and certainly not the most important factor, but it is factor. "If you only give yourself two 'at bats' to hit a home run," says Chuck," you're making it more risky than it needs to be. Even Barry Bonds needed ten at bats to hit a home run." Founders are no different.

At the same time, just because you've raised money doesn't mean you need to spend money or spend it *now*! Be diligent about how and when to spend the money. Early on, you need to manage both expectations and cash by the minute. Every decision you make is a chance to figure out McClure's three things: product benefit, customer fit, and path to profit. Some will be right. Most will be wrong. Assuming you can manage cash, the question then becomes: How do founders handle the emotional toll of trying to learn in a capital-constrained environment? How do you manage your own psychology?

Chuck quotes Hamlet, "Nothing is good or bad; thinking makes it so." As an entrepreneur, some decisions work out and others don't. Luck plays a huge part in whether or not you succeed. Luck *does* favor the prepared, but preparation and hard work do not necessarily guarantee that you'll get a break. Chuck adds, "Don't get overexcited about the wins or overly discouraged by the failures. Failure is part of the process of building something great (you now know what *not* to do).

It's not any individual aspect of your life [wins or losses] that makes up your life; you have a *body of work*. Think long-term. If you're going to fail, don't fail catastrophically. Give yourself another *at bat*."

Managing a White-Hot Vision with a Sub-Standard Product

When you are in the early days of any venture, you have to get good at selling people on the dream. Because you are so early, your product, team, strategy, and support are all going to be sub-standard. "But," Chuck says, "the vision needs to be white hot." There is a tension between selling people on the vision and being honest with current reality. You've got to believe even when the product sucks. And, let's be honest, early on, your baby is ugly. It gets cuter over time. But your vision can remain the same. The challenge is in balancing a white-hot vision with a sub-standard product.

"I'm not a fan of 'fake it 'til you make it,'" says Chuck. "If you are transparent with your early customers about what you know and what you *don't* know, they will be willing to work with you to figure it out—particularly if they see that what you are working on is a solution to a pain point they have. If they also see you making progress on your product and that you are keeping your word, they will rally to give you the benefit of the doubt. And they will stay with you once you land on a plan that works.

"The best way to meet expectations is to set expectations. Set honest expectations. It's not about ego; you're doing what it takes to make the idea successful. When we were first pitching customers on OpenTable, we'd say that we wanted early customers' fingerprints all over the product. We wanted them involved. And, we really followed through with that promise, which helped us create extremely supportive customers at the beginning.

"When you are starting out, you need to find customers (early adopters) who are experiencing the pain so *intensely* that they will be willing to put up with a sub-standard product. You've got to find those who are hurting the worst. Being transparent about the flaws in your product or your model can work wonders if you do it correctly. If your idea is big enough, people will take a risk on you. As the product gets more sophisticated, everyone can celebrate and feel like they had a part of it. I hated the expression we *deal with* our customers. I liked saying that we *work with* our customers. They were our friends, partners, and confidantes."

Early on, your customers are more than the people you sell your products to. They are co-product developers, co-marketers, and co-designers of the dream. They want you to solve the problem as much as you want to solve it for them. Invite them in. Bring them along. Let them help you succeed. Be transparent. Be inclusive. Be committed to figuring it out. These same principles apply to building your internal team.

Vested in My Success: Smarter Than Me. Different Than Me. In It With Me.

Nick Rosa, co-founder and managing director of Sandbox Industries, has helped incubate his fair share of companies. "One mistake I see entrepreneurs make sometimes," observes Rosa, "is not doing the age-old, proven technique of hiring people smarter than themselves." This happens for all sorts of reasons. Among them, sometimes it's really hard to hear people tell you that your baby's ugly. People smarter than you will tell you. But wouldn't you rather have those people smarter than you working *with you* than working for your competitors?

"When it comes to building a team," says Chuck, "I always

tried to hire people who were smarter than me. I am also a big believer in diversity. I appreciate different perspectives, and I want them around the table when it came to decision-making." The founders are the leaders, no doubt, but it doesn't necessarily mean that it is their way or the proverbial highway. Chuck commented, "I believe that leaders should work *for* their team members, not the other way around. Their job is to remove what is getting in the way of their team's success. I wasn't afraid to hire someone that was smarter than me. I have three jobs as a founder: 1) to create the vision that everyone goes after; 2) to remove obstacles for my team; and 3) to make sure we are pursuing the best ideas to get to our vision. There are so many skillsets needed in a company these days. One person can't do it all. I want to make sure we get it right as a company, and everyone helps to accomplish that. The more you are micromanaging the business, the less influence you have.

"This is a hard pill to swallow for the founder with a white-hot vision. They believe to their core that this business *needs* to exist and they have put it all on the line to make it so. Therefore, they have a tendency to want to keep tight watch on everything that happens during execution. They want to have influence on every part of what is happening. It is an understandable desire, but can be a destructive one as well if implemented."

Chuck explains his point visually: "Picture a Venn diagram," says Chuck, "Let's say that you have six people on the team. If you micromanage all of your employees, it would be like all six circles being directly on top of each other because you (as the founder) are overlapping all of your influence onto someone else's domain of responsibility. Conversely, if you aren't micromanaging, picture another Venn diagram—this time with six circles spread out and overlapping only slightly around you and each other. Your influence is *much* greater when you allow people to do the work you hired them for, and so is the influence of each of your team members. The more latitude you give your team, and more autonomy you give them, the larger influence you have."

The job of a leader is to keep people on track and to keep them motivated toward the optimum goal of the company. The job of a founder is *not* to make sure everyone is pleasing the wishes of the founder. Chuck recalls of his experience, "I made sure our team knew they didn't work *for* me, but we worked *together. After all, we were a team.* I hate '*that's not my job.*' Early on, everything is everyone's job. I wasn't willing to ask someone to do something that I wasn't willing to do myself." If you subscribe to McClure's definition of a startup, why be the only one who is learning? It may be the founder's vision, but it's not the founder's company. In Chuck's experience, "If you think as an entrepreneur you are working for yourself, you need to think again."

As a founder of a high-potential startup, and contrary to folklore, you don't work for yourself. You work for everyone else: your customers, your employees, your investors, all those who benefit from your existence in the world. You are in service to others. You need them to make your vision a reality. As Thomas Edison once observed, "vision without execution is hallucination." At the same time, that vision will likely change. After all, startups are learning organizations. You may think you have a good idea, but you don't really know until someone is willing to pay you for it. Your vision is worthless until it is worthwhile. And your vision may change. That's okay as long as you're able to recognize and—more importantly—*admit* when your vision isn't working. Be prepared to deal with doubt.

Dealing with Doubt

Contrary to the popular imagery of startup life, startups are stressful work environments (also fun, yes, but a stressful variety of fun). There are many moments of doubt. If you're human, you've questioned decisions you've made. In stressful situations, you've likely questioned them even more. Doubt can kill you but so too can blind confidence. Voltaire said it best: "Doubt is uncomfortable, but certainty is ridiculous." Startups live in the space in between doubt and certainty, between fear and hope. The trouble is that "Doubt," to quote Buddha, "separates people. It is a poison that disintegrates friendships and breaks up pleasant relations. It is a thorn that irritates and hurts; it is a sword that kills."

As a startup founder you need to be mindful of doubt creeping in. There are two things you can do mitigate this risk: 1) hire those who are comfortable with uncertainty and chaos, and 2) manage doubt as soon as it arises.

With regard to recruiting those who are comfortable with uncertainty, there is perhaps no better example of this than the early-twentieth century explorer Sir Ernest Shackleton and his Imperial Trans-Antarctic Expedition of 1914–1917, a period now known as the Heroic Age of Antarctic Exploration. In 1914, not long after setting sail from England and arriving in the frigid waters near Antarctica, Shackleton's ship, *Endurance*, became trapped in pack ice and sunk. Shackleton and his crew camped on the ice and waited for the spring thaw, at which point they navigated lifeboats 720 nautical miles to the uninhabited island of South Georgia. "With ship and stores gone" and after a series of treacherous crossings over the course of the next 18 months, Shackleton and his crew would arrive safely at home in England. The greatest testament to Shackleton's leadership: all 27 of his crew survived. No one died. (Though they did eat the dogs).

Some attribute Shackleton's astonishing success in part to his early anticipation of potential difficulties. When recruiting crew for the expedition, Shackleton posted the following job description: "Men wanted for hazardous journey. Small wages, bitter cold, long months of complete darkness, constant danger, safe return doubtful. Honor and recognition in case of success." While the job listing may be apocryphal, Shackleton was a master of managing doubt. He knew that when people start to doubt, they look to one person: the leader. Shackleton, however, wanted people to also look to themselves. And so he recruited for it. If you, as a startup founder, can attract those who are willing to undertake such a journey, God bless! If not, you, as the leader, need to be mindful of what you say, what you choose not to say, and how you act when you hit rough patches in your business. And you *will* hit rough patches. Many. And so the second thing you need to be prepared to do—beyond recruiting those who are comfortable with uncertainty and chaos—is to manage those moments of doubt.

Chuck suggests the following: "There often comes a moment when a founder's *vision well* goes dry. People start doubting. The founder may even start to doubt that the vision is the right one. There is a tension between whether the founder should re-cast the vision or re-motivate the team around the original vision. Then there is also the tension of whether a change is necessary to the strategy or even the product itself." How should you think about reconciling this tension? How do you know which way to go?

"As a founder," says Chuck, "I was way more concerned about *getting it right* then I was about *being right*. I didn't care if ideas originated from me, or from a partner, or from an employee. You need to be open to other people's feedback and hear it, but in the end, you need to make your own decision.

You must assess whether or not you are looking at the situation in the right way. Are you looking in the mirror and asking: 'What is the best decision for the health of the company?' and then following through with the answer? Are you objectively looking at all the information that is coming to you from a variety of people with no bias? Once the founder lands on a decision, then the founder needs to be able to rally the troops in that direction with confidence, with pure belief that it is the best way to go. This has to be done from an authentic place where it is about *getting it right* not about *being right*. There were plenty of moments at OpenTable that we doubted. I started the company in 1998, but I wasn't 100% sure it was going to work until probably 2007. So, I experienced that moment many times." It takes a decade to become an overnight success.

Designed for Impact

Speaking of success and looking to the future, Chuck reflects, "I'm a big believer of the authenticity of ideas—not trying to trick people into buying your product, but having a product that people actually want, something that they actually believe in. Some people build businesses only to make money. While making money is a necessary part of building a business, to be successful in the future, it can't be the only reason. If money is the only reason you are doing it, you won't have direction and conviction to make the tough decisions. If you aren't authentic about the idea and the problem you're solving, I believe the chance for success is significantly less. To be competitive in the future, impact has to be baked into your business model and operations." Chuck uses the word impact to describe entrepreneurs whose businesses are designed in the context of social consciousness. These are for-profit businesses making the world a better place. Chuck believes that these businesses are not only viable businesses, but competitive ones. In fact, he believes that all businesses in the future must become impact businesses if they wish to remain viable. Says Chuck: "If impact is not designed into your business model, you will be uncompetitive in at least four ways: human capital, natural capital, financial capital, and customers.

"In regard to human capital, people increasingly want to work for companies that reflect their passions. That is not just about money. It's about making the world better. If you are not at least attempting to have impact, the best people will go elsewhere. In terms of natural capital, businesses built using virgin and non-renewable resources will also be increasingly uncompetitive. From a financial perspective, there is a dramatic increase in the amount of investment dollars that are looking to have impact and that number will only grow. So if you are not doing impact-related work, investors will look elsewhere. And of course, let's not forget customers. People are getting picky on where and how they spend their money and with the ever-increasing transparency of a connected world, those options will become clearer and clearer."

As Chuck makes plainly clear, impact cannot be an afterthought or a clever marketing scheme. It must be part and parcel of your business model to be sustainable. Authenticity is not only about being honest with yourself and others about the problem are you attempting to solve. It's about the sustainability of resources and profits. You can make money while making good. But success takes more than an authentic idea. It also takes founder skills.

A Penchant for Problem-Solving & A Bias Towards Action

"The two things that make an entrepreneur someone I want to work with," says Chuck, "are when they are action-oriented and open to feedback. I'm a big fan of getting things out into the wild and seeing what customers want. I'm not a big fan of whiteboard talk. I also don't believe in the term *expert*. If you claim you are an expert, I think you've decided to stop learning. It means you've arrived and you don't need to do any more. Henry Ford said it best:

None of our men are "experts." We have most unfortunately found it necessary to get rid of a man as soon as he thinks himself an expert because no one ever considers himself expert if he really knows his job. A man who knows a job sees so much more to be done than he has done, that he is always pressing forward and never gives up an instant of thought to how good and how efficient he is. Thinking always ahead, thinking always of trying to do more, brings a state of mind in which nothing is impossible. The moment one gets into the "expert" state of mind a great number of things become impossible.

This sentiment is echoed in Zen Buddhism as *shoshin*, or beginner's mind. Question assumptions, challenge orthodoxy, and be prepared to learn. This requires being open to the opinions of others. As Chuck suggests, "You may know a lot, but if you think you know it all, you're in trouble. The world in which we live is dynamic, and it is changing fast. Always be open to new opportunities to learn. No one has built the exact business you are building with the exact resources available to him or her at the exact same time. So, no one is going to know *exactly* what to do in your situation, and following someone's specific advice is not usually the best course of action. Talk to others and get their perspective, but let the customers and the market speak as well. After all, that's who you're working for."

Maintain a beginner's mind. Don't worry. Be scrappy. Keep the vision white-hot as you evolve the product from sub-standard to world class. Enroll as many people in your success as possible, including your early customers. And be prepared to manage doubt. After all, if you don't believe in your vision, how can you expect anyone else to? Worse yet, if you refuse to change your vision after it has been proven wrong by customers unwilling to pay for your idea, you need to be flexible and honest enough with yourself to be able to re-frame a new vision. If, or when, you need to do this, remember, you need to bring others along. They signed up for your original vision and now that you are asking them to head in a new direction, don't assume they will be as fired up about this direction as they were about the old (wrong) direction. Take your time. Be deliberate. Communicate your new vision and the reasons for change clearly, and then get back to work. You have a business to build.

CHAPTER TWO

EXTREME BOOTSTRAPPING

"There's no road map. There's no formula. It's a mindset. We want the shortcut. We want the secrets to success. Success comes from within—an undying and relentless hunger for success."

Mark Lawrence, Co-founder & CEO, SpotHero

EVERYONE IS FAMILIAR WITH THE IMAGE of the bootstrapper. Duct tape in one hand. Ramen noodles in the other. Jeremy Smith, co-founder & COO of the popular on-demand parking app, SpotHero, defines bootstrapping as: "Financially hacking your life to allow yourself a desired lifestyle while you grind day in and day out in search of Ramen Profitability." Few have mastered the art of the lifehack more than Smith.

In this chapter, we'll talk about:

- Bootstrapping as a lifestyle
- Checking your ego at the door
- Inspiration happens when you least expect it
- Crowdsourcing (the new way and the old way)
- Never taking your eye off your bank account
- Abundant and cheap forms of startup capital
- The importance of a technical co-founder

A Master's Degree in Financial Hustle

"I got my degree in financial hustle," says Smith. "After grad-
uating from college in 2008, I worked for a once-prominent
technology company on the verge of being pushed out of
the market they created. In my time there, many people lost
their jobs or worked in fear of the same outcome. Luckily,
my situation wasn't really that bad. I had a nice salary, free
rent, no debt, and food at my parents' house. That allowed
me to stockpile a good cash surplus, which I would later use
to change the course of my life.

"In late 2009, I met Mark Lawrence (my close friend and
now business partner), who convinced me to leave my plush
suburban basement. I don't know what I was thinking the
night I gave up paradise for a garden apartment in Chicago's
Bucktown neighborhood. It wasn't long after moving in that I
became tired of the three hour commutes, layoffs, and having
to make 'face time' at the office. But then a great thing happened, I got laid off!"

"Once notified," recalls Smith, "I got paid two weeks' salary plus severance (eight more weeks salary in my case). I then
cashed in my accrued paid time off (PTO) and started collect-
ing unemployment. The combination of the two weeks, severance, PTO, and unemployment yielded the same financial
take-home that I would have gotten by working for a half a
year at normal salary. Getting laid off was the best thing that
could have happened to me."

Sometimes having no other choice is exactly the thing
people need to get started. It is no coincidence that over half
of the Fortune 500 were started during recessions, including
GE (1890), IBM (1896), Disney (1923), Microsoft (1975),
and Apple (1975). Creativity loves constraints. It always has.
It always will. In the case of Jeremy Smith, a severance package
would later become seed capital for starting his own business.

BOOTSTRAPPER'S WISDOM #1:
Bootstrapping is a Lifestyle, Not Just a
Funding Mechanism

"After leaving corporate," recalls Smith, "I took five months off to enjoy life and find direction. At some point in that time I got into online sales and tried some pretty crazy things. One time I went to the bank and pulled out 75 $2 bills that I ended up selling on an eBay auction for $185! I even received positive feedback from the buyer, WTF? I pushed the envelope even further by going into baby bottles, steel canisters, textbooks, electronics, designer dresses and belts, and dog clothes. I didn't care because it was a ton of fun and I started to learn the opportunities in running my own small business."

His personal life started changing as well. "Mark got me into hosting couch-surfing guests. In any given week I would wake up to a crew of travelers sleeping in my main room. These guests became my built-in group of friends to explore the city with while I lived on funemployment. Most of them were bootstrapping poor so I got used to doing all the fun free things to do around the city. I got into salsa dancing, biking the Lakefront Trail, hitting the beach, going to museums, cheap standup shows, and a whole bunch more. I got pretty into all the free hacks this city had to offer. I moved into free drinks and food all over the city by checking out websites like brokehipster.com. You would think this would get old, but those were some of the best days of my life. I could get everywhere, explore, and eat at most places for free.

"The free movement occurring in my life was an important factor in shaping my social consciousness and my beginning in giving back to everyone else. I hosted, cooked, and acted as a tour guide for all of my couch surfers. When I moved out of that apartment, I posted all my old stuff, food, and clothes for free pickup on Craigslist. In general I would offer a helping hand in any situation I could. I love working out and so I would help all my buddies move out of their apartments too. They loved the help and always had things leftover that I would then take to my place. That helped me outfit an entire apartment with furniture and electronics for two years. Now that I was a world-class vagabond, I was ready to enter the world as a bootstrapping entrepreneur."

BOOTSTRAPPER'S WISDOM #2:
Check Your Ego at the Door

Starting a new business requires more than an idea, talent, and capital. It requires some serious soul searching and willingness to make significant life tradeoffs. For Smith, like many entrepreneurs, this required checking his ego at the door.

"I moved to Lakeview with a roommate," recalls Smith. "We paid only $800 a month! My first entrepreneurial endeavor was not a tech startup but rather at a local pizza shop. After getting Razr'd from aforementioned declining electronics company, I knew I wanted something social, funky, and that had free food. I picked up a job at Ian's Pizza, a business that I still believe has huge nationwide potential. I wanted to start my own restaurant and I decided to learn the business from the ground up. I found myself working the overnight shift (10PM–5AM) for minimum wage. That was a tough undertaking for someone who is the quintessential morning person.

I always ate on the job, and would even trade local restaurants for their food and beer. I noticed that at the end of closing shifts there was always a bunch of uneaten pizza that would get thrown out. It would always kill me to see that get thrown out knowing how badly others needed it. I decided to start biking to work and I would carry home two to three filled pizza boxes on my handlebars after shifts. I set up a text message/Facebook alert system to start informing my friends about the influx of new *meal capital*. Over the five-month period of working at the shop, I was supporting three different people who relied on making frequent pizza pickups from my house. It helped them afford living in the city and allowed them to pay the bills every month. I was helping others bootstrap without realizing it. I really valued my work experience at the pizza shop for two reasons.

"First, it gave me the confidence to get over worrying about what people thought of me. It was a very weird situation serving pizza to people from my not-so-distant past. Peers I graduated college with would walk in and see me behind the register. I even had ex-coworkers come in one time. They yelled 'I don't believe it!' when they saw me. You really have to swallow your pride and remember that you are doing it with the aspiration of achieving something better in the future. Luckily, I grew out of my fear of other people's thoughts, and I have become comfortable in my own skin.

"Second, by working at the pizza shop, I got to see what it was like to be around winners. In my old job, many people around me hated their jobs. That ambiance was infectious. At Ian's, I worked with young kids who had aspirations of being business owners, and they took pride in all the little things they did. The business was very successful and still is because all the employees act as if they own the shop (kudos to their team). That got me thinking, 'Why couldn't I do something similar?'"

BOOSTRAPPER'S WISDOM #3:
Inspiration Can Come From Anywhere, Anytime. Look. Listen.

"While all this craziness in my life was happening," recalls Smith, "that's when car 'mishaps' started. I got my car towed twice, had my driver's side mirror kicked off by what I suspect were drunken goons. I got 15 parking tickets just for street cleaning violations. In a little over a year, I had collected somewhere in the range of $5,000 in parking violations. The frustrating thing is that I don't really like rules, but I like spending money to break the rules even less! The parking system was proving that I had to change my ways or I'd go broke. As the co-founder of SpotHero, it's now well known that I got a bunch of parking tickets, but there were a few other things that also caused me to hate it so much.

"At my apartment, I noticed this parking spot that was never used. And so, I asked my landlord if I could use it from time to time. Sure enough, not only did he say yes, he gave me the spot for free! *If you don't ask, you'll never know what can happen!* Of course, at this point, given my master's degree in financial hustle, I thought, 'Well, now that I have a free parking spot, why not make some cash on it!' I decided to rent out the spot.

"I lived near Wrigley Field. During Chicago Cubs home games a spot like mine would sell for $30+. Additionally, I lived next to a church that sold parking during home games. So I did what every smart lazy person would do and I made a deal with the guy at the church to direct cars to my spot. I would get $20 each game and he would get whatever else it goes for on top of that. Simple, right?

"One time, after returning from an epic West Coast road trip, I was expecting to get home to ten home games worth of accrued parking spot cash. What I ended up getting was a measly $40. I laughed at the guy and said, 'You've got to be joking.' Now, I might be able to intimidate some, but this guy was 6'6", 330 pounds, and built like a fridge, so I wasn't about to impose my will upon him. At least it was enough to cover the lunch I was heading over to eat.

"That same day I came across a few of my fellow parking

spot salesmen arguing over who had the right to advertise renting their parking spot on the corner. It's very popular for all the residents to stand with signs on the street selling spots in their garage, however this time it got ugly. The situation got me thinking: 'Would those guys be fighting if people could reserve their parking spot online?'

"I felt like I was hit by a thunderbolt and I hurried over to meet Mark for Thai food. I pitched the idea and he loved it. That was all I needed to convince me to go for it. It was the moment that had finally pushed me over the edge to try something totally radical, which was to build my own website. I didn't know it at the time, but this would be the craziest, most confusing, motivating, emotional, and financially challenging endeavor I would face up to this point in my life.

"Fast-forward a few months. I had now become an official entrepreneur. I left the pizza shop, had a partner (Mark), and even had a logo. We had decided to build our company. We had no clue what we were doing, or how we would do it, as we were both technologically inept. We incorporated, dumped cash into a mutual account, started a blog, and began working out of crappy apartments with an unreliable Internet connection. That setup lasted for a good six months and carried us until we had—brace yourself—our very own splash page! Before the splash page ever dropped, we needed to figure out how to get a logo."

BOOTSTRAPPER'S WISDOM #4:
Crowdsource It (The New Way & The Old Way)

"You'll need a logo for your company. Crowdsource it. Get it done on sites like 99designs and Crowdspring," says Smith. "They're awesome. They have tons of talented designers and they'll refund you if you are unhappy. Win-win! The logo came out so well that I went and got my site designed through crowdsourcing as well. I had no idea what front-end coding even meant, so I was puzzled when I was just handed back some pretty looking PDFs. (Okay tech crowd, you are free to laugh at me now for being a total moron. Oh well, at least I had something)." Crowdsourcing is a game changer. No doubt. Before you do anything, first stop and ask yourself whether or not there is a crowdsourced solution.

Crowdsourcing is not only a technology movement. It's been around since business has existed. The old-fashioned name for it was *get out of the house, talk to people, and ask around to find people who can help you*. In Smith's case, this involved getting social in the entrepreneurial community. "I reached out to a buddy of mine from college who runs a design company and I asked him to code everything up," Smith recalls. "His shop was very busy and had plenty of clients, but I was able to get him to do all the work for half off. I told him that he would not only be helping a friend but that I would remember what he did when our company made it big. I really hope I get the opportunity to pay him back properly! Our next task was to hire a developer to build it all.

"We went to our friends and family and came across a talented developer in Cleveland who seemed too good to be true. He had built startups before, wanted something to work on, and was willing to take a payment based on our company sales. We learned a great lesson from our early stage negotiations. Everything is negotiable. You can structure deals however you want. There is no *one way* things have to be done. We owed him about $10,000, and started to pay him back each month. This had the added benefit of not having to convolute our equity as well.

"While we dragged along on the technology side, we worked on making connections and learning about our community. We scavenged Meetup.com and Eventbrite to find anything related to websites that could help us learn. In the early days we would go to six meet-ups a week: SEO/SEM, Chicago Python, something about UI/UX, Lean Startup Circle were all events we would seek out. All the events were free or a few bucks and always had pizza and beer. The more people we met, the more people we were introduced to that could help us. Going to those events (particularly the Technori events), was priceless."

BOOTSTRAPPER'S WISDOM #5:
Never Take Your Eye Off Your Bank Account. Keep Hustling.

The thing with bootstrapping is that it never really ends. You don't just bootstrap to get started. You need to be diligent about watching your cash flow like crazy. Says Smith, "As we developed more, my funds started dwindling. I was no longer on unemployment, didn't have tip money or free pizza to fall back on, and I had just sunk a little over $10,000 into getting my business going. Luckily, I'm a good negotiator and I found a source of income right in my own home.

"I had always wanted to give Airbnb a try after having hosted so many couch surfers in my life. The setup was great. I slept on the couch. My Airbnb'ers slept in my room. While Airbnb had been a great way to fund my living expenses, there was still this company that I was pouring a lot of time and cash into. Luckily, I found yet another way to hack the system. This particular hack was awesome because it allowed us to continue to bootstrap our business without any additional money coming out of our pockets."

BOOSTRAPPER'S WISDOM #6:
Startup Money Is Out There. Go Get It.

"If you look around online," suggests Smith, "you will see

that there is always some competition giving out cash to a young startup. It usually requires an application, a viable business and/or some type of presentation. I've spent a good week or two straight as an entrepreneur just completing applications, so I'm good at it. In addition to these competitions are programs like Techstars, YCombinator, and Capital Factory. They all require a detailed yet concise application explaining your company. I've saved almost all of my applications and have done them so many times that I can complete laborious applications in one-tenth the time with exceptional quality. I know the quality was awesome because we ended up getting interviews at all three of the aforementioned programs. Something must have been working! We also got rejected by all three!"

It is worth noting that Jeremy, Mark, and the SpotHero team did not make the cut for Techstars Chicago the first time they applied. They were encouraged to apply again the following year. They made progress on their business, applied again, and were accepted. They are now one of our shining stars and one of Chicago's great startup growth stories.

"We also won money," recalls Smith. "We won $15,000 from the City of Chicago for winning best transportation app. This led to media mentions just by the nature of winning. This helped us create the buzz that everyone had talked about. After our win, we reached out to our friend who runs one of the most prominent parking blogs in the United States, and he distributed the information to all of his media contacts. That landed us in the *Huffington Post* and got us an exclusive four-minute video on Fox's *Good Morning Chicago*. Those media mentions got parking companies to pay attention to us.

We then got a call from a startup competition in Cleveland. And so, we drove down. The audience was filled with VCs and entrepreneurs. We pitched. They all immediately identified with the pain point we were working on and saw the scalable opportunity we provided. As a result, we won another $5,000! From there, we were then one of four companies selected to pitch in front of Daymond John, FUBU founder and television personality from ABC's *Shark Tank*.

Jeremy Smith, Mark Lawrence, and Daymond John are cut from the same cloth. In John's experience, "If you can't prove your concept when you're broke, you won't be able to prove it with money either." SpotHero started out as broke as they come. And it has benefited them greatly. Smith and Lawrence have built and continue to operate their company with as much frugality today as before they raised capital. John calls it 'the power of broke' (also his book title). "The philosophy of *The Power of Broke*," says John, "is, whether you're running a Fortune 100 company or you are just starting out, you have to be creative and determined, and you have to make sure that instead of other people's money, you use other people's marketing, mind power, manpower, and manufacturing." Sometimes having nothing to lose is exactly what you need.

BOOTSTRAPPER'S WISDOM #7:
A Technical Co-founder is Critical

Not everyone can code. That's okay. You don't need to know how to build a product in order to build a business. Although if you do want to learn (and learn fast), a place like Starter League is a great option. Co-founded by Mike McGee and Neal Sales-Griffin, The Starter League is an immersive, beginner-friendly school in Chicago. As they point out: "We've taught lawyers, baristas, nurses, and people from all walks of life how to code, design, and build web applications."

That said, remember: Steve Jobs did just fine. But, of course, without Steve Wozniak, his odds would have been significantly reduced. Teams build businesses. At their core, startups need two people: someone who can build and someone who can sell. Sure, there are all sorts of other skills you will need over time (and relatively quickly), but at the very beginning you need a product and the ability to get a customer to buy it. For many would-be digital technology founders who are not technical, an early challenge is finding and attracting tech talent. This was no different for SpotHero.

Recalls Smith: "The biggest company challenge for us at the beginning was finding the right technical partner. Mark and I labored for ten months with a product that was as MVP as humanly possible. The technology limped along so slow that the first sales we ever made actually had to be transacted outside of the SpotHero system! We had customers bringing cash to our *house* and we would literally walk the cash over to the person selling their parking spot. We did this just to get people to start using our service.

"We had to claw to make sales, but we had something that was working and people started paying attention. We had cycled through ten different test runs with programmers, ranging from Chicago's best, to interns, to our Bangladeshi programmer friends who made our map scroll up and down. At one point I decided that I would try my hand at learning code to see if that would make a difference. The problem was that coding school was going to cost me $6,000 that I didn't have. So I went into to super hustle mode. I had 12 friends refer my application, which took $3,500 off the cost of the class and I raised $2,500 on my own by asking people to donate to my cause online. When all was said and done, that $6,000 class didn't set me back a penny! It was a great experience to go, but I know now that I'm not a coder. I was a disaster.

"Then I got a LinkedIn introduction to our third founder, Larry. Someone randomly had remembered meeting me at our networking events and thought we should meet. That *run in* went better than we could have ever imagined and now we have a technical partner that we love, who is smarter and more motivated than the two of us. With a technical co-founder, the product grows so much faster. You don't have to pay someone else to build a mess that you pass along to another person, and they help balance out any of the existing founders who are there. We made sure not to be greedy and gave him a sizeable portion of our company. He is as much a founder as Mark or myself, and everyday I'm glad to have him on my team.

"Bootstrapping is a game. When there is something you want, you need to dig deep. It's not glorious, but it can be done. Get creative. That resourcefulness you will learn will grow and become part of your life. I strongly believe that you should never pay full price for *anything* and it's helped our company minimize our expenses. Each day we bootstrap further we are learning more about our character, proving out our business, and staying humble.

"The time will come when we need to back our business with the right resources and I'm determined to stay as efficient with my spending then as I am now. I saw what happens to big corporations when they lose track of spending and the impacts on their culture and demeanor. I spent days cancelling out unused telephone lines that ended up in millions of dollars saved to a company that had to axe half of its staff in the 2008 financial collapse. I've also been on the side of a bootstrapping company where every last dollar is crucial to staying alive. Along this time I've learned how to do more with less and how it can lead to a lifestyle that few pictured was possible. So the next time you see me will probably be over free pizza at a meetup and don't be surprised if I stay late to carry the leftovers home."

CHAPTER THREE

CREATING AND HIRING FOR CULTURE

"We asked ourselves what we wanted this company to stand for.
We didn't want to just sell shoes. I wasn't even in to shoes.
But I was passionate about customer service."

Tony Hsieh, Founder, Zappos

ACCORDING TO Gallup's *State of the Global Workplace* study, only 13% of employees worldwide are engaged at work. One in eight workers (roughly 180 million employees in the 142 countries studied) are "psychologically committed to their jobs and likely to be making positive contributions to their organizations." More disturbing is the fact that 63% of employees are "not engaged" or "lack motivation and are less likely to invest discretionary effort in organizational goals or outcomes." And worse yet, 24% are "actively disengaged"—meaning they are "unhappy and unproductive at work and liable to spread negativity to coworkers." That's 900 million people not engaged and 340 million people actively disengaged around the globe. Why does culture matter? *That* is why culture matters. And not just any culture but rather a culture that embraces innovation and measured risk-taking. Sir Richard Branson makes clear what he believes a business must do in order to create a culture of innovation. Says Branson, "a business has to be involving, it has to be fun, and it has to exercise your creative instincts."

In a startup, you cannot afford to *not* be deliberate about culture. Imagine running an early stage company where only 13% of people feel engaged. Of course, startups—unlike larger, established firms—often have a cultural advantage insofar as they have no other choice than to engage all employees in everything and anything that needs to be done. As a result, working for a startup generally tends to be a more creative vocation. After all, you're in the business of creating stuff that does not exist. That said, be careful. Those large, so-called lumbering companies that some like to mock used to be the cool, nimble, innovative kids on their respective blocks. Early stage companies are not immune.

In this chapter, we'll talk about:

- Where company cultures comes from.
- How to create a culture of innovation.
- How to hire for the culture you want to create.
- How to sustain that culture as you grow.

Creating a Great Product Isn't the Same as Creating a Great Culture

You must be as intentional about the culture you create as you are about the products you make. Don't assume just because you're a startup founder that people will be *as engaged* as you are or that they will maintain their enthusiasm as the company experiences growing pains and hits bumps in the road. And there will be bumps in the road. Many.

Company culture is a mashup of values and beliefs that show up every day in every way in which a company operates. In a startup, culture is everything. Zappos founder Tony Hsieh once quipped: "Your culture is your brand." He went on to explain, "Our belief is that if you get the culture right, most of the other stuff—like great customer service, building a great brand, and passionate employees and customers—will happen naturally on its own." Get culture right and success will follow. So where does culture come from and what can you do to ensure success?

How to Create a Culture of Innovation

In the early stages of a company, culture is a direct outgrowth of the *founder's* beliefs and values. As a company grows, a founder's values will attract early management team members, including co-founders and non-founder CEOs, who share those values. Over time, culture becomes a reflection of all the people who work at the company and how they interact with each other and with customers, suppliers, investors, and the broader community. Culture is not an accident. It is an outcome of very deliberate hiring, leadership, and operating practices. If you're a jerk, you will create a company of jerks who will likely treat each other—including your customers—like jerks. Rule #1: Don't be a jerk.

Effective founders and startup CEOs take culture very seriously, but they also find ways to have fun. After all, starting anything new is difficult enough, so why not have fun trying? Like Hsieh and Branson, among the culturally astute is Amanda Lannert: the smart, talented, inspiring, and self-described *sometimes* funny CEO of The Jellyvision Lab, an offshoot of the interactive gaming company Jellyvision, Inc. It's safe to say her attentiveness to culture is working. Under Lannert's leadership, Jellyvision has doubled its revenue three out of the last four years and has grown to serve hundreds of mostly Fortune 1000 clients.

Jellyvision, Inc. originally made *You Don't Know Jack* and *Who Wants to Be a Millionaire* using virtual, online game show hosts. The Jellyvision Lab separated the same *virtual host* concept to apply it to different concepts such as a virtual salesperson, teacher, guidance counselor, and others to expand the idea of interactivity. They work with large companies and organizations to make very complex things like health insurance benefits easy to understand. Jellyvision is a Chicago-based company that is known for its A+ talent and its fun culture. Lannert suggests, "You'll never forget a presentation made by the Jellyvision team. They are funny, smart, witty, intuitive, humble, and gracefully honest with clients. It truly is a differentiator."

Lannert suggests, "It is important to clearly define what culture is. It is not a slogan on the door. It is not whether or not you have a foosball table. It is a reflection of your people, your process, and your policies. More simply put, it's how the people you hire and retain treat each other and your products day in and day out. Culture emanates from the way employees talk, walk, lead, and interact with customers. It is an extension of their personality, habits, and values." Says Lannert, "It seems to me that the values, quirks, pet peeves, and working habits of the initial leaders become engrained, and are formative for early stage companies. Typically, what the CEO believes is most important, especially in the early days, will become the culture of the company."

These beliefs are informed by what founders and nonfounder leaders think are important. Different founders and different leaders value different things. The things they value tend to show up in how they run the business. For some founders, it may be the product. For others, it may be customer service, fiscal responsibility, or risk-taking. According to Lannert, "These are all things that the founder or CEO has an opinion on and acts upon and the company inevitably follows that action with its culture. Culture is a factor of how you treat people. It sets a tone for the people you hire and how they act toward each other. So founders really need to put their best foot forward even in the early days."

At Jellyvision, like many companies, much of its culture is a reflection of the personality of its founder, Harry Gottlieb. Lannert joined the company in 2001 and had the opportunity to work directly with Harry in the early days. When asked about Gottlieb, she reflects, "He was a kind, funny, thoughtful, and brilliant man. He thought critically and with imagination, but really valued a laugh; therefore, we still do today."

Gottlieb wrote down the values early on so that people knew them, but that wasn't what instituted culture at Jellyvision. As Lannert suggests, "Writing company values on the wall or on the company letterhead is probably as valuable as wallpaper in terms of having a healthy productive culture. Employees need to see the values lived out in real life settings. Harry's behavior formed the Jellyvision culture. It wasn't a laminated document or words on placard. It is whom you hire or whom you don't hire; what you work hard for and what you ignore. It is how you solicit ideas from others or don't. It's how people treat each other, share information, make decisions and mistakes, day in and day out. As a founder or CEO, you need to ask yourself: How do you communicate? Who do you ask for opinions? What do you celebrate? What do you get worried about? How do you share that you are worried? Or, not share it at all? That is the stuff the truly sets the culture of a company."

Hiring for Culture

In the early days, when you are cash-strapped and unable to pay competitive salaries, you really have only two tools to attract the best talent: equity and culture. People join startups for different reasons, but among them is a very personal feeling that they "fit in." They believe in the mission that the company is on, the product the company sells, and perhaps most importantly the culture that the company has created. As a founder, you are not only competing with the competitors in your category, you are competing for talent. Don't wait to work on culture. It's never too early to start thinking about it and, more importantly, to start living it.

Several years ago, when I first met Desiree Vargas-Wrigley and Ethan Austin, co-founders of the crowdfunding platform Giveforward (a Techstars company), I was taken aback by their commitment to culture. They had come to my office to pitch me as investor in their seed round. I loved the problem they were out to solve and I loved their business model, but what struck me most was a comment Ethan made *after* their pitch. He said they were really serious about their culture and went on to explain their values. As much as he was engaged during the pitch, he physically lit up when he spoke about culture and leadership. This typically would come as no surprise. Culture is a big deal. Many companies talk about culture. Founders believe in it. People know it is important. But what struck me about Ethan's enthusiasm for culture was the simple fact that, at that time and in that moment, Giveforward had one employee. *One.* And she had just recently become a salaried employee after working for 18 months as an unpaid intern. Ethan spoke about culture not as if they had *one* employee but as if they had *one thousand* employees. I invested.

Today, Giveforward is the leading crowdfunding site for medical expenses. They employ 29 people and have a Net Promoter Score (NPS) that rivals Amazon, Apple, Harley-Davidson, and Zappos. NPS, a measure of customer loyalty, is a direct reflection of a company's culture. Essentially, a company's NPS is the difference between those customers who enthusiastically recommend the company (promoters) and those unhappy customers who enthusiastically detest the company (detractors). The average company has a Net Promoter Score in the 5 to 10 percent range (meaning they're barely breaking even, on a net basis, between the customers that love them and those that hate them). Many firms (and entire industries for that matter) have negative Net Promoter Scores (you know who they are). In contrast, Giveforward's Net Promoter Score is 80! *Eighty!* Based on analysis by Bain, companies that achieve long-term profitable growth have Net Promoter Scores two times higher than the average company and grow at twice the rate of their competitors. All those who poke fun at culture as a flavor-of-the-month initiative, do so at your own peril. Culture matters, a lot.

Amanda Lannert shares a similar commitment to culture at Jellyvision. "You need to lead by example," says Lannert. "Be a public and visible model of the behaviors that you want to see in your company. And, hire like-minded people. This may come at the expense of diversity, but it is more important to hire people that represent the way you like to work than it is to make sure they are maximally competent. Hire for common values and then give people room to interpret and embody them in their own right." Hire for competency and for culture. Both matter. As Elon Musk has observed, "My biggest mistake is probably weighing too much on someone's talent and not someone's personality. I think it matters whether someone has a good heart."

At Jellyvision, Lannert says, "We want people who are *interested* and *interesting*. We do a lot of work to make the boring interesting and the complex simple. So, during the interview process, we ask people to tell us three things about themselves that would surprise us. People who have lived an interesting life are much more likely to be open and agile to new things and experiences. They also are more fun to have in the workplace." According to Lannert, hiring the right people that match your desired culture is one of the most important things you can do in the early days of your startup. Therefore, they ask questions like: *What do you want to be when you grow up? How do you learn new things?* Lannert continued, "We do care about skills—we have an audition where candidates can show us what they can do and not just tell us what they can do (there is a big difference)—but, we spend our interviews trying to figure out how an individual thinks and processes the world. It's more about personality.

Founders often ask if culture can be taught. For example, if someone is the perfect fit for a position based on their competence, but lack chemistry, is it worth it to hire them and teach them how to work in your culture? Lannert has an opinion on this, "There are many things I think you can teach, but they are mostly around functional skills. You can't teach work ethic, attention to detail, and humility. You either have it or you don't. If you have it, you might have a really successful career here. If you don't, you definitely won't."

Jellyvision is primarily a communication company, so Lannert says that they care deeply about an individual's ability to write. She commented, "To me, writing is a sign of intelligence. Great writers are typically very smart people. It's hard to fake really good original writing. Therefore, we have people put together the best cover letter they have ever written as a component of our application. Also, by having people write an extensive cover letter it helps us find the right candidates, because the people that are humble enough, and care enough, to take the time to do it are the right kind of people. I put very little stock in resumes. It's hard to tell what an individual did, versus a team, and you can't tell *anything* about the environment—was it a high performance environment or was it nearly impossible to get anything done? These things matter, and resumes don't provide helpful context. Moreover, I don't think *human beings* come through on a resume. Therefore, I put a much heavier weight on a cover letter because the candidate is able to tell me more about who they are."

Lannert says they hire for DNA. "We always hire potential over experience. Resumes and historical knowledge will only serve you for six weeks. Then, what you've done in the past doesn't matter. All that matters is what you are *going* to do. Someone who has learned how to learn is more valuable to me than simply someone who has been to the rodeo a thousand times before." Lannert doesn't believe that past experience is the best indicator of future success. She believes that who you are, how you think, and what excites you about your work is the best predictor of your ability to perform. Lannert added, "No two companies are the same, no two bosses are the same, no two projects are the same, and no two clients are the same; therefore, you DNA makeup will determine your ability to perform.

"In a startup phase, people need to get along. Harry (the founder) and I once asked the question, 'Do we have to want to go to lunch with every person we hire?' And, we determined that the answer is YES. You work too hard and too long to not work with people you like to be around. I don't think it is worth it to hire someone you don't enjoy to be around. Of course there are those times you think you are hiring the perfect fit and they prove not to be. Lannert observes, "Nobody bats a thousand when hiring. Part of growing an organization is learning how to identify people that *aren't* a fit and then removing them with grace and speed. You can usually tell in the first thirty days whether or not someone is a fit. So, we have instituted a 30-day review and a 90-day review, which allows us to flag people that aren't working out. It also helps us provide very early and written feedback to the employee so that they have a chance to adjust."

In order to increases your chances of getting it right, Lannert says that posting fantastic job descriptions is a great place to start. She said, "The most important marketing for your company early on is your job descriptions. Tell your story, galvanize people who are like you, and they will galvanize you back. Great job descriptions are beautiful, compelling advertising pieces to help you attract the people that will help you become successful."

Startup culture begins with a founder's beliefs and values, but in order to scale a company you must be thoughtful about scaling your culture. This cannot be done if it is only a founder's beliefs. It has to be what everyone believes. At some point, the organization will become too large (hopefully) to have the founder at every meeting, on every sales call, in every product review, and so on. By hiring for culture, fostering it, and living it every day in every thing that you do, you will be able to remain agile and creative as you grow.

CHAPTER FOUR

THE ART OF DOING THINGS DIFFERENTLY

"Whenever you find yourself on the side of the majority,
it's time to pause and reflect."

Mark Twain

JASON FRIED STARTED 37signals in 1999 as a web design firm—*just* web design. He and three friends each put $10,000 into the business and began doing custom design work for small, medium, and large companies. Fried recalls, "We were always focused on doing one thing well. Most web design companies were offering full service (hosting, design, backend, etc.). We just focused on making the site *look* better." 37signals built a great reputation for doing that one thing well, its business took off—even surviving the dot-com bubble in 2000 and 2001.

Five years after starting their web design business, on February 5, 2004, 37signals launched a project management tool called Basecamp. Within a month, they had a hundred paying customers. Hundreds more followed. As Fried recalls, "Within a year, Basecamp was generating more income for us than our web design business. We had a hit! So we stopped designing web sites and went all-in on our software business.

Soon we started hearing stories of Basecamp being used in schools, governments, churches, consulting firms, publishers, and just about every other industry on earth. The stories keep coming to this day and we keep growing. Today, 11 years after Basecamp first hit the market, nearly 15 million people have worked on a project with Basecamp! And every week, thousands of companies sign up to use Basecamp."

Today, Basecamp is the world's #1 project management tool (and they've reached the top nearly exclusively through word-of-mouth). *That* is a story worth knowing more about and a founder worth listening to. In this chapter, we'll talk about lessons from 37signals, Basecamp, and Jason Fried, notably:

- Managing what you want versus what your customers want
- Reinventing how you work
- Attracting the best talent
- Scaling trust
- The art of the long view
- Starting a business to stay in business

One note: Basecamp (the product) is now also Basecamp (the company). 37signals is no longer. However, throughout this chapter, we'll refer to 37signals as the company that launched Basecamp and Basecamp as their now-famous product. When appropriate, we'll also refer to Basecamp (the company) as it relates to their current business post-name change.

Solving Their Own Problem

As 37signals grew, they eventually needed a better way to manage projects. Fried recalls, "We wanted to keep track of things, and seem professional to clients. We looked around for a project management system, but we couldn't find one; so, we built our own." As they began to use it with clients, their clients would ask how they could start using the same thing. It was designed just to serve an internal need that they had, but as they saw other organizations express the same need for a similar system 37signals knew they had a product. "So, we polished it up," recalls Fried, "put some prices on it, and called it Basecamp." Basecamp is now a widely used project management system, especially by web development and design firms. "We have always focused on doing a few things well," recalls Fried, "and we have always focused on not trying to deliver every feature that we can think of. We wanted a simple system that solved our organization problem. It didn't have bells and whistles. It just worked."

Entrepreneurs, like Fried, who create products designed to solve their own problems are referred to as *user entrepreneurs*. Why are they special? In terms of success, user entrepreneurs punch well above their weight class. According to the Kauffman Foundation, while user entrepreneurs represent only 10.7% of startups, they account for 46% of businesses surviving past the 5-year mark. The question is why do they have better odds of success? First, they're intimately familiar with the problem they are attempting to solve (after all, it's *their* problem). And, secondly, they are hell bent on solving it (again, it's *their* problem!). Keep this in mind when starting your business. Venture capitalists call it domain expertise. It helps to think outside the box by knowing what the box looks like. This is not to suggest you have to be an expert. History has shown that you don't need to be an expert in the category in order to disrupt it, but you do need to know the problem really, really well. If you don't, you'll likely be blindsided by some detail you didn't know, overbuild the product with features that don't matter, or create something that no one wants.

Take time to understand the problem. And make sure you solve the right one. And do it simply. Like Basecamp, less is often—if not *always*—more.

Using the same approach of simplicity, agility, and speed, 37signals can also be credited with the creation and open-sourcing Ruby on Rails which is one of the most popular and fast growing coding platform available today. Fried recalls, "We didn't know it was going to take off the way it did. And, we didn't care. The approach and the technology made sense to us, and we used it. So, we thought we'd share it with the world. Over time, we started doing too many things at once. When you do that, projects end up sitting untouched for too long. The key to keep things progressing in your company is to devote enough time to critical tasks to keep momentum going in the most important areas. Therefore, we are in the process of selling off our non-core products so we can focus the most on what we want to focus on."

What You Want vs. What Your Customers Want

Once you figure out the right problem to solve, the question is: can you get paid? After all, solving a customer's problem is only half of *your* problem. The other half is figuring out how to make money. Do you give it away and sell audience? Charge for it? Offer subscriptions? Allow customers to pay what they want? Seek sponsorship? The options are endless. Fried suggests the following:

"When we originally launched Basecamp (the product)," recalls Fried, "we introduced it as a free version where you could upgrade. A few years ago, we took that away and introduced a 60-day free trial on the paid plan, and that has worked well for us. Now, we are re-considering. Bottom line: It's okay to experiment and change your mind. Don't take anyone's word for it. You can't apply what worked for another company to your company and expect it to work identically. You have to try it for yourself, and see what happens, being ready to adjust."

In the early days of a startup, it is hard *not* to chase the money. When you chase the highest paying customer, you can often drift off course of the original vision by pleasing the needs of one customer while ignoring the needs of millions. Basecamp has taken a very unique approach in their pricing to prevent this drift. Fried reflects, "We've always been very careful to not allow customers to pay us more than $150 per month. The reason we do that is that I don't want to be beholden to the person who has the most money. When you're getting started with your company, you'll have a high paying customer come to you and say, *We like your product, but if you add this, this, and this, we'll buy it.* And, then they don't buy it. They say they want more—so, you deliver it for them. And, they still don't buy. You are constantly chasing that high paying customer and losing track of the original vision you had for the product. You're chasing dollars that you might never get. And, even if you do get the money, they'll want more from you. Therefore, the reason we don't allow customers to pay us more than $150 is so that no single customer can sway your business. The aggregate of the customers can, but no single customer can."

Basecamp has since launched an annual subscription that is actually more than the month-to-month plan that they also offer. *How can that be,* you may ask? Typically, you would expect to get a discount if you pay all upfront. Fried reasons, "What we discovered is that there are some customers that want to pay by check. They aren't price sensitive; they are *process* sensitive. Their company isn't set up to pay via credit card, so they would gladly pay more if they could pay by check. You don't always have to get discounts. In this case, it was more important to understand our customers' 'process' and optimize around *that*, even if we have to charge more."

Solve problems you understand. Be ready and willing to adapt. Try things. See what works. And be careful not to fit your product for each and every customer or you'll end up fitting no one. Customers may love it, but if you can't make money, you won't.

Reinventing How You Work

Beyond Basecamp (the product), Basecamp (the company) is also known for taking an unconventional approach to managing their organization, among them remote work and recruiting. There has been a lot written and discussed about the advantages and disadvantages of a remote workforce. While many have steered clear of it often citing questions about accountability, communication, camaraderie, and efficiency, Basecamp has made it a hallmark of the way they run their business. In fact, Fried wrote a great book on the topic, *Rework*, in which he espouses a number of unconventional approaches to work. Fried is a firm believer in remote work largely because it has worked for them. He has the evidence to prove its benefits.

"We started 37Signals in Chicago with all of us local. But, since then, we have valued a virtual workforce. Our first hire out of our core team of three was in Denmark. Our second hire was a guy in Utah. Our third and fourth hires were in Chicago. And, then our fifth hire was in California. The advantage of a virtual team is that we weren't interrupting each other all day long. No casual chats that were interrupting our work flow. We realized that whenever we were together physically, we got a lot less done. We had unnecessary meetings. Therefore, I believe it's totally possible to build a company with a virtual workforce. In order for it to work, you have to find people who are comfortable working in that environment (and are okay working alone in their basement)."

Fried suggests two primary reasons why he believes in remote work. "First," says Fried, "We want to respect people's lives outside of work. We want people to live where they want to live. For example, we have a guy on our staff that lives on a farm in Tennessee. Traditionally, he would have to move to a big city to have a job at a firm like Basecamp. And, he would hate that. Now, he gets to live on a farm and work his dream job. And second, we want to hire the best people. We don't want to limit our selection pool to people who are local, or who are willing to be local. By embracing a remote, virtual workforce, we can literally hire the best talent in the world—with no complication."

Fried does not deny that there are potential downsides of remote work. He cites several of the most common concerns. "First, there is a management challenge," Fried offers. "How do you keep track of people, communicate well, and motivate in a virtual workforce environment? Second, there is a relational challenge. How do you build team camaraderie over a videoconference? Third, there is a culture challenge. Not everyone is cut out to work in a remote, virtual workforce environment. People who come from a more corporate, office culture usually find it very difficult to adjust."

If, however, you have a virtual workforce, like Basecamp, it is important to treat every person with the same amount of relational touch. "For example," according to Fried, "at Basecamp, whether you are in the office or not, we all use videoconferencing for meetings, so that the people who are not in the room don't feel a degree of separation. Everyone is on an even playing field. Sometimes, companies only solve the *work together* challenge by renting office space. But, what if you took what you would have spent on office space every month and spend it on travel to get the team together?" Basecamp, like many great innovators, is as creative about how it works as it is about what it makes. Given the war for talent and the highly competitive nature of software development and technology, you can't compete on product alone. After all, it's people who make the products. Keep in mind: We live in a world where the very best software developers now have agents. Attracting and retaining the best talent takes more than a great product. It takes a great company.

Attracting and Retaining the Best Talent

In addition to deliberately building and managing a virtual workforce, Fried has also taken an unconventional approach to recruiting and employee benefits. The default of many tech companies is to go into the hiring process with equity as the hook. It is common practice, but it doesn't have to be the *only* way to get the right people. Fried offers, "At Basecamp, we pay people really well, treat them right, give them perks, and make work an awesome thing in their lives. For example, we pay for people's hobbies (e.g., flight school). We also pay for people's vacations every year (not just give them vacation time). I'm way more interested in paying people with experiences and real cash *today*, than the hope that they *might* get something down the road. Don't just throw equity around. Once someone is an owner, you can't get rid of him or her. There are a lot of people out there that are super talented and just want to work on something cool. You don't need to overpay for the *best of the best* developers to build a team. You can find great talent who are still in school. Give people a chance. You might get lucky."

Scaling Trust

Given their unorthodox approach to management, it should

come as no surprise that culture is of utmost importance at Basecamp. Fried says, "I have always felt that culture is the byproduct of consistent behavior. For example, if you want ideas to be celebrated in your culture, then *you* have to celebrate new ideas *consistently*. Behavior matters the most. Whatever you think is important, you need to act that way *consistently*. People follow the leader. This is especially true in the early days. People will look to the leader to set the tone for the company. As the company gets bigger, this gets harder."

One of the ways Basecamp has worked to establish a high level of trust is that they allow their customer service people to do whatever they feel is appropriate to make customers happy. Fried explains, "We have a sign in our customer service center that says, 'No reasonable request will be refused.' Therefore, as long as a customer has a reasonable request, we equip each person with the ability to do whatever they think they need to do—without asking permission—in order to make the customer happy." Building this approach into their culture has instilled a mindset that employees do not need to *check with their manager* to refund money, for example. It permits a culture of trust and not one of fear. "If I have a huge list of rules," says Fried, "people will think I don't trust them to use their minds and to determine the best thing to do."

Culture is a deliberate thing. You have to be intentional. Hiring is one of the most important things you do to create the culture you want. Take your time. Hire not only for competence but also for culture.

The Art of the Long View

One explanation of why Basecamp and Fried have put so much effort into reinventing how they do what they do is their perspective on time. "I think too many entrepreneurs are thinking that they won't be in their business for a long time," says Fried. "Therefore, they make decisions that have the short term in mind and not the long term. Founders who plan to be in their business for the long term behave differently, and ultimately, build better businesses. Jeff Bezos says, 'Invest in the parts of your business that will never change.' For example, no one will wake up one day and say, *I wish shipping was slower and more expensive.* Therefore, Amazon has invested relentlessly in distribution centers, logistics, and customer support. It will take a long time to pay off, but that is okay for a founder who is in it for the long haul. If a founder is looking to flip the company, they are more likely to use a Band-Aid where surgery is required." People who tend to focus on their customer typically stay in business longer. If you plan to only be in a business for a few years, then you are more likely to *not* focus on your customer because they don't matter as much. If on the other hand, you want to around for the long haul—maintain your focus on the customer.

Don't Confuse Starting a Business with Staying in Business

People often say that it's hard to start in business, but it's not. It's hard to *stay* in business. Creating and building is the easy part. It's the maintaining and growing parts that take the most grit, skill, and discipline. If you don't see things through, you'll have a bunch of half-baked ideas. Fried suggests, "When you raise money, you learn how to spend money. When you don't have money, you learn how to *make* money. I would exhaust all options to fund growth through *making* money before you decide to *raise* money. It will build discipline to help you stay in business when things get tough."

Basecamp's success is a testament to what is possible when a founder not only listens to the market, but also listens to himself. Know what you want from your business. Know what kind of culture you want to create. Keep your head down. Keep it simple. Do the work. And someday, like Jason Fried and Basecamp, you may look up and discover that millions of fans are standing in ovation. That's what happens when a product—and a company—just works.

CHAPTER FIVE

THE UNIT ECONOMICS
OF YOUR DREAM

"There are three types of accountants: those that
can count and those that can't."

Anonymous

"THE BUSINESS WAS CRATERING," recalls venture capitalist and serial entrepreneur Joe Dwyer. "I was asked to come in and help out. Although I had no knowledge of the industry, I did have knowledge of *unit economics*. After quick analysis, I learned that while the business was making $2,375 in revenue per customer, it was spending $4,295 to acquire each customer. We were losing nearly $2,000 every time we closed a sale. Imagine what the board said when I walked in and told them I was going to ramp down sales. The problem was that our sales approach was too expensive. And worse yet, the team didn't know it. In order to turnaround the business, we needed to entirely reinvent how we went to market to acquire customers."

This is not an uncommon reality among startups. Most startups spend more than they make. As Troy Henikoff, managing director of the Chicago-based Techstars program observes, "Early on, you'll do anything to get those first customers. You may spend five times what you know you should be spending to acquire them in order to prove out your business model and test your assumptions. But you don't scale that!"

In Dwyer's case, the business he walked into had done just that: scaled an unsustainable (and perpetually unprofitable) sales strategy. Dwyer wasn't entirely surprised by his findings. "It's shocking how many startups don't understand the unit economics of their own businesses," observes Dwyer. "It is just about impossible to manage an early stage business without it."

In this chapter, we'll talk about:

- Benefits of unit economics
- What unit economics tells you about your business
- Putting unit economic to work in your business

What Unit Economics Helps You Do

Unit economics helps leaders do a number of things, among them:

1. Know what to change (and what not to change) to improve and grow
2. Determine how best to price your products/services
3. Figure out what you're willing to pay to acquire & service a customer
4. Know how you're doing versus similar businesses
5. Create a reasonable financial forecast of your business at scale

Failure to Change What Isn't Working

The problem with an aggregated financial view for a startup is that losing money in the aggregate is *normal*. "All that financial accounting will tell you is what you already know," says Dwyer, "you have very few assets, you're hemorrhaging money, and your balance sheet sucks. It is so consistent with what all startups look like and it is not meaningful. It does not tell you what's going on."

In the aggregate, you may answer the question of why you're losing money by stating the obvious: *we've overestimated sales and underestimated costs.* But does that simply mean you should sell more and spend less? Of course, but the more meaningful questions are what sales are the *right* sales and what costs are the *right* costs. Not all customers (and costs) are created equal.

When startups don't know their unit economics, they fail to change what isn't working and, worse yet, they change things that *are* working. "For example, one of the most common errors startups make," Dwyer observes, "is that they add new features to their products. Usually adding a feature is a *really* bad idea. Simplicity rules. But if you don't know what is creating value or what it costs to create value, you really have no way of knowing if adding that feature makes sense or not. Unit economics can help you figure this out. Without it, it is virtually impossible to make good decisions and to remain competitive."

Determine How Best to Price Your Products/Services

With better line of sight into the unit level costs of your products, you are in a much better position to determine the best price for your products (and not lose money).

Figure Out What You're Willing to Pay to Acquire and Service a Customer

Assuming you have an idea of the lifetime value of your customers, by attributing costs at a unit level, you will be able to determine the range that you will be willing to pay to acquire those customers and also to service them post-acquisition.

How Are You Doing vs. Similar Businesses?

Unit economics are critical in providing reference points. If I simply told you the price of a house, how would you know if it was worth it or not? You wouldn't. But if I told you the house was selling for 2x others in the neighborhood, you'd have a much better idea. Unit economics normalizes data. Price per square foot is a unit you can use to make a decision.

In the stock market, price-to-earnings (P/E) ratios are unit economics. They tell us the relative price of a unit of stock to its earnings. With this information we can compare one stock to another with some level of confidence.

With unit level data, as a founder you can begin to answer questions such as:

- What is the typical bounce rate for a business like mine?
- What should I expect to pay in order to acquire individual customers?
- What is the most effective customer acquisition channel for us?
- What variable costs should I reduce?
- Others?

What Is Our Financial Opportunity At Scale?

The point of a startup is to scale to mass-market adoption. But, you can't do that on guesswork. With unit economics, you can compute break-even analysis as well as begin to model what the future can look.

How to Use Unit Economics

Central to unit economics is a cost accounting concept called contribution margin. Not all margins are created equal. Notably, gross margin is not the same as unit contribution margin.

Gross Margin = Revenue – Cost of Goods Sold (COGS)

Unit Contribution Margin = Unit Revenue – Unit Variable Cost

Gross margin tells you the difference between your revenue and your cost of production or acquisition. It does not include variable costs and therefore does not give you an accurate picture of what you may need to change in order to improve your business and grow. And since a lot of things don't work in startups, you need as much data as you can get on your business.

Unit contribution margin, on the other hand, attributes all variable costs to each unit sold thereby giving you much better line of sight into what is driving your success (or lack thereof).

"For example, imagine you are a manufacturer of beer," Dwyer offers. "In order to operate a beer business, you have employees, a facility, raw ingredients, huge brewing vats, equipment, bottles, packaging, etc. In order to sell your beer, you have a marketing team, distribution and channel partner expenses, etc.

Let's say you sell your beer for $3/bottle and it costs you $1/bottle to brew it. Your *gross margins* would be $2/bottle.

From a *unit contribution margin* perspective however, you would also include *everything* it costs you to make and sell that bottle of beer to the end customer:

- How much do you spend to market to/acquire a customer per beer bottle?
- How much do you pay retailers per beer bottle?
- How much do you spend on equipment maintenance

per beer bottle?

- Others?

Are your margins *still* $2/bottle? Not even close.

As Dwyer suggests, "By understanding the impact of *all* business activity on *each* bottle of beer that you sell, you will find fascinating inefficiencies and/or opportunities that your competitors may not be paying attention to. Without it, you are running blind."

As a reader of this book, you are probably not making beer. But if you are, God bless you! In your case, you are likely building some sort of application, platform, product, or service that has different types of metrics such as downloads, upgrades, shares, subscriptions, repeat visits, viral loop, and customer lifetime value—to name a few. However, the principles of unit economics applies regardless of the business you are in.

How to Put Unit Economics to Work

Here are six things Dwyer suggests in order to implement unit economics as a decision-making tool in the management of your business, all of which can be done using your head, a dry erase board, and Excel.

1. **Systems**: value creation activities
2. **Zoom**: the frame of reference for analysis
3. **Value**: how your business creates value for the customer
4. **Flow**: stages of value creation
5. **KPIs**: key performance indicators
6. **Modeling**: building future scenarios based on data

1. Systems: value creation activities

Systems are all the activities your business engages in to create value. A systems view can help you better understand how best to attract and retain customers, allocate your marketing spend, make improvements to customer service, add (or delete) features, and determine how to fix what's not working. With this view, you'll begin to home in on the types of things that you should be monitoring, tweaking, and improving.

"For example," Dwyer offers, "consider the various systems of the daily deal site Groupon. One system involves salespeople acquiring merchants that, in turn, lead to the design of deals. Another system involves the relationship between consumers, offers, and merchants. Another could be customer support. For example, let's say you had a less than satisfactory experience with a deal, but it was handled well at customer support. That could be a huge source of value creation (or loss) for the business. Customer satisfaction is a system. Merchant loyalty is a system. And so on."

Each of these systems are of course related, but they can be studied in isolation. There are an infinite number of value creation systems in all businesses. As Dwyer suggests, the best place to start the application of unit economics is to map out these various systems such that you can then move on to the next step, Zoom.

2. Zoom: the frame of reference for analysis

Zoom (as in "zoom in" or "zoom out") creates your frame of reference to isolate the unit you wish to measure. Units can be very high-level or extremely granular. "For example, Groupon may look at a unit as a neighborhood, a city, a region, a country, or more granularly as a specific deal," says Dwyer. "Each is a varying level of zoom. The appropriate level of zoom can change based on the objectives of a company, or the role of the individual in the company."

As a startup founder, you need to be diligent about what level of zoom you choose to apply to your business and at what time. Zooming "out" too broadly too early could be fatal if you don't have a more granular view of individual customer profitability for example. You may scale yourself to the grave, spending more to acquire customers than you will ever be able to extract from them. On the other hand, as Dwyer suggests in regard to Groupon, "If you're heading towards an IPO, it might be best to focus on city roll-out versus the economics of a single deal. Zoom provides the flexibility to conduct your analysis at any level. Timing is key."

3. Value: how your business creates value for the customer

Next is value. Dwyer suggests, "Be explicit about the value you are creating and for whom. What does your product do to create value for the customer?

"For example, on one level, you could say that Groupon creates value by offering a discount over typical retail pricing. On an emotional level, you could say that Groupon enables customers to do something they couldn't have afforded otherwise. From a retailer's perspective, value could be getting consumers they couldn't get before. For a restaurant, it might be filling empty tables or incremental meals sold. By using a broader Zoom on the entire business System, you could imagine Groupon developing initiatives to improve merchant retention or the customer experience, and so on."

The goal of continually studying how you create value is vital for startups because value shifts over time. What your customers may have valued when you launched may have changed. Or since you launched, new competitors may have introduced products or services that have since leapfrogged your original value proposition leaving you in the dust. Look no further than Kodak, the Sony Walkman, or Barnes & Noble for evidence of value creation systems that are no longer as relevant as they once were.

4. Flow: stages of value creation

Related to Value is Flow (or how value is created). As Dwyer illustrates, "Flow helps you understand how customers flow through your system—the equivalent of beer going from non-existent to in a bottle. With Flow, you can then look at things such as acceptable conversion rates per stage of customer acquisition (e.g., page views required to drive clicks to submit to return to upgrade to refer, etc.)?" Flow puts the System view in motion.

5. KPIs: key performance indicators

"Once you know exactly how you create value, then you must measure it with tenacity," says Dwyer. "What is measured is improved. If you don't measure something, there is no chance it will improve. However, that doesn't mean you should measure everything. A lack of focus can dilute your influence on the metric."

There are an infinite number of things you could measure. The question is what *should* you measure: customer price of acquisition (CPA), average revenue per user (ARPU), churn, customer lifetime value, conversion, and so on. Whichever you choose, steer clear of vanity metrics. Vanity metrics are those measures that sound good but aren't something you can impact or that matter. Page views, for example, matter only if they translate into customer actions (e.g., signing up, registering, buying, etc.).

According to Dwyer, "We typically start by measuring

between one to three metrics. And then you can track, tweak, and improve. You will be shocked at the results."

6. Modeling: building future scenarios based on data

Finally, if you know you have a positive contribution margin, and you understand the exact method to create that value, then you can reasonably plot a plan to scale.

"By using unit economics," Dwyer advises, "*you're not always going to be right, but you're going to be a lot less wrong!*"

Being able to clearly explain your unit economics to an investor will put you miles ahead of a competing company that is not able to do the same. It inspires confidence that you have not only built a good product, but you have built a good business that just gets better with time. And, with increased competition, an advantage wouldn't hurt you.

And, according to Henikoff, "If you can convince investors that the unit economics work, you win."

CHAPTER SIX

GETTING CUSTOMERS TO CARE

"We listen to our customers, but what we mean by that is that we listen to sales. Ultimately we have a lot of respect for the market but we look for what is saleable and we build it. Oftentimes, entrepreneurs think too much about this stuff. You really just have to have some empathy for your customers and figure out what is saleable. When we say listen to the market, we mean what is the market willing to buy?"

Rishi Shah, Founder & CEO, ContextMedia

"MANY PEOPLE SAY ADVERTISING IS DEAD," observes John Kenny. "But, storytelling is still alive and kicking. We're living in a world where big data means we're constantly bombarded with information; we're overtargeted but underengaged. It's all about getting people's attention, and then harnessing that attention toward behavior change."

Kenny heads up strategy at FCB, a leading ad agency in Chicago. FCB provides brand expertise and marketing campaigns for everyone from blue chip companies to the Fortune 500 to startups. Key to their success is the relentless focus on creating behavior change in customers.

In this chapter, we'll talk about:

- The difference between getting customers' attention vs. getting them to act
- How to get people to change behavior (and buy your products)
- Five proven techniques to encourage behavioral change

It's All About Behavior Change

It's one thing to get a customer's attention. It's another thing to get them to buy and yet another thing to keep coming back. Many customers are perfectly happy with the status quo (even though they may complain about it now and then) and habits are hard to break.

As Kenny advises, "Research tells us that 40% of our behavior every day is done by habit. Therefore, if you're doing anything worthwhile with marketing, you've got to be working on trying to change people's habits. If you can get them to change their habits in favor of your product or service, you've struck gold. The question is how do you get people to change behavior? How do you get customers to care? Among the possible tactics, Kenny suggests, "Short form video is and has always been one of the best way to motivate behavior change. We've seen it with the 30-second ad, and now we are seeing it with online videos that have sparked viral marketing campaigns. We see short form video as a persuasive technology, but that is not the only way to create behavior change. These principles can be incorporated into any of your marketing tactics. The more effective you are at acquiring attention and turning it into habit change, the more profitable you will be as a company."

According to Kenny, sparking behavior change is the only way that you can sustain a return on your marketing activities.

But, you can't just decide one day to create behavior change. It requires intentional effort, creativity, and a discipline to achieve the desired result. Beyond the creative use of media, Kenny outlines five core components that they focus on at FCB to drive behavior change in customers.

Component 1: Appeal to great needs.

"The world is getting on fine without you," Kenny says, "Why should I spend my time with your product or service? In today's world of the Internet everywhere, smartphones in our hand, televisions everywhere we go, and social networks abounding, we are so overwhelmed with options. Therefore, we are used to making trade-offs and blocking out the noise. Due to the sheer volume of marketing messages we receive everyday, marketers need to do more than just inform of us the benefits of their product. Customers skeptically ask, *Why should I engage with you?*"

In order to get someone's attention, there are a handful of things you can do.

First, you can use *norms*. Norms are what people normally do. It is their routine, their habits, their way of life. Kenny says, "Research tells us that people are four times more likely to do something when it is framed as being consistent with something that they have already done, or already do.

"Second, you can appeal to people's *ideals*. Help people achieve what they are already trying to achieve. For example, Listerine produced a classic, extremely effective ad several decades ago that is still used as teaching material for marketers today. They created an ad that showed a woman alone at a cocktail party, couples surrounding her, and then a big quote saying 'Always the bridesmaid never the bride. How's your breath today?' The ad alluded to the fact that maybe the girl couldn't find a husband because she had bad breath and didn't know it. If you think about it, no one knows they have bad breath and no one will tell you that you have bad breath. Think about the marketing challenge. Listerine was selling a product for a need with no evidence that the problem existed. But, it appealed to an ideal that every girl in that era was trying to achieve. 'How's your breath today?' The ad implied she wasn't getting married because she had bad breath. Another example is an ad campaign launched by Morton Arboretum designed to encourage people to plant trees in their yards. The ad read: Do you know that trees increase the value of your home?"

Kenny adds, "Sometimes, it's okay to give people the wrong reason to do the right thing. Don't give them reasons why *you* think they should change, focus on what reasons they think *they* should change."

Third, you can appeal to people's fears by using *threats*. Kenny suggests, "Fear is very, very effective. People have inherent fears and learned fears. Both work magical wonders when designing an ad campaign. For example, Hyundai used this tactic very effectively in an ad. Most people think of themselves as above average. Automotive research tells us that 93% of people think they are above-average drivers. It's not arrogance, rather we simply reason that our mistakes behind the wheel have something to do with external influences (it's often the other guy's fault). When we see other people drive poorly, we blame them." Kenny asks, "So, if you are managing the Hyundai brand, how do get people who think they are above-average drivers to buy safety features for their car when they think *everyone else* needs those features?" Kenny cites a Hyundai television ad that shows teenage kids attaching themselves to a car via a bungee cord and then shooting themselves into the air attached to a tower. The voiceover in the ad then goes on to say: "Six million young adults will get their driver's license this year, better get yourself a safe car." For the 93% of people that think that they are better than average drivers, this ad told them exactly why they should fear the roads and, in turn, why they should buy a Hyundai. As the saying goes: it is easier to sell painkillers than vitamins. Sure we know vitamins are good for us, but making the pain go away (now) is more motivating.

Component 2: Create Memorable Triggers.

Beyond figuring out a customer's *great needs*, you then must remind customers that they have the need. You need to be very deliberate about making your story as memorable as possible. Kenny suggests, "Memorability isn't just about recall. In other words, to create advertising that is memorable is not just about helping people remembering your ad. Research tells us that the easier something is to remember, the more likely people are to believe it as true." Make it easy for them to remember you. Promoting an endless array of product features is the fastest way to induce sleep. Keep it simple. Make it memorable.

Marketers have the tendency to over inform their audience. It's a natural mistake. We think, *If I can quickly outline all the ways this product or service is better, and convince people to buy it, the chances of them actually buying it go up.* Ironically, that is wrong. Kenny adds, "Someone is more likely to buy something when given one good reason to buy something versus ten good reasons." People won't remember the ten reasons they should buy something. They will remember one. If you give them ten, they won't remember any. If you give them one, they might remember it. Therefore, what is the *one* reason that your product matters and should be bought, used, or invested in?

We have a hard time remember abstract concepts or

numbers. There are several ways you can get people to remember your product. "First," Kenny suggests, "You can use the *bizarre* tactic. As humans, we remember bizarre associations, people, places, and humor, especially rude humor. We're not good at remembering concepts or numbers," says Kenny. "It is more important to be irrationally distinctive than it is to be rationally better. For example, the chocolate brand Cadbury produced an ad several years ago with a gorilla playing the drums to a famous rock song. For 25 seconds of the 30-second ad, that is all it was: a gorilla playing drums, and then the Cadbury logo came up at the end of the ad. It said nothing about the quality or taste of the chocolate, but Cadbury experienced a significant sales increase. Why? People remember things that are bizarre."

Second, you can use *humor*. People love to laugh. They love humor, especially rude humor. Kenny referenced an example: "You may be familiar with the Kmart campaign called 'Ship My Pants.' Kmart wanted to advertise that you could elect to ship anything in their store directly to your home for no charge. It is not hard to persuade people that the idea is good, but it is hard to get people to remember to use the service when they're in the store. Therefore, Kmart designed a campaign that played off the very rude but very memorable humor of 'ship my pants,' 'ship my drawers,' and 'ship my bed.' The video got 25 million views, and the campaign was very successful." Humor makes your message more memorable and sharable.

Finally, you can use *people*. Dos Equis has done a masterful job with this tactic by using "The Most Interesting Man in the World." Kenny suggests, "Whenever you hear or see Dos Equis, you think of the guy with the grey hair and beard who is literally invincible. It is simple, beautiful, memorable storytelling." Tony the Tiger (Frosted Flakes), a little green lizard (GEICO), and the duck with an attitude (AFLAC) are all great examples of this.

In terms of memorability, Kenny suggests, "When you are trying to sell a client, you can always make your case based in business principles, features, cost savings, functionality, etc., but people remember stories. Stories not only make your message memorable, they make you credible. People feel they can relate to you and to your brand. Memorability doesn't just drive conversion; it drives credibility."

Component 3: Offer Simple Actions.

You have their attention, and they remember you. Now, you want them to act. You want them to invest some time and money in your product. You want them to act. So how do you drive action?

First, you must make things *simple*. This is a recurring theme in product, but it also applies to marketing. It must be very clear and straightforward for the customer to understand exactly what you want them to do. Kenny suggests, "You can focus on motivating a customer or you can focus on simplicity. Simple almost always beats motivating." For example, during the devastating earthquake in Haiti, the TEXT HAITI campaign did this superbly. The campaign asked people to simply text "HAITI" to 90999 to donate $10. Would people have given more if the campaign did not limit donations to $10? Maybe. But, it didn't matter, because that would have over-complicated the step of *action* for the individual. By having only one (accessible) amount for people to give, it eliminated the need for them to decide how much to give. Kenny advises, "Reducing friction from the customer experience is a very different creative endeavor than storytelling. But, it is just as important."

Second, like making the message fun, you can also make

the action fun. No one would say that dumping a cold bucket of water on your head is fun necessarily, but posting the video of yourself pouring a cold bucket of water on your head *was* fun. And, that is what the ALS foundation wanted. It was fun, contagious, and simple enough for anyone to do. Kenny cites Google. "Early on at Google, they turned a demo into a game with the *I'm Feeling Lucky* button. It was like playing a game with Google to see if they knew what you were searching for. Little did many know they were getting a demo of their search engine and one that also was compelling them to use it again." Kenny continues with perhaps the best marketing advice for all those who have fallen madly in love with their own products: "Don't overthink how interesting you are. You're not. Make things simple and fun."

Third, in addition to simplicity and fun, you can make things *sequenced*. Kenny says, "If you have a complex choice structure, be sure to break it down into simple steps." Chipotle does this well by having customers first pick a vehicle (tortilla or bowl), then a meat (chicken, steak, or pork), and then choose from a limited set of toppings. The customer doesn't need to make all the decisions at once. There are thousands of ways to build a burrito at Chipotle, but they have made it simple and straightforward. Sequencing actions make the overall commitment easier for customers to make. Baby steps.

Fourth, use *comparisons*. Kenny says, "When people are learning about a new product or service, they will subconsciously try to compare it with something they are familiar with. They will say (or think), *Oh, it's like BLANK*. Using this principle, Mini Cooper designed a campaign where the Mini Cooper CEO challenged the Porsche CEO to a race. Porsche accepted, and Mini Cooper lost terribly. But, it doesn't matter because they shifted the point of reference in the customer's mind from Mini Cooper being an expensive compact car to a cheap sports car. Kenny suggests, "Comparisons help you make easy choices."

There are several other ways to inspire action in customers:

Social proof: Who else is using the product? For example, video game *Dead Space 2* ran an ad showing the horrified reactions of a series of moms to the gore of the game. Social proof in this case was that mom would hate the game. The result: kids loved it.

Completion: Simply, people don't like to start things they feel that can't finish. Make it easy for them to complete whatever task you need them to take.

Scarcity: Scarcity is a marketing hallmark. Think no further than the McRib. Limit the opportunity to get the product.

Price: People associate higher price with better quality (true or not). For example, beer brand Stella Artois once ran a campaign called "Reassuringly Expensive" that included a coupon that customers could redeem in order to pay 20% *more*. They ran the coupons in discount-oriented community newspapers. It was the only ad that promoted a higher price. The coupon read: *Bring this coupon and pay an extra $1.25 for your next Stella Artois*. It fits the brand. Stella Artois is about quality. It must be because they suggest I pay more.

Immediacy: People disproportionately value immediate benefits over long-term benefits; thus the saying it's better to sell painkillers than vitamins. How do you get people to wear seatbelts, quit smoking, lose weight or save for retirement? You need to make the long-term benefits have immediate benefit. For example, save more and be entered into a contest to win *something* today. Make future benefits more accessible today.

Component 4: Give Surprising Rewards.

Now that you have customers taking action, how do we get

them to move from trying something once, to it becoming a habit?

First, people like to get stuff they don't expect. A surprising reward that is hopefully unrelated to their need. Rewards that are unexpected are 3x more motivating than rewards they know they are going to get. There was an experiment done several years ago that had kids enter a room, sit down at a table, and draw on a blank piece of paper. Half the kids were told at the beginning that they would get a piece of candy as a reward for drawing and half the kids weren't told they would get a reward at all. When the researchers tracked habits after the experiment, they discovered that the kids who got the surprise reward spent 3x more time drawing the next day than the half that got an expected reward. Kenny suggests, "People stay more loyal when they get a surprise reward. Typically, it needs to *enhance* the customer experience not undermine it. For example, if you give me 50% of my money back after I've made a purchase, it undermines my enjoyment. A lot of customer experiences are heavy-loaded with the good experiences on the front end. The start looks great but the checkout looks awful! In designing a great customer experience, how the experience *finishes* is more important than how it starts. So, consider introducing a surprise toward the end of the experience. People are so jaded by business pitches and presentations. For example, $10 off at the beginning typically means that it was probably *built into the price* in the mind of the customer. Therefore, surprise them at the end." If you do something for them that they do not expect, they will respond more favorably.

As Kenny suggests, marketers often feel like they have to dangle something shiny to drive action or discount the price of their product. "Don't always resort to discounting for your reward program," advises Kenny. He goes on to explain the overlooked opportunity marketers often miss. "The human brain responds 2,000 times more to the human smile than to a piece of *chocolate*. But, most reward programs are based on chocolate." You don't need shiny objects to market your product. Your product is your shiny object. Make it great.

Component 5: Invite Engaging Investments.
Once you've connected with a need, become memorable, have gotten them to act, and surprised them with a reward, now ask them to do something for *you*. You want them to become more than a customer. You want them to become an evangelist for your brand. How do you do that? Just as Richard Branson advises making work engaging for your employees in order to spark innovation, so too can you make your customers' relationship with you engaging. One such way to drive engagement is through allowing your customers to be more engaged in the product itself. The logic is that the more people spend time customizing their experience, the more likely they are to stay with it.

"Take IKEA, for example," suggests Kenny. "When customers spend the time and energy to build their own dresser, or desk, or couch, they feel a greater sense of pride of ownership, much more than they would if they just carried it in the door." They are invested in the experience. It's not IKEA's furniture now. It's their furniture. They have pride of workmanship. "Another example," suggests Kenny, "is giving blood. When people are given a choice of which arm they want to surrender to the nurse, they are less likely to report pain and more likely to come back and give blood again." In marketing circles, this phenomenon has become known as the *IKEA effect*, and you should harness its power. The power of giving consumers choice in their experience with your product produces pleasure for them that is remarkable.

Turning Ideas into Products and Problems into Profits

Everyone has ideas. Today, with technology, nearly anyone can turn those ideas into products. However, your goal should not only be to turn ideas into products. It should be to turn problems into profits. Inventors build products, but innovators build businesses. In order to turn your product into a business, getting customers' attention is only half the battle. You must also get them to act. Behavior change is the goal, but it's not easy. Have the tenacity to think through every detail of your customer's experience: reducing friction, being unique, and making things as simple as possible. Remember, the world is getting on fine without you. Convince them otherwise and you'll reap the rewards.

CHAPTER SEVEN

BRAND WHAT YOU STAND FOR

"It's a complicated and noisy world, and we're not going to get a chance to get people to remember much about us. No company is. So we have to be really clear about what we want them to know about us."

Steve Jobs (1997)

JOHN BATTELLE, chairman & CEO of NewCo, describes brands as "what people say about you when you are not in the room." He adds, "and that room has gotten extremely big and extremely digital." Experienced brand strategists have always understood that brands belong to customers. You may have an opinion, but your customers ultimately determine whether or not they agree with or accept or want to engage with that point of view.

Brands are about much more than messaging. A brand is a relationship your customers have with you. To quote Pam McKissick, formerly president of TV Guide: "A brand is a like a date. If you have a good time, you'll remember the name and number." That relationship is formed through not only messaging but through the product experience itself. Your product is your best salesperson. Your user experience is part of your brand experience. And brand matters, a lot.

In this chapter, we'll talk about:

- What all great brands do well
- What it means—as a brand—to have a point of view
- Developing a point of view
- Telling your story

What All Great Brands Do Well

One of the most valuable brands on the planet is Coca-Cola. In describing the value of the Coke brand to the franchise, a Coke executive once explained it this way: "If Coca-Cola were to lose all of its production-related assets in a disaster, the company would survive. By contrast, if all consumers were to have a sudden lapse of memory and forget everything related to Coca-Cola, the company would go out of business." By the end of 2014, Coca-Cola's brand was valued at $81.6 billion, ranking it the third most valuable brand on the planet. After 13 years of dominance at the #1 spot on Interbrand's list, in 2013, Coca-Cola was knocked off by two relative newcomers, technological juggernauts Google and Apple. But brands don't just happen. They are deliberately designed and manufactured ideas. After all, functionally speaking, Coke is sugar water. Apple is plastic, glass, and software. Or is it? Not only is *brand Apple* a beautiful idea, the brand itself played a leading role in one of the most stunning business turnarounds in history. It's a history worth knowing and a history worth repeating. Here's where brand Apple came from, why we love it today, and what you can learn from it.

When Steve Jobs returned to the helm at Apple in 1997, recall the company was not doing well. It had posted a net loss of $161 million. In addition to expense reduction and a focus on gross margin improvement via new products, SKU rationalization, and an aggressive restructuring plan, central to Apple's resurrection was a very deliberate and now famous focus on their brand.

Shortly after his return, Jobs took the stage in his black mock turtleneck and khaki shorts to announce what they were going to do with the brand. He went on to lay the foundation for what the world has come to know and love about the Apple brand. His words, on that day, from that stage, should be required reading for anyone and everyone in the technology business. And so we share them here with you.

"A great brand needs investment and caring if it's going to retain its relevance and vitality. And the Apple brand has clearly suffered from neglect in this area in the last few years. We need to bring it back. The way to do that is not to talk about speeds and fees. It's not to talk about MIPS and megahertz. It's not to talk about why we're better than Windows. The dairy industry tried for twenty years to convince you that milk was good for you and its sales went like this [Jobs points down]. And then they tried '*Got Milk*' and its sales went like this [Jobs points up]. *Got Milk* doesn't even talk about the product. As a matter of fact, it focuses on the *absence* of the product.

But, the best example of all is Nike. Remember, Nike sells a commodity. They sell shoes. And yet when you think of Nike, you feel something different than '*it's a shoe company.*' In their ads, they don't ever talk about the product. They don't ever tell you about their air soles and why they're better than Reebok's air soles. What does Nike do in their advertising? They honor great athletes and they honor great athletics. That's who they are. That's what they are about. Apple spends a fortune on advertising. You'd never know it [audience laugher]. And so, when I got here, Apple just fired their agency, we were doing a competition with twenty-three agencies that, you know, four years from now, we'd pick one. And so we blew that up and hired Chiat\Day...we started working about eight weeks ago.

And the question we asked was: 'Our customers want to know who is Apple? And what is it that we stand for? Where do we fit in this world?' What we're about isn't making boxes for people to get their jobs done although we do that well. We do that better than almost anybody in some cases. But Apple is about something more than that. Apple, at the core—its core value—is that we believe that people with passion can change the world for the better. *That's* what we believe. And we've had the opportunity to work with people like that. We've had the opportunity to work with people like you, with software developers, with customers who have done it—in some big and some small ways. And we believe that, in this world, people can change it for the better. And that, those people who are crazy enough to think that they *can* change the world, are the ones who actually do.

And so, what we're going to do in our first brand marketing campaign in several years is to get back to that core value. A lot of things have changed. The market is a totally different place than it was a decade ago. And Apple's totally different. And Apple's place in it is totally different. And, believe me, the products, the distribution strategy, the manufacturing are totally different, and we understand that. But values and core values—those things shouldn't change. The things that Apple believed in—at its core—are the same things that Apple really stands for today.

And so, we wanted to find a way to communicate this. And what we have is something that I am very moved by. It honors those people who have changed the world. Some of them are living. Some of them are not. But the ones that aren't—as you'll see—you know that if they would have ever used a computer, it would have been a Mac."

The audience erupts into knowing laughter as they know it's a perfect fit for their brand. After all, those values *are* their brand. Jobs continues:

> "The theme of the campaign is *Think Different*. It's honoring the people who think different and who move this world forward. It is what we are about. It touches the soul of this company. And so, I'm going to go ahead and roll it and I hope you feel the same way about it that I do."

A black and white video image of Albert Einstein appears on the screen against dramatic music, followed by images of Bob Dylan, Martin Luther King, Jr., Sir Richard Branson, John Lennon with Yoko Ono, Buckminster Fuller, Thomas Edison, Muhammad Ali, Ted Turner, Maria Callas, Mahatma Gandhi, Amelia Earhart, Alfred Hitchcock, Martha Graham, Jim Henson with Kermit the Frog, Frank Lloyd Wright, and Pablo Picasso.

As the images roll past, the narrator, actor Richard Dreyfuss, reads:

> "Here's to the crazy ones. The misfits. The rebels. The troublemakers. The round pegs in the square holes. The ones who see things differently. They're not fond of rules and they have no respect for the status quo. You can quote them. Disagree with them. Glorify or vilify them. About the only thing you can't do is ignore them. Because they

change things. They push the human race forward. And while some may see them as the crazy ones, we see genius. Because the people who are crazy enough to think that they can change the world are the ones who do."

No MIPS. No megahertz. Apple created a brand that mattered and continues to matter. It took a stand. It has meaning. It has a point of view.

Creating a Point of View

The notion of a brand having a point of view—of standing for something—is and always has been the central premise of good brand strategists, among them Suzanne Muchin, co-founder and principal at Mind + Matter Studio. "How do you build a brand that matters?" Muchin asks. "Because it *does* need to matter. As a founder, you should want what you do to matter to someone. And so, what does it mean for your brand to matter?"

According to Muchin, brands that matter need to do three things really well:

1. Have a *point of view* that turns heads (a sharp, pointy opinion);
2. Communicate a *narrative* that connects deeply with customers;
3. Establish a meaningful, authentic vision.

"Your brand," says Muchin, "is a point of view told through narrative that establishes a meaningful and authentic vision. You need to get *great* at telling your story to investors, customers, partners, and prospective employees. People often confuse branding and marketing. Branding is about knowing exactly who you are as a company. Marketing is about telling that story in a way that people will care. You cannot do well at marketing unless you've nailed branding. If you have customers of any kind, you need to brand."

Muchin warns founders to stay away from the false assumption that branding is a pitch, a list of products and services, a marketing strategy, or even a purpose statement. "A brand is not a logo or slogan," she suggests. "A brand is a point of view." Muchin approaches branding as a unifying idea, an enduring identity, a narrative, and content strategy. "Having a point of view is the secret ingredient to a great brand strategy," she suggests, "because it forces you to stand for something bigger than any particular product or service. A point of view is one that is portable, and carries through to the voice of your company across all mediums. We make sure that every company we touch has a clear idea what they are really up to—what they are all about. It's an inside-out process. And if you get it right, it's addictive to everyone from your employees to your customers. No one outside of your company will ever be able to tell you what your brand is about. It's the founder's job. Market research is good input, but it won't brand your company. Your brand is your decision. You need to ask yourself: Why do people need to know this information? And why are we the ones that should be talking about it?"

In Muchin's experience working with startups, she observes, "Startups are typically in a hurry to put a logo and slogan out there, and haven't done the hard work of thinking through their strategy, their perspective, and their unique corner on the world. Too many startups jump right to social media skipping over the need to define their brand strategy." As Muchin suggests, "You will not be successful without a brand point of view, or a brand *opinion*. A point of view is a unifying set of ideas designed for internal use. It influences the messages your brand takes to market. Unless you claim a distinct point of view (that no one else has), it's not sharp enough."

Your point of view statement should posit something provocative enough to make someone stop in his or her tracks. If it doesn't do that, then your point of view statement is not sharp enough. Muchin encourages founders to push themselves. She says, "I'd rather see you go too far out with your point of view that it makes people who hear it uncomfortable than to not go far enough. If you do that, we can always pull you back in." A point of view is something that should immediately make people question whether they agree or disagree with your position."

Telling Your Story

"Once you've established your point of view," suggests Muchin, "your next task is to build a great narrative. Essentially, when talking about your product, your service, your cause, or your company, you need the audience to nod their heads, and not stop. How do you captivate their attention to the extent that they put down their iPhones, and start to really tune in?

First, *set up the problem* in a compelling way. For example, you may say, *There are too many people experiencing (X problem)*, and then go on to explain why the stakes are too high to leave the problem unsolved. Too many companies tell their story like they are selling it to a robot. Companies and computers don't feel pain, and they don't make the decisions. People do. You have to believe that your product solves a high stakes pain point for people, and then explain it in a way that will allow your audience to resonate with the pain on a personal level.

Second, *nail your opinion*. Get good at framing things as an opinion. It's okay to say that you have a different take on how a problem should be solved. You have to be able to have an opinion about why the other solutions in the market aren't solving the problem and why their solutions aren't working."

Third, *communicate your distinctive solution.* People need to understand what you're doing about the problem, why it is a *unique* solution, and why *you* are uniquely equipped to solve it. Cast a vision about your approach that is irresistibly compelling.

Fourth, *tell me why I should care.* Explain your company, product, or service in a way that makes the customer feel a sense of connection to you. Even if they can't relate personally to the specific customer, they can feel why customers would care so much. And, only then do you earn the right to mean what you care about."

Apple, Coca-Cola, Disney, Google, Intel, Louis Vuitton, McKinsey, Mercedes-Benz, Pepsi, Volkswagen, and others have proven time and again that brands are not made by accident. They are intentional works of art. To be successful, your brand must not only establish how you are uniquely relevant to solving your customers' problems, it must also reflect what you believe as a founder and as a company. Before you fall in love with your product, take the time to take a step back and recognize that your customers are thinking, feeling, judgment-forming people. And, as Jobs did years ago, think through what you are really about. What do you value? What do you believe? What is your purpose in this world? If you can connect your brand with those thoughts, emotions, and judgments, you'll win the sale and keep them coming back for more.

BUILDING A USEFUL
FINANCIAL MODEL

"Profit is a matter of opinion. Cash is a matter of fact."

Anonymous

WHEN THE DOT-COM BUBBLE BURST in the late '90s, it wiped out $5 trillion in market value for technology companies. By 2004, more than half of the Internet companies started since 1995 had disappeared. No wonder the #1 song of 2001 was Lifehouse's "Hanging By a Moment":

> *There's nothing else to lose, there's nothing else to find*
> *There's nothing in the world that can change my mind*

It may have been a good year for an American rock band from Los Angeles, but there could *not* have been a worse time to be a cash-starved startup from Chicago. Yet Troy Henikoff had already made the trip to the Silicon Valley to raise money for his online payroll processing company, SurePayroll.

"In 1999," Henikoff recalls, "we decided it was time to move payroll online. Our business model was simple. We were going to spend $400 in direct marketing to get customers whose lifetime value was $5,000. *That* was the business.

That was our plan. And so we took our pitch out to the venture community. Our first meeting was on a Monday morning with a big name venture firm on Sand Hill Road. There were ten VCs in the room and four of us. Two slides into our pitch one of the partners stopped me and said, 'Which one of you is the payroll expert?' As experienced entrepreneurs, we each responded by saying the same thing, 'Well I had to run payroll at my last company...so did I...and so did I...and....' With that, the partner responded with 'You guys don't know what you don't know! This meeting is over.'

Troy and his team were then exited out of the room.

"And so we needed a *second new plan*," Henikoff recalls with bulldog determination. "The first thing we did was scour the industry for a payroll expert and within a few weeks we found one and hired him. In April 2000, we then went back out to Sand Hill Road. We had great meetings on Monday, okay meetings on Tuesday (although, during the meetings, everyone was on their Blackberrys), but by Wednesday we learned that the market had been dropping by 350 points a day. We then knew why they were on their Blackberrys the day before! The VCs saw that the end was near and they were scrambling to save what they had already invested in. By Friday, they were cancelling meetings with us. It was the week the bubble burst. And so, we needed a *third new plan*.

"Plan number three was to fund with the best capital there is: *customer capital* (aka revenue). And so we did a deal with CitiBank. At the time CitiBank had 300,000 small business customers and wanted something that was sticky. Payroll is sticky. It could keep customers from switching to other banks. And so we co-branded with them to provide CitiBank small business customers with online payroll services. In each monthly bank statement that CitiBank sent to its 300,000 small business customers, they would put a slip of paper (an ad) with a big (800) number in red letters (a call to action) asking people to call to enroll in SurePayroll. We were fired up! Think about it. This was not junk mail. These were the opposite of junk mail: *bank statements*. 100% of the 300,000 envelopes would be opened, likely by the business owner, the CFO, or someone who had responsibility for making the financial decisions for services including payroll. This was the best marketing we could get. This was going to be the break that we had been waiting for. And so, we staffed up! We hired a bunch of temporary employees to answer the phones the day the statements were to be mailed. There was *no way* the four of us could handle the volume of 300,000 customers calling in to sign-up for our service. I don't remember exactly how many *calls* we got but I'll never forget how many customers we got from that campaign: *two*.

"That led to our *fourth new plan*. This time we were going to go with a sales approach versus marketing—inside sales-people working the phones. This changed our financial model from $400 in direct marketing spend in order to get a cus-tomer with an lifetime value of $5,000 to $1,200 in sales costs to acquire customers with an LTV of $4,000. This was an entirely new model, but the numbers worked. Like CitiBank, Wells Fargo Bank had been processing payroll for many of its small business customers because knew that customers who used more of their products and services (checking, savings, payroll, etc.) tended to stick around longer. The year was 2000 and it was time to move from legacy systems to processing payroll over the Internet. Wells Fargo sent out a request for proposals (RFP) from online payroll providers. As the RFP process progressed we were optimistic. The field was narrowed to just three companies and we were the only one with the technology already working and in-market. However the other two companies were *much* more experienced at payroll.

We were still novices.

"Meanwhile, in parallel, our fundraising was progressing. We had a syndicate from Chicago that was going to be led by Kettle Partners and Mark Achler. At one of our meetings, Mark inquired about our progress and since I was in sales mode, I told him that I thought it was going well and that we were going to get the contract. I had not even finished my sentence before I realized that I had just made a big mistake. Mark immediately replied with 'Bring me a signed agreement with them and we'll sign the term sheet.'

"And so we needed a *fifth new plan*. We had to get Wells Fargo to work with *us* in order to get the venture capital investment to work with Wells Fargo! If we couldn't get Wells Fargo, we would be out of business. And so we dramatically cut our pricing in our response to the RFP and won the business. In fact, we even ended up getting Wells Fargo as a co-investor in our $8 million Series A round that we closed on January 6, 2001."

There is an adage in the venture business: entrepreneurs *will* the world into existence. At its core, entrepreneurship is a fancy word for *hard work*. To quote Elon Musk, "Optimism, pessimism, *fuck* that! We're going to make it happen. As God as my bloody witness, I'm hell-bent on making it work." Like Musk, there are few entrepreneurs with as much will power as Henikoff. The question is, beyond will and hard work, how did Henikoff recover and, to use Musk's words, "make it work?" Apart from the VC meeting that had ended prematurely at slide two, how did the conversations go with the subsequent investors in the wake of the dot-com bubble?

"Risk aversion was running rampant among the venture community," recalls Henikoff, "and so in every pitch, inevitably investors would ask us to talk more about our financial model. Specifically they wanted to know more about our assumptions and apparent risks. I'd say, *Great, I would love to talk more about our model. In fact, I've got a very detailed structure of how it was built. Let's schedule 90 minutes with you, me and your associate and I'll walk you through it.* They'd typically asked if I'd just send the model to them. Never do that. I'd say, *I want to save you time* (make it matter for them, they are your customer), *believe me, it would be much better if I walked you through it so that we can address your questions as they come to your mind. And then, I'll leave a copy with you.*

"Typically, they'd agreed and so we'd meet.

"By showing we had good rationale behind each component of our projections based on what we had learned from our several new plans, it demonstrated we had command of our business and a sophisticated understanding of how to drive performance and solve problems when they occurred. This made an inherently risky investment seem less risky. We were able to shine not only because of the problem we wanted to solve but also because of how thorough we had been in constructing our financial model and communicating it to investors. We knew what hadn't worked and what would likely work, given assumptions and experience.

"As a result, at that point 100% of the people who sat down with me to walk through the financials either wrote a check or offered to write a check." (*Read that sentence again. 100%*). Henikoff's tenacity (and his model) ultimately paid off in 2011 (11 years from being kicked out of a VC's office on Sand Hill Road) when rival Paychex acquired SurePayroll for $119 million (an 8x return to shareholders).

What's important to learn from Henikoff is that while his business was the result of will and determination, their nine-figure exit all began and evolved with the aid of an evolving financial model, a model that Henikoff continued to tweak, improve, and adjust accordingly based on what he and his team had been learning in the market.

It's why—to this day—Henikoff advises all of the founders he backs as a venture capitalist and those he mentors to invest the time to build and then update their financial models regularly.

In this chapter, we'll talk about:

- Definition of a financial model (what it is and what it isn't)
- Purpose of a financial model
- What investors want to see (and what you need to show them)
- Why cash > profit
- 17 rules of thumb when building your financial model

What is a financial model?

"First, as a founder, you need to understand that your financial model is not the same as your financial projections," says Henikoff. "A lot of startup founders make this mistake. *Your projections are the outputs of your model. Forecasts are not models.*" Projections are useful for existing businesses with existing business models that have been proven over decades to work, but not for startups that are *trying to figure out what works.*

"For example," explains Henikoff, "if you were running a business unit for IBM, each year you would be told to provide a pro forma. And so, you'd add 4% to everything you did last year and hand that in. That's putting it simply but that is sort of how it really works. In a startup you don't have a clue. Everyone knows your forecasts are wrong. But your financial model is not a forecast. It's your business."

What is the purpose of a financial model?

Your job as a startup founder is figure out what the drivers of your business are. You're not a Fortune 500 company that already knows what drives performance. You are, hopefully, an aspiring Fortune 500 company in the making. A financial model is the best (and the least costly) tool you have to figure it out. It provides a number of benefits for your startup, including the ability to:

- Run 'what if' scenarios
- Communicate with investors in their language
- Iterate quickly and cheaply
- Identify what you should focus on and what you shouldn't focus on
- Determine what are the real drivers of your business

1) Playing 'what if?'

A good financial model allows you to represent how your business really works on a spreadsheet and create scenarios to understand the impact of decisions you could make. For example, *What if we hired another sales rep? What if we increased price by 15%? What if we decreased marketing spend 10%? What impact would these decisions have on our business?* You don't have to actually *do* these things to understand their impact on your business. You can model them.

2) Speaking their language

Financial modeling is not only a mathematical exercise. It's a communications exercise. If you can't explain your model you likely can't explain your business, at least not to an investor. "Investors speak a particular language," explains Henikoff. "If you are going to communicate with them, you have to communicate in their language. Their language includes income statements, balance sheets, and cash flows. That's what they really care about. That's what they know. A big piece of financial modeling is about you understanding how to speak their language not just the spreadsheets, but how you communicate your ideas.

As Henikoff advises, "Once you've made it clear in your pitch that you realize the projections are estimates of what would be (given certain assumptions), then the conversation with the investor can focus more on how *wrong* the projections are versus whether or not your business is a viable business or not." Everyone knows your projections are wrong, including you. Be honest. It's meant to encourage discussion. You want investors to ask questions. That is your chance to show them you know what you're doing.

"When I was out sharing the model for SurePayroll," recalls Henikoff, "I would open every meeting with the same thing. I'd say: *The only thing I know for sure about the model I'm about to show you is that it's wrong.* This allowed me to illustrate to them that I know the model is based on assumptions and that the meeting was a chance to talk about the assumptions. I'd say: *This is my best shot at what the next five years are going to look like. Let's look at the assumptions.*" The worse thing you can do when pitching an investor is to get defensive of your model. After all, no one can predict the future. But you can make relatively safe predictions given conservative assumptions. It's fine to let the investor know your model is built upon assumptions.

3) Iterate quickly and cheaply

Another benefit of a strong financial model is that it allows you to figure out where the failure points are. You don't need to fail in the market when you can fail on a spreadsheet. As Henikoff advises, "A good financial model will show you whether or not you have a business worth pursuing, much less investing in." Use it to test assumptions quickly.

4) Determine what to focus on and what not to focus on

Much like understanding your unit economics, a sound financial model allow you to determine what to focus on and what not to focus on. For example, as Henikoff has observed, "Part of the reason we are entrepreneurs is that we like to control our destiny. We tend to gravitate to the details to the things we can control; things like rent and free furniture. That's great and all, but that's not going to add value. The thing you need to be maniacally focused on is revenue and the costs of getting that revenue." Your financial model will make this glaringly obvious to you if it is not already.

5) Determine the drivers of your business

The ultimate goal of a financial model is that it will eventually help you figure out what drives success in your business. By creating *what if* scenarios, you can play around with increasing or decreasing spend on marketing or sales, increasing or decreasing pricing, adding or subtracting a specific channel partner or reseller and see what the impact would be on your overall costs of customer acquisition and thus, in turn, how much capital you will need to raise to fund your venture, and so on. After a while you will begin to identify contradictions, inconsistencies, efficiencies, and ultimately levers that will drive growth.

What Investors Want to See (and What You Need to Show Them)

"What do investors really care about most?" asks Henikoff. "You might say your underlying assumptions, expenses, profit, or the exact date and time you're going to run out of money. They are all important, but they are not the *most* important. Through my years of experience as an entrepreneur and now venture investor, I will tell you that nine times out of ten, venture investors look first at *revenue.* Revenue generation is the most important part of the business to the investor.

"Expenses can always be managed, cut, and changed. You might say, *But we just signed a $10,000 per month lease on some office space.* That is a fixed expense. No it's not. There is no such thing as a fixed expense. If things go terribly wrong and you need to get out of the lease (respectfully), you can find a way. If you believe the revenue line, you can believe the rest can work itself out. Unfortunately, revenue is the most difficult thing to predict, the most difficult thing to control, and is also the reason most businesses fail.

"As an investor in startups, when you show it to me, I know that the revenue line is bullshit. But, I want to see how you came up with your numbers. Also, I want to see what direct costs are involved in creating that revenue. For example, you customer lifetime value needs to be more than your cost to acquire that customer. Not right away, but eventually. Display a thoughtful process of how you came up with your revenue line and you will have driven the ball to the red zone with the investor."

Cash > Profit

Keep focused on cash. In an early stage company, cash is more important than profit. As they say, profit is a matter of opinion, but cash is a matter of fact. As Henikoff explains, "You have flexibility about when you record expenses. *'Do I expense the computer I just bought now or depreciate it over three years?'* If you take an expense up front, you'll show less profit today. If you take it over three years, you'll show less profit over three years. Two accountants could look at a similar business and come up with two different profit numbers. Profit can be made to look however you want it to look. It is an opinion."

Cash, on the other hand, is not an opinion. You can't argue how much cash you have. You have it or you don't have it. "As a startup, cash is like oxygen," says Henikoff. "The moment you run out of cash, you're done. Ultimately, there is only one reason investors will give you cash. They expect to get more in return while minimizing their risk. People think of venture investors as big risk takers. They're not. The best venture investors are good at minimizing risk in an inherently risky environment." Your goal with the financial model is to help them think they're minimizing their risk.

Rules of Thumb in Building Your Financial Model

While there are endless finance and accounting books, here are some general guidelines on building your financial model that are most relevant to early stage companies. Think of these as rules of thumb, those things that are most important that aren't highlighted in books (and in many cases don't show up in books at all!).

1. Start with assumptions (e.g., size of market, comps from other businesses, published industry averages, your mentors' experiences running their own businesses, etc.).
2. Then build your income statement.
3. Fully-load your numbers. For example, when you have employees, running at full scale, you may think you have an employee at $50k but you may be overlooking expenses (state income tax, federal, FICA, 401(k), etc.). In which case, you're missing 30% of the real number. That's what it is. It's always 30%. Again, remember, this is your opportunity to demonstrate clear and logical thinking. If you think it's only $50k

for example, you'll look naïve and it will raise questions about your abilities.

4. There is no such thing as a fixed cost. Call them indirect expenses. Anything and everything is negotiable. Nothing is fixed. You don't want to create that mindset. Again, remember, cash is oxygen.

5. When you're working with complicated financial models, label all of your assumption cells. They are much easier to interpret (e.g., SalesPerRep not cell "D16").

6. Do not hard type any numbers in your detail pages. Nothing is hard typed with the exception of things that are absolutes (e.g., 12 months in a year, etc.).

7. Every time you add something, you need to think through what other costs will be associated with adding it. For example, every time you add a sales rep, you need to add the associated commissions, computer, desk costs and other expenses for that rep.

8. You can't outsource building your financial model. You can hire an accountant to help you construct it, but you need to be heavily engaged. You need to do the work.

9. The person who built your financial model has to be in the investor presentations. The only thing worse than not knowing how your financial model works is in proving your ignorance in front of a potential investor! If you don't know it, have someone in the meeting that does (and it can't be your outsourced accountant).

10. Don't use financial models off the Internet. You have to build them from the ground up. You'll only end up wasting time trying to shoehorn your business into someone else's financial model that you do not really

understand. And it will be obvious.

11. Every month take two hours to tweak your model based on what you're learning. And then, once a year build a new model from the ground up. By dedicating two hours per month to tweak things and understand what the real drivers were, then by the time you need to build your next model, you'll be up to speed and so much smarter!

12. As you learn, put in the actuals and see how they compare to your forecasts. You'll find out what assumptions were right and which were wrong. This will help you going forward.

13. When investors ask you where you got your numbers, you need to have good answers. Did you use comps of other companies? If so, who were they and why are they the right comps? Whatever you do, don't use some large publicly traded company to determine your numbers. Who cares if Walmart only spends 0.4% of revenue on marketing? You're not Walmart. You're a startup. You'll spend 1,000 times revenue on marketing in the early days.

14. Early stage investors generally will not run Net Present Value calculations. They will however ask for your data. Typically they'll take your bottom line and plug it into their tools and run their own analytics.

15. You *can* get too granular. You should have the back-up there if it is requested, but you don't need to show it all at once. Put it in your Details page. For example, a rule of thumb is to have 18-20 rows on each statement (each row can then have a ton of backup). But keep the statements relatively clean and concise.

16. After you've built the model, step back and do a sniff test. For example, can one sales rep actually cover 200

stores in 15 minutes? Is that even physically possible? Just because it works on a spreadsheet doesn't mean it will translate into real life.

17. Emerson Spartz told me the best lists were odd-numbered lists, thus why this one is here. (You'll get that after you read *Chapter Twelve: The Science of Going Viral*).

Starting a business is hard enough. Don't make it harder by making mistakes in the market that you could have learned on a spreadsheet. Sure, some things you'll only learn by launching. But, contrary to popular startup folklore, you don't need to fail in order to learn. You can learn to avoid failure. Nick Rosa of Sandbox Industries puts it best: "It's okay to make mistakes. Just don't make the same mistakes. Make new mistakes." One way to avoid mistakes is to surround yourself with mentors, advisors, and other entrepreneurs who have experience and have likely already made the mistakes. But another way is to model scenarios to determine the likelihood of something working or not. A good financial model is not only a way to figure out how to *make* money; it is a great way to figure out how not to lose it. Math works.

CHAPTER NINE

LEGAL ISSUES FOR ENTREPRENEURS

"The life of the law has not been logic; it has been experience."
Oliver Wendell Holmes

ESTHER BARRON IS THE Harry B. Reese Teaching Professor of Law and the Director of the Entrepreneurship Law Center in the Bluhm Legal Clinic at the Northwestern University School of Law. She plays an active role in advising startups out of Techstars and elsewhere, helping them on a variety of important topics and documents in their early days. Having worked with startups for such a long time, she has seen how important it is for new ventures to understand certain legal issues from the beginning.

Although there are many important legal issues for entrepreneurs to consider, the three topics discussed in this chapter are critically important for startup founders.

In this chapter we'll talk about:

- Trademark Law
- Contracts
- Hiring Workers

Trademark Law

Your brand is a trademark and it is important for your new company to protect its brand through trademark law. It can be one of your company's most valuable assets. Says Barron, "Think about Nike. They make good shoes, but perhaps not that much better than anyone else could make if they tried. But, the fact that Nike is the only one who can put 'Nike' or the *Swoosh* on their shoes gives them an enormous brand advantage, allowing them to charge a higher price. If Nike had no trademark protection on the word 'Nike' or the swoosh design, their brand would likely be worth significantly less than what it is today."

The best time to think about trademark law is when you are first starting your business. Sometimes, founders believe they may want to change their branding eventually, and therefore don't do any trademark work up front. The downside is that your company could take off (with its current branding in place) before you have a chance to do that, and then it may be too late. Barron adds, "Changing your mark would be costly in more ways than one because customers would have loyalty to a brand name you are changing. I've met with founders who decided not to pursue trademark protection early on, and later regret it. On their second or third companies, that's one of the first things they do!"

You want to think about trademark law from two perspectives: offensive and defensive. The offensive perspective is thinking through the proposed name of your product or brand to see how likely it is that you could *obtain* trademark protection—is it a strong mark? The defensive perspective involves a search and assessment of potentially similar marks being used by third parties in related industries in order to determine how likely it is that you could *defend* your trademark if someone sues your company for trademark infringement down the road.

Offensive Perspective

The goal is to pick a name for which you can obtain trademark protection so that you can stop others from using that name (or something close) in a related industry. The test for trademark infringement is "the likelihood of customer confusion." Barron suggests, "If another company is using your brand name in a way that causes customers to be unclear whether the source of the product or service is your company or the other company, it is grounds for trademark infringement." Some names or marks are entitled to stronger protection than others (see our discussion below on the continuum of strength for different types of marks).

Defensive Perspective

Companies should also focus on the defensive perspective because they don't want to be forced to change their name or brand down the road. Finding out a year after launch that another company already had trademark rights in your brand and can essentially force your company to "cease" using that particular name can cause massive damage to the value of your company. Entrepreneurs do not want to have to redo efforts in creating brand good will and customer recognition, which is what can happen when they are forced to change a brand name and basically start over from a marketing angle. VCs interested in investing in a startup almost always care about trademark protection.

Acquiring Trademark Rights

You can acquire trademark rights simply by using the name or mark in commerce without doing anything further. These rights are automatic and are called *common law trademark rights*. However, the rights are limited to the geographic area in which you are doing business. Federal trademark rights are stronger and broader.

Getting a federally registered trademark is relatively easy and cheap, especially considering the value it provides. Application fees to register a mark with the USPTO are currently either $275 or $325 depending on which application form you choose. "The only times I would not automatically recommend pursuing a federal trademark registration," says Barron, "is if (i) my client intends to stay local (in which case common law rights exist without registering), but which is pretty rare these days, (ii) I believe the application will be rejected on account of the fact that the proposed mark is "merely descriptive" or otherwise not able to be federally-registered, or (iii) if I think the application will likely be rejected based on a conflict from a prior registered mark in a sufficiently related industry and know my client would still choose to move forward with that name (which I would not recommend)."

Knockout Searches

When picking a name, you may ask your legal team to do a "knockout search." Your legal team will then conduct online searches on the proposed names you are considering to determine what third parties may be using similar marks in related industries. The purpose of the knockout search is to eliminate names that have obvious conflicts. Law firms generally charge between $500 (on the low end) to $3,000 per searched name, so choose your list wisely—otherwise, you can spend a lot of money. You can do free basic trademark searches on www. uspto.gov for registered marks and Google for marks that may not have been registered, but still could have common law rights. Says Barron, "If you haven't spent six to eight hours researching whether or not you think you can get trademark protection for your mark, you haven't done enough. A Google search alone won't suffice. A GoDaddy domain search won't suffice either."

You'll never have a 100% clean search. However, if you want even more information, you can order a commercial search report that provides additional information that might not be available through online searches alone. "If you do find a company that is using the same or a similar name," advises Barron, "you should ask the following questions:

1. How close is the mark?
2. How strong is the mark?
3. How similar is the industry?
4. How similar are the customers?
5. How big is the company?
6. Do they have a federally registered mark?

Then, based on the answers to those questions, you can make a business decision on whether or not it's a good strategy to proceed with trying to register the mark with the USPTO. Knowing early where you stand in relation to your ability to get trademark protection is important!"

The Continuum of Strength for Marks

Generic Terms
You cannot get trademark protection on generic words. "For example," says Barron, "if you call your company Water, and you are selling water, you can't get federal trademark protection. Note though if you call your company Water, and you are selling hand lotion, you may be able to get federal trademark protection."

Descriptive Marks

Descriptive marks are not entitled to immediate trademark protection. If the mark describes the product or service, the company must first establish what is called "secondary meaning," which basically means the customer recognizes the mark and connects it to the product or service. "For example," offers Barron, "the application to register Vitamin Water (water infused with vitamins) was initially rejected by the United States Patent and Trademark Office (USPTO) when the company filed for trademark because it was considered a descriptive mark."

From a business standpoint, having a descriptive trademark can be attractive because you don't have to explain the product to customers. It is obvious what it is. However, from a legal perspective, trademark rights are more difficult to acquire and more complicated to protect.

Suggestive Marks

A suggestive mark suggests meaning but doesn't explicitly state it. Esther offers, "A Techstars company, SpotHero, I believe is a suggestive mark. It does not explicitly state what the product or service does ("parking spot reservation system")—it needs more explanation." Suggestive marks are often a great compromise between marketing and legal goals. They suggest some attribute of the product or service, but are still relatively strong marks."

Arbitrary Marks

An arbitrary mark is using a word (or series of words) that are real things, but not used in the traditional or expected way. "For example," says Barron, "Apple is an arbitrary mark in the context of selling computers and phones. However, apple would be generic (and thus not entitled to any trademark protection) in the context of selling fruit. Using "apple" to identify a computer is arbitrary, and is entitled to strong trademark protection."

Fanciful Marks

A fanciful mark is one that is completely made up. Twitter would be an example. Xerox would be another. The name of the product or brand is completely unique and has no reference to an actual word. "These trademarks are the strongest kind that you can have," suggests Barron, "because infringement tends to be obvious and irrefutable."

> **Side Note #1:** Slogans can get trademark protection as well. For example, "Just Do It" from Nike.

> **Side Note #2:** Once you start using your name in public for your product or service, you are eligible for a common law trademark, which means that you are "claiming rights" for the name of that product. When doing this, you can use the TM without actually having a federally registered trademark. You can only use the ® if you actually have the registered trademark issued to you by the USPTO. So, why would you go to the trouble of getting a registered trademark? TM, among other things, only gives you local protection in the market in which you are operating."

Contracts

Contracts can be great assets and they can be great liabilities. Barron strongly encourages founders to take the time to fully understand every contract they are signing or considering signing. It can be a matter of life and death (for your company, in most cases). Barron suggests, "The boilerplate stuff is really important! Don't skip over the end of the contract with all the stuff that looks like standard information. That could contain the most important part of the contract and potentially should be negotiated." Here are a few areas from Barron's experience where there can be "tricks" in the boilerplate sections of a contract and how she advises you manage these issues.

Term: Pay careful attention to the term of the contract. Look for "automatically renewable unless 30 days' notice." If you don't remember to give 30 days' notice that you don't want to renew the contract, it will automatically renew and you'll have another one or multiple-year term added to the contract. Contracts should only be term agreements with no automatic renewal unless it is to your advantage to have them automatically renew (e.g., your business provides services or licenses software and for the most part you are going to want to retain your customers year-over-year).

Ownership: Pay careful attention to who owns the work that you or an independent contractor created. Look for "your intellectual property is yours, unless we make modifications" because they will always make modifications. If they do, then it is theirs. It can be the smallest modification, and it could fall under this clause.

Choice of Law and Venue: People think, "who cares," because all the laws are the same. This important part of a contract determines where a court proceeding would happen if there were a lawsuit filed. So, for example, if the company you're working for happens to be in Texas, then any dispute would be resolved in a Texas courtroom. That means you'd need to travel there and engage legal counsel licensed to practice law in Texas. So, if they sue you, you are less likely to fly to Texas and refute it. So, I recommend instituting an "If I sue you, I'll go to you and if you sue me, you come to me" clause. This prevents frivolous lawsuits where the other side of the contract can take advantage of the geographic hassle.

Indemnification: This provision typically requires that you pay for bad stuff that happens to the other side on account of your actions or breach of the contract. Sometimes you can't get it out of the contract, but at least you can make it reciprocal. Often, the company will want to just take it out. Ask for reciprocity in contracts. It usually defuses things.

Personal Guarantee: Try to never do it. Always look for them. They are often hidden in contracts (such as, for example, equipment leases). It removes all the personal limited liability protection you got from setting up your corporation or LLC. You are now personally liable for any debts the company incurs related to the personal guarantee. You may have to do it with bank loans, but try to avoid it in all other contexts.

Limitations on Liability: This puts a "cap" on what you can owe the other side if something goes wrong. A good rule of thumb is to institute a limitation on liability that is equal to the amount you paid them or they paid you. For example, if they pay you $20,000 to do a job and something goes wrong, the most you can ever owe them is the $20,000 they paid you to do the job. If you don't have a limitation on liability clause in the contract, the liability may be unlimited.

Contract negotiation is all about leverage. If you really, really need this contract, then you may not want to negotiate too hard. If you are a startup looking to enter into a business relationship with a Fortune 100 company, you may have to live with their form contract that, in all likelihood, will be rather one-sided in their favor. That's fine. But, at least be aware of and understand the risks you are taking.

Hiring Workers

Startups typically want to hire people as independent contractors and not employees because they think it is cheaper. That can *sometimes* be true. But, oftentimes it is in your best interest to hire employees. "Also," says Barron, "there is a legal distinction between employees and independent contractors so it is important to classify workers correctly. This is true even if someone wanted to be treated as a contractor and you are in agreement. If they don't fit the legal requirements of an independent contractor, you could be in big trouble. There are long standing public policies in place to protect workers. For instance, you have to pay someone minimum wage. So, the government won't allow companies to pay people as independent contractors to avoid paying minimum wage or offering other required protections and benefits. If it is obvious that you are using contractors to implement that tactic, you could be fined an amount that definitely makes it not worth it."

The IRS sets forth the most commonly used test on how to classify workers (Google "SS8 form" to help determine whether or not a person is a contractor or employee). You can complete the form before hiring the person and send it in, it will tell you how you should classify the worker. You can also just use the form to gain insight on how the IRS would view the worker.

Says Barron, "There are three basic considerations that you can apply to determine whether or not someone is an employee or a contractor (from a legal standpoint):

- *Financial Control*: How are you paying them? If you are paying them by hour, then it looks more like employee. If you are paying reimbursements for work tools (computers, phones, etc.), it looks like an employee. But, if it is a set amount of money for specific deliverables under a certain timeline, then it looks like a contractor.
- *Behavioral control*: Telling them how to act, where

to be, when to be there, how to do their job, how to dress, etc. looks more like an employee. An independent contractor relationship tends to be based on timeline and deliverables. Therefore, you don't care where they work, when they work, or if they are wearing pajamas.

- *Relationship of the parties*: One of the best ways to show that an individual is an independent contractor is to demonstrate that they are doing work for other companies and organizations. If they are working only for your company, then it looks like an employee. If they are working 40+ hours per week only for your company, the argument that the individual should be classified as an employee becomes even stronger."

There is nuance in how to handle a contractor and an employee when it comes to intellectual property. "When someone is an employee, you may automatically own what they create," says Barron. "When someone is a contractor, they typically own what they create (if they don't sign something saying that they don't own it or assigning it to you). So, when you hire someone to design your website, logo, create content, etc., make sure they sign something saying that *you* own the work once complete. If not, you only have a license to use what they created."

With employees, you need to do tax withholding, pay worker's comp, abide by employment laws, etc., so it is understandable why startups want to hire contractors. However, hiring employees can create more loyalty, you can control their behavior more, and you own what they create. So, there are great reasons to do both, you just need to weigh which one is best for the role and for the position (making sure it meets all the legal requirements).

Internships

If someone is an employee, you have to pay them at least the government-mandated minimum wage. You can't have them work full time, call them an intern, and pay them $0, even if that is what the intern wants (to add to their resume, for example). There is a Federal act that lays out six standards of how an intern can be classified as an intern.

(Source: http://www.dol.gov/whd/regs/compliance/whdfs71.pdf)

1. The internship, even though it includes actual operation of the facilities of the employer, is similar to training which would be given in an educational environment;
2. The internship experience is for the benefit of the intern;
3. The intern does not displace regular employees, but works under close supervision of existing staff;
4. The employer that provides the training derives no immediate advantage from the activities of the intern; and on occasion its operations may actually be impeded;
5. The intern is not necessarily entitled to a job at the conclusion of the internship; and
6. The employer and the intern understand that the intern is not entitled to wages for the time spent in the internship.

"Basically," explains Barron, "an intern needs to be a sacrifice for the company, not an asset. A company isn't getting free work; it's more of a burden than anything." You are teaching them something, helping them grow and learn. You're the one doing the work.

While there are many legal issues you should discuss with your attorneys as you start and scale your business, at a minimum protect your mark, always know what you're signing, and be careful in how you account for those who you hire to do work for you. As Barron points out, however, the best legal defense is a good offense. *"Be nice to people,"* she says. "Ninety percent of lawsuits filed are a result of a simple action that did not get handled well by a manager. Being good to people, returning phone calls, emails, etc. can save you lots of time and money in the long run."

CHAPTER TEN

OPTIMIZING CUSTOMER ACQUISITION

"The currency of an early stage business isn't revenue or profit, it's learning."

Kent Goldman, First Round Capital

"WHEN BUILDING THINGS FROM SCRATCH," says Joel Grossman, SVP of Technology & Operations at Leapfrog Online, "most businesses today (specifically tech businesses) have a lot of internal complexity and they interact with human beings who demonstrate complex behavior. The intersection of what you're building and how people interact with it is a pretty complicated thing. When it comes to acquiring customers for your business, the most important thing you can do is to understand what's taking place. The challenge is not building it, but *understanding* it."

Leapfrog specializes in web conversion for large corporations in telecommunications, financial services, home services, and other industries.

In this chapter, we'll talk about:

- The importance of having a good conversion equation
- Building a testing culture
- Understanding your conversion funnel

From Prospects to Customers

In order to develop effective strategies for converting interested consumers into committed customers, Grossman maintains three core principles.

Principle 1: Have a Good Conversion Equation

There is a huge amount of information coming at you as a founder. You need to know what is most important. You need a way to separate signal from noise. One way to do that is to build systems that can help you *understand* what is going on in your business; systems that can help you learn. And these systems must be designed around metrics. Otherwise how will you know what's working and what's not?

According to Grossman, there are two metrics that matter most in early stage companies:

1. Cost of customer acquisition (cost of acquiring new customers)
2. Lifetime customer value (how much money you make on a customer over time)

Each marketing tactic will vary in its effect on *cost per acquisition* (CPA). According to Grossman, "The cost spectrum ranges from Super Bowl ads (very expensive) to customer referral (free)." Although nothing in life is really free. It's *free* because you've built a great product that people love so much they have to talk about it. Advertising is simply the price you pay for being unoriginal. But in competitive markets, you need to advertise. You need to get the word out. The question is: What are you willing to pay to acquire customers? The answer to this is largely dependent on how much money you can make on those customers over time. Says Grossman, "It might make sense to pay a lot for a customer initially if the

LTV is high (at least as high as the acquisition cost). Don't look only in the short-term."

The goal of a great customer acquisition strategy is to spend the least to acquire the most customers with the highest LTV. It's not about acquiring *any* customer. It's about acquiring the *right* customer; customers whose lifetime value will far exceed your cost to get them as customers.

Troy Henikoff puts it simply. "If CPA < LTV, you have a serious business. If CPA > LTV, you have a serious problem." The only reason you would accept CPA costs to be larger than your LTV is if your CPA costs decrease substantially over time with scale while your LTV remains the same or increases. If you can get this equation right, you can bootstrap your way to success. Growth is always best funded by revenue. The irony is that the better you do this, the less venture capital you are going to need to raise, and the more people are going to want to invest in you. Get this equation right before you start spinning up volume. Losses aren't good. Accelerated losses are worse.

Principle 2: Build a Testing Culture

"One of the most important thing you can do as an early stage founder," says Grossman, "is to build a testing culture. It should be a cultural imperative to test like crazy. You will have plenty of times when you are being pressured to make a decision, you have a feeling in your gut, your team really wants a specific thing, your customers are telling you something, etc. There will be plenty of opportunities to be swayed. Therefore, you need to get in the practice in having your team 'make a call' based on an experiment." The scientific method has been around since Aristotle. Use it. It works.

The Testing Process

> *Step 1*: Generate Hypotheses. "I think that if we do x, y will happen."

> *Step 2*: Establish an Overall Evaluative Criterion. "What is the one thing that will make your hypothesis valid or invalid?" Not five things.

> *Step 3*: Test. Rinse. Repeat.

"You want to make experiments dependent on small things that are contained," says Grossman, "not generalities. Create pass/fail tests with objective outcomes. You can't say, *We are going to test how well these 5 words convert...* You always get an answer, but it doesn't tell you anything. That is a bad test. If you can't decide what is pass and what is fail before the test, don't do it. A better test would be, *We think that $100 in CPC marketing on Facebook should result in five new customers.* If you don't meet the goal, the experiment failed.

If founders disagree on the validity of an idea, *don't* argue. Just test it. Always test it. Stop talking about it; try it. Data has the right answer. If you don't do this, you'll always follow the *HIPPO* (highest paid person's opinion). A culture of testing is essential to avoiding that from happening. Fights are now opportunities to learn. Resolve disagreements with a test!"

Principle 3: Understand Your Conversion Funnel

A *conversion funnel* is a framework that describes the specific steps you take to sell your product. Every business has its own conversion funnel.

In Grossman's experience, "Sometimes, founders look at this like a linear process (a sequence of web pages) which is almost *never* the case. A conversion funnel is non-linear. Customers in today's world have a variety of inputs impacting their buying decisions all happening at the same time. The sale is not happening in a vacuum. People don't follow a particular course for every purchase decision. So, you can't control the path. But, you can start to acknowledge patterns of how it happens and try to optimize your product and conversion process to be conducive to the patterns that cause conversions. You need to make measurements of the individual steps that are required to close a sale. For some businesses (typically B2C products), the conversion process is all constructed on a website or mobile app, and then the measurement of those steps is pretty straightforward. For other businesses (typically B2B products), there is a much higher need for a relational touch (a phone call, meeting, etc.).

Don't just pick a tool to start 'measuring stuff.' Decide what you want to measure by determining how people become your customer. Identify the steps, groups of steps, and overall series of steps. They're like notes, chords, and melodies that contribute in different ways to the conversion song. Once you've got the melodies, you can figure out how to record. Pick a tool that measures exactly what you need to know to optimize that process. It does you no good to pick a popular analytics tool and start measuring what it measures. You need to have a direct measurement need connected to *your* specific selling process and then measure that metric maniacally.

Pay a tremendous amount of attention to the things that *feed* conversion—the top of the funnel—where people start looking for your product or things related to your product. One of the founders I worked with was trying to decide between spending on SEM and in-person visits. Her product was in the education space. She realized that a seemingly unexceptional bureaucratic position in the ecosystem of her market played a major role in helping her target consumer make decisions. Sometimes it's an individual person; other times it's media content or a conversation. Try to identify life events, company events, cultural events, times of year, etc. that affect the amount of people who might be looking for your kind of product or solution.

Then you need to ask yourselves a number of questions: Are you aligned with those events? What are the potential paths in and out for your product? When could someone bail out of your conversion funnel? Why would they do so? What can you do to fix it? It's often just as important to understand the things that are seemingly unrelated.

For example, I've sold a lot of cable TV and high-speed Internet service in my career. Typically, cable companies have specific territories where they are allowed to sell cable. We noticed that in apartment buildings, there were often overlapping territories; so, customers were trying to sign up for service but getting denied because they tried signing up for a service with a company that didn't own their territory. Therefore, they'd ditch the prospect of getting cable. We figured out ways to identify these customers and get them routed to the appropriate provider.

Look for big opportunities to drive big conversion. Don't always try to convert the low-hanging fruit. Is that the best ROI? One hundred small customers might not be worth one big customer each month." Although, keep in mind, this depends on your business model and your point of view as a founder. Recall Jason Fried and 37signals strategy of not relying on any single customer and maintaining their $150 per customer target. All businesses are different. Do what's right for your business.

And then, according to Grossman, "Figure that out and optimize for the best strategic option and know where the big risks are that could cause huge decrease in conversion. One thing to watch for is when there is increasing and decreasing commitment levels. Those are often early indicators of conversion or abandonment. Pay attention to where and when they leave. Distraction plays more of a critical role than you would ever believe. People don't have any sense of connection to context."

"For example," offers Grossman, "Pay attention to *day of the week* and *time of the day*. If there is a significant spike in people who are casually shopping on a tablet on Sunday afternoon, understand why that is happening. Pay attention to initial visits versus return visits and try to figure out why they come back. Pay attention to where they come from. Pay attention to new people versus existing relationships (cheaper to upsell). And be careful. When looking at these things, be sure to not fall in love with the results. Fall in love with the idea of understanding *why*. It is very easy to fall into the trap of feeling like you *know* what is going to take place when for example you increase logo size, eliminate the need for a credit card, or add a step in the process, etc. But is it *always* the case? The environment is complex. So, *always* test assumptions with experiments.

"In an early stage business, you are trying to understand how your market works. What are the things that affect it? How do customers behave and respond to different environments? Conversion funnel thinking is not an activity to produce defined outcomes; it is a process of experimentation and discovery that eventually leads to business results."

When in doubt, test it. But, as important, when you are absolutely certain you *think you know* what will happen, definitely test it. Remember, early stage companies are in the business of learning.

CHAPTER ELEVEN

THE GAME OF SEARCH (SEO)

*"You have to learn the rules of the game. And then you
have to play better than anyone else."*

Albert Einstein

"IF YOU ARE FROM Chicago (or even if you're not)," recalls
Loud Interactive founder & CEO Brent Payne, "you have
vivid memories of the Chicago Bulls' huddles where Michael
Jordan gave an electrically-inspiring pep talk to his teammates,
then all players put their hands in the middle of the circle,
and finally they all chanted, 'Game time, hoo!' It was awesome. Even if you were not a Bulls fan, it fired you up. Most
importantly, it set the context that this was a game that meant
to be *won*!

Most of us grew up playing games as kids. Whether it
was sports, chess, or video games, we all know what it is like
to compete. We know the pain of loss, and we have tasted
victory. If you take a moment to reminisce, you'll likely stum-
ble upon some great childhood memories. As we get older,
our playfulness starts to turn into seriousness. That's a good
thing for the most part. What would happen if the world were
run by a bunch of ten-year-olds? There would be lots and lots
of Pixie Sticks in the break room. Age and maturity bring

responsibility, competency, ambition, drive, and accountability. Life and work get serious. But, where is the play?

Starting a company can feel like play. It's like building a Lego structure with *much* higher stakes, but play nonetheless. But because of high stakes, the game can turn serious quick. It should. But, there is one area of building a startup that should always be considered a game—your search engine optimization (SEO).

In this chapter, we'll talk about:

- The difference between organic search and paid search
- The Google referee
- Learning to play the game (the goals)

The Accidental Expert

Payne is recognized as one the world's most renowned SEO experts. But his story is also one of an entrepreneur who's built a successful business by solving a real problem.

"I fell into this SEO stuff accidentally," recalls Payne. "Fifteen years ago, I was a 100% commission salesmen for a company that manufactured flash memory cards. We weren't the best company (or product) in the market, but I still had to 'sell the sizzle' and figure out how to get the product sold. Being relatively new to the sales force, I had to stake a claim to a set of accounts. I decided to ask the CEO of the company for the online-only accounts. At the time those consisted of Amazon.com, Buy.com and 800.com. He said 'no' and imparted wisdom upon me that the Internet was a fad that would soon pass. I begged him by telling him that I felt I could be the #1 salesperson within a year if he let me at least have Amazon.com. He finally agreed but told me if I failed to become #1, he'd fire me. So, the pressure was on.

"It took three months to get Amazon to call me back, then

two months to get products uploaded, so I only had seven months left to become the best salesperson in the company. Considering I was competing with seasoned salespeople with accounts like CompUSA, Circuit City, and others, it was going to be a difficult task. After uploading the products, I was getting no traction. So, I *had* to do something to keep my job. I decided to change the product sales copy and even resorted to using user features like So You'd Like To and Listmania to create massive inbound links from within other areas of Amazon to get my products some attention. One day, when Amazon placed the largest order in the history of our company, I discovered that I had accidentally figured out SEO and I was #1 in AltaVista, Lycos, Excite, and a small new search engine called Google.

"Payne became the #1 salesperson at the company through grit, determination, and creativity and—like many entrepreneurs—a bit of luck. But he didn't stop once it worked. He realized he was on to something big. And so, he fine-tuned his approach purposefully for success. Brent explains, "This stuff really works. As founders, I know that you have a million things going on. But, it's worth paying attention if you want to get over those first hurdles in your startup."

Organic Search versus Paid Search

Did you know that each time you perform a search on Google, it returns two types of results? These search results can be classified as organic or paid. Paid search advertisements, also known as Pay-Per-Click (PPC), are the results set apart at the very top and right side of your browser. Paid search ads are usually differentiated by shading or bolded font. Companies must bid and pay to have their ads displayed in one of the top positions when a user searches for certain keywords.

One major misconception about SEO is that a company

can simply pay to have its website displayed at the top of search results. But this is only true for paid search. SEO, on the other hand, is the method of getting a website to rank organically at the top of search results, using a combination of factors. How highly a website ranks in organic results is mainly determined when Google indexes a site, its content, and the relevance of keywords.

"There are several benefits to having your website appear at the top of organic search listings. Historically, search engines and consumers alike trust organic or natural search results over paid search results, as they tend to be more credible and are generated by usage and popularity. Organic SEO can also be done at little to no cost if you know how to play the game right, while companies must shell out major moolah to compete for the top ad spots in paid search. So, how do you play the game right? Well, first you need to understand how the Google referee works."

The Google Referee

"The whole point of SEO is to get Google to like you," says Payne. "If Google likes you, people will find you when using Google's products/services. There are a lot of tips and tricks to make that happen. You can read blogs and books, watch YouTube videos, or talk to some experienced friends who have successfully worked the system. The problem is that as soon as strategies are successful, they start to become obsolete. It is not in Google's best interest to let you get an unfair advantage. While it's important for Google to offer relevant search results to their users, it's equally important to make sure those results aren't too heavily weighted to one source. After all, if Google's top paying customers could reach #1 on the search results organically and not *pay them money* to be there, perhaps they'd choose to stop advertising with Google altogether.

As soon as Google sees the strategy you are using to drive a disproportionate number of people to your website, they will assign legions of engineers to the task of plugging the loophole. *This is what makes it a game!* It's always changing. What worked yesterday won't necessarily work today. You typically have to start from scratch on a quarterly, monthly, daily basis. Remember, it's a game and it's fun! It's not fun if you don't look at it from this perspective; it can be a frustrating hassle. So, make it a game with your team, and you will see attitudes change for sure. The game is about getting traffic. You need traffic. You can't live without it. You just can't have customers without traffic. And, you can't have traffic without kick-ass SEO," says Payne. "It's plain and simple. Show me a startup that doesn't pay attention to their SEO strategy, and I'll show you a startup that isn't trying to win. It's critical and you must pay attention. First, you need to understand how search engines work."

Here are the basics of what Google uses to evaluate your website and determine whether or not to put it atop the results. Again, keep in mind that it's a game. "These things are constantly changing," advises Payne. "You need to stay on top of what's moving beneath you feet."

1. ***Popularity***: How many links are going to your webpage? Are you trusted by a lot of websites? Have many more people found your website to be useful?

2. ***Authority***: How many links do other pages have linking to *them* that then link *to* your page? In other words, it doesn't matter that your grandma's blog is linked to your company's homepage nearly as much as *The New York Times* linking to your company. In fact, *The New York Times* linking would *really* matter. Furthermore, generally, .edu, .mil and .gov websites

give you more authority because those websites aren't allowed the .edu, .mil or .gov designations unless they can prove they truly are an education (.edu), military (.mil) or government (.gov) organization.

3. **Relevance**: How relevant is the webpage to the search query? For example, if someone searches for *poodles* and you sell *yo-yos*, you would not be relevant.

4. **User Signals**: What makes search engines a great user experience is that they work. They give you what you want (generally). According to Google's Privacy Policy, "Google uses cookies to track user trends and patterns to better understand our user base and to improve the quality of our service."

Understanding how each of these elements affects your company is key to becoming better at SEO. When your ideal customer searches the web to solve a problem, what will make you most relevant, authoritative, relevant, and in their taste spectrum? The goal is to be the #1 search result for your ideal customer.

"Does being the first search result matter?" asks Payne. "Yes, very much. 40% of people click on the first link in a search result. 20% click on the second, 10% on the third, 5% on the fourth, 2.5% on the fifth, and 1.25% on the sixth through the ninth search result. About 3% of people click on the last link on the search result page. Sometimes it's better to be last on the page than fifth on the page.

Nearly 90% of users don't go past the first page of search results. Therefore, if you're not on the first page, you're missing out on most of the opportunity. Being first on the first page matters because you are 32 times more valuable than being eighth. It's important to note, this isn't including the few paid advertisements at the top or on the side of the search results. People do click on the paid ad results, but not nearly as much as organic search results. And in terms of where people go: Google is the only search engine that really matters because that is where the vast majority of Internet searches worldwide are done.

One hole today with Google though is in regards to social media content. Google doesn't get much data from social media sites like Facebook, Twitter and others because Google has a competing product of their own called Google+." In Payne's opinion, "Until they get rid of Google+, they aren't likely to get the data pipeline that other smaller search engines like Bing enjoy. Ironically, despite Google+ being a relatively small social media site, Google+ is pretty powerful in regards to SEO on Google. For example a much less popular piece of content in Google+ typically receives a much more favorable search results placement than a more popular Twitter post (go figure)."

Learning to Play the Game: The Goals

As Payne suggests, "Every game has goals, and winning at the SEO game is no different. There is no point in giving you the tips and tricks that work today because those tricks probably won't work by the time you are reading this book (remember, that's what makes it fun). But, we can establish a framework of goals that will help guide your strategy to be successful over the long run."

In order to create your framework, Payne suggests you commit to the following goals.

Goal #1: Build Your Site Right.

"The game starts with how you build your website," says Payne. "Google cares mostly about the HTML structure and doesn't pay as much attention to all the bells and whistles on your

CSS or elsewhere. You need to ask yourself: does your website make structural, hierarchical, contextual sense? Are there specific instructions that tell Google how to crawl your site? Is everything on your site correctly and explicitly labeled? If not, why not?"

As Payne points out, the strategies to win the SEO game are always changing. But, here are some basics from Payne's experience of what Google loves in a built website:

- Well-thought-out, clearly labeled structure
- Rich content (informative text, great photos and helpful videos)
- Instructions on what your site is about
- Instructions on why your site is important
- Websites with a lot of unique and relevant pages
- Active content with the latest information on a topic

Goal #2: Pick a Precise Target.

"One might assume that SEO is all about focusing your strategies around the highest traffic keywords," says Payne. "That helps, but that doesn't create as much traction as you think. Betting the ranch on a few specific search queries is not a good strategy for new or smaller websites. For example, you would think that *wedding dresses* is a great keyword to organize your website around if you are new site selling, let's say, wedding dresses. That's true, but there are a thousand other companies already doing that *and* people typically don't search for that term—ironically. They search more specifically, e.g., *wedding dress designers in Chicago*. You need to optimize around more specific phrases and create powerful, useful content appropriate for the more specific phrase on your website, not just wedding dresses in general.

The more specific you are in targeting niche searches with

each individual page of your website, the better traction you will get with SEO. Granular targets are typically more successful than broad shotgun-like strategies, especially if you can leverage the strengths of those more detailed pages later in your strategy to target the more broad terms.

Goal #3: Have a Voice.

You need to establish a unique, identifiable voice in the market. An opinion. When you establish a well-thought-out opinion, people start to notice and ask you to speak up more often (if your opinion is valid). As you speak up more often, you set yourself up as an expert. Experts do well in search.

"Get yourself quoted in the press," advises Payne, "write a blog post, guest post on someone else's blog, participate on a live webinar, engage actively on social media, etc. The more places on the web (in your market) where you are present, the more those venues are going to post quality links back to your website, and the more your opinion gets shared with new networks, which helps with SEO. Most people believe that if you're on the front page (or top result), you are the authority for that information."

Goal 4: Build a Web of Influence.

You need credible sites to post a link to your webpage on their webpage. This creates credibility and popularity. The more links you have pointing to your website, the higher you will show up in search results. However, all links are not created equal. The *quality* and *exclusivity* of a link is very important.

Explains Payne, "Industry experts call it *link juice*, and you need some. There is only so much link juice out there to go around. Imagine that I have a big pitcher of margaritas and I'm planning on sharing it in a bar. If there are only two of us in the bar, we're both going to get hammered. If there are 100 of us, none of us will even get a buzz. It works the same with links. If you get *The New York Times* to post a link on their front page to your website, that's great. But, if they are posting a list of 1,000 websites, it doesn't matter nearly as much." Payne continues, "A great way to get a link is still to prepare a press release. But, make sure it is something that can attract real attention from journalists and their readers. Your press releases should be written in a way that would make journalists want to write about it. No one cares about features or launches. Think about *What is unique and wildly interesting?* And then tailor this approach as granular as possible. Don't try to send one press release to hundreds of journalists. Customize it to a specific journalist for optimal results.

Press releases are a great way to bring strong links into your site. Marketwire.com is a great resource to post press releases. Ask for a link in your press releases. Getting links is a primary objective, but don't be a jerk. If you are getting into communities (and interacting in social media), build relationships and *give* before you ask anything or drop a link."

Goal #5: Be Good, but Not Too Good.

"There are some smart people at Google," Payne quips. "They are just like school teachers. They can typically tell if a paper is *too good.* If it's too good, they will know that you are likely cheating. It works the same with Google." Great SEO strategies only work for a while, and then Google catches on and fixes it. They make money from paid search and so they have a huge incentive to make sure organic SEO tricks don't work. You want to look like you're doing awesome, but you are still within normal. Don't be too good at one thing. Otherwise, Google will notice your SEO weighting isn't balanced and will possibly penalize you. Do a bunch of different things. There are hundreds of ways to improve SEO performance, so don't just do one or a handful of things." Spend your time and money on a wide array of strategies to reach your specified target customer.

Optimizing your company's website(s) for superior SEO performance takes time, experimentation, and patience. It won't happen overnight. Building credibility, authority, and popularity in a very loud market is not an easy task, but a worthwhile one. Stay at it, and always adapt to the game. Remember: it's supposed to be fun.

CHAPTER TWELVE

THE SCIENCE OF GOING VIRAL

*"When people laugh at Mickey Mouse, it's because he's
so human. That is the secret to his popularity."*
Walt Disney

THE WORDS PROJECTED ON THE SCREEN behind him set the tone for what's to come. *Hi! I'm Emerson Spartz. I want to change the world.* Emerson Spartz speaks with the cadence of a man on a mission. He talks fast—*really* fast—as if his tongue is in a race to catch up with his brain. His tongue has no chance. Spartz wastes no time, knows what works, and is generous in sharing it. He—along with his team at Spartz, Inc.—has turned the art of virality into a science, a science he began studying at a very early age.

At 12 years old, Emerson Spartz convinced his parents to let him drop out of school to homeschool *himself*. A month later, he created a website called MuggleNet, a Harry Potter fan site that quickly drew over 50 million page views per month. "I had to grow up really fast," Spartz recalls. "Through MuggleNet, I was managing a part-paid, part-volunteer staff of 120 people. I learned how to code, how to write, how to lead, how to edit, and how to design. We published three books, one of which became a New York Times bestseller. The success of MuggleNet allowed me to represent the fans at a press conference with J.K. Rowling. It went extremely viral because she rarely does interviews."

Spartz combined his early success with an insatiable appetite for the study of influence, which became the foundation of his company. Spartz, now 27, is co-founder of Spartz, Inc. along with his wife Gaby, she too a once-precocious 12-year-old founder. Her site, Daily Cute, is a website of images of baby animals. As Emerson recalls from when he met her as classmates at Notre Dame, "I hit the jackpot!" Both MuggleNet and Daily Cute are now two of what is a growing portfolio of Spartz Media websites and apps that collectively draw over 17 million readers and over 25 million followers on Twitter, Facebook, and YouTube.

Spartz now launches a new property once every six weeks. Among the properties he's launched over the years are GivesMeHope, Memestache, OMG Facts, Unfriendable, As Failed on TV, SmartphOWNED, Dose, in addition to new mobile apps in gaming (Blanks) and dating (Twirl). Spartz now has nearly forty people working for him full-time including data scientists, web developers, and editors. Together, Spartz, Inc. media properties educate, inspire, and entertain over 100 million people every month.

Spartz is in the business of virality. Using predictive science to measure viral potential, Spartz can predict the likelihood of a piece of content going viral or not. Thus far, Spartz Media has a 90 percent success rate. Spartz refers to his proprietary algorithm as an "awesomeness meter."

In this chapter, we'll talk about:

- The science of virality
- Making stuff go viral
- Really useful techniques you should use

The Science of Virality

Virality, in nature, comes from the study of how diseases and epidemics spread throughout people and groups. The same is true of the way messages, ideas, and information can spread through social networks. "We discovered the science of virality [in media content] by basically trying a bunch of things and seeing what works," says Spartz. "Then, when something worked, we did more of that and less of the other stuff that didn't, eventually discovering effective ways to correctly posture a message for virality." When done right, virality can be a huge source of influence for your startup (and your success). Before trying some of the proven techniques that Spartz recommends, there are two concepts that you need to know: *viral coefficient* and *cycle time.*

Viral coefficient (how many people they tell)

Viral coefficient measures the likelihood that someone who has received your message will share it with others. "For example," says Spartz, "think about the virality of a joke. If I tell you a joke and you, in turn, tell two others the joke and then they tell two others, and so on, you have a viral coefficient of two." A viral coefficient above 1.0 is good because it means that an idea or message will inevitably grow because each person that hears it will always spread it to at least one more person (> 1.0 = exponential growth). If, on the other hand, your coefficient is below 1.0, then your message will gradually diffuse over time and eventually die to zero (< 1 = flat or incremental growth).

Cycle time (how long until they tell someone)

Viral coefficient measures sharing. *Cycle time* measures how long it will take someone to share your message with the next person. "So, for example," says Spartz, "if your message has a viral coefficient of 1.0 but it takes a month for that person to share your message, it will stall virality because there is no velocity to the message. Shorter cycle time equals faster virality. Cycle time is somewhat dependent upon the content itself. For example, a photo has a very short cycle time. When someone sees a photo, they decide to share it or not *in that moment.* They don't go back two weeks after seeing a photo and then decide to share that photo. On the other hand, games or apps generally have longer cycle times because people tend to share those over time as they use them."

These two measurements, viral coefficient and cycle time, are critical to the performance of your message. According to Spartz, it doesn't take much to influence the trajectory of your success. "Oftentimes," says Spartz, "if you can increase your viral coefficient by as little as .01, you can make a dramatic impact on the virality of your message." Of course, in order to increase your viral coefficient and improve cycle time, you first need to measure how viral your content is *today.* As we discussed in the chapter on unit economics, you can't improve what you don't measure. Everything you focus on and measure will improve.

In its simplest form, you can measure virality by how many users you acquired on your own versus how many came without any effort on your part. As Spartz asks, "How many people showed up beyond those who you directly reached out to? Say you sent a message to 1,000 people and 5,000 *showed up.* The 4,000 you didn't directly contact were probably reached virally." Once you have this benchmark data, you can then work to create content that has better odds of going viral. Here are the things you need to keep in mind in designing for virality.

Making Stuff Go Viral

There are two key strategies to increase the virality of your message: *emotion* and *bribery*.

First, let's talk about emotion. According to Spartz, "In general, you have to be awesome to be viral. More emotion equals more awesome equals more viral. High valence emotions are the best kind of emotions. These are the ones that make you feel *up*, such as surprise, humor, or personal interest. To get people to share, you have to get enough of those emotions. You can elicit an emotional response with bits of information, pictures, videos, or headlines that literally make you lean forward in your seat. And, it doesn't have to be positive emotion. Anger is one of the most powerful emotions that can be harnessed for virality."

Here are a few of the proven techniques for engaging human emotion in order to get people to share, share often, and share quickly. You, of course, need to figure out how these principles would apply to your content. By the way, if you think you are not in the media business, think again. All businesses today are media businesses. If you have customers that you need to communicate with, you are in the media business. If you have a brand, you are in the media business. It doesn't matter if you sell hotel rooms, duct tape, or dental floss. All brands are now media brands. If you produce advertising content, sales brochures, marketing messages, or any messaging that is intended to win the attention of customers, you are in the media business.

In regard to emotion, there are several proven techniques that work in media. It's worth noting that whichever you choose, advises Spartz, figure out ways to use one or more of these techniques in tandem.

- Piss people off
- Use cute animals, humor, or nostalgia
- Promote personal identity
- Ride the coattails of what's hot

1) Piss People Off

Anger is a high valence emotion. "At Mugglenet," Spartz recalls, "I would get 150 emails a day, most of which were from nice people, but I'd also get emails from assholes. And so, I created a *Wall of Shame* for the assholes where I'd publish their hilarious emails. It created a firestorm of activity and spread like wildfire among our users because people on the site felt like they got the chance to be part of the *shaming of the assholes* by sharing and commenting on the assholes' emails. After a while, it became our most popular section. Get people emotionally engaged in your business and they will be your biggest promoters."

2) Use Cute Animals, Humor, and Nostalgia

People like to laugh, feel inspired, and remember good times. "For example," says Spartz, "we published this fact on OMG Facts and had incredible results: *You can't hum while holding your nose closed.* Go ahead. Try it. Was I right? You can't do it. It was fun. It made you laugh. This became irresistible to share." Make people laugh. Remind them of fond memories and good times. Then associate yourself with the humor and nostalgia.

3) Promote Personal Identity

"Before sharing anything," says Spartz, "everyone asks themselves, unconsciously: *If I share this, will it make me look cool?* It's the reason why no one shares porn. It doesn't make you look cool. People *do* share *New Yorker* articles, even though few people read them entirely. In fact, heat maps show that the many *New Yorker* article visitors never scroll down. They read the headline and a few sentences. And then, they share it. It makes them look cool, educated, and interesting enough to have read the whole article. Help people look smart, funny, and cool and you win."

4) Ride the Coattails of What's Hot
A shortcut to creating something that's viral is not to create something from scratch. Says Spartz, "Think about how viruses work in nature. You could try to engineer the DNA from scratch or you could use an existing virus, mutate it, and expose it to a new group of people." Content, suggests Spartz, works the same way.

"People have this really weird notion that innovation requires making everything from scratch," says Spartz. "Every founder believes what they are doing is unique, fresh, and innovative. And, that's great. But, don't overestimate the uniqueness of your business. Chances are high that there has been, is, or will be someone else trying to do something very similar to what you are doing in the way that you are doing it. Therefore, at first, I'd suggest spending 80% of your time researching what other people have done successfully, and unsuccessfully. Through tools like Alexa (shows where your competitors get their web traffic and how much traffic they get) and Topsy (shows what posts went viral), you can learn from strategies that have already proven to be successful.

There is unnecessary pressure in startup world to be overly *innovative*, but that results in a lot of people wasting time, money, and energy reinventing the wheel. You don't have to be original in every part of your business. You don't have to manufacture energy if it is already there. An example is Retailmenot. They have a huge Facebook page. How did they do it? Rather than simply posting, let's say, a discount for 20% off of dog food, they would say the same thing (20% off dog food) but then they would go and find a really cute dog photo, perhaps off of the top of Reddit, and they'd post that irresistible photo of the cute dog along with the message. More people would see the photo and associate the post with the photo. One note of caution: If Justin Bieber's tweet goes viral, it's not necessarily because of the content, it's because of him. There is a difference. Look for differences between content and authorship. Just because it worked for Justin Bieber doesn't mean it will work for you." Emotion sells. It always has and it always will. If you want to create content that is prone to going viral, engage people's hearts.

Give People Incentives to Share (aka "bribery")

Beyond emotion, the second tactic you should be using is "incentivized sharing." Spartz refers to this loosely as bribery (not technical *bribery*, but rather providing incentives for them to care). "Bribery is a strong word," admits Spartz, "but it's basically what is happening. *Retweet this for a chance to win...* or *Tweet #hashtag to receive a [fill in the blank]*. It's okay to do this. If you are a business, there is no shame in dangling some bait in order to spark behavior and tip virality. I typically tell people to write down a list of all the things they want people to do (tweet this, hashtag this, sign up, recommend, etc.) and then write down a list of all the ways that you can bribe people to do those things (receive a coupon, get a month free, enter a chance to win, etc.) Then, start experimenting with combinations from each of the lists. When you find something that works, go with it.

Emotion and bribery drive virality. Virality helps to drive awareness to your business. And, if done right, it can be one of the most cost-effective marketing tactics you can execute.

Really Useful Techniques You Should Use (Spartz's data shows they work!)

Social media is great for awareness and thought leadership. If you want people to know about your sale, your campaign, your video, or your new announcement, social media can help you out. Of course, once they get to your website, mobile site, or app, you need to convert them to becoming buyers. That's another set of issues. Spartz Media predictive analytics engine has put data to human behavior. They know what will work and what won't work in the context of social media and content. Below is a list of things that the data has shown to work and work well.

- Use Facebook. For most people, Facebook *is* the Internet. Don't believe the bullshit that people are leaving Facebook. FB, Twitter, Pinterest, LinkedIn. They work.
- Facebook loves photos/videos. Most content you upload should be a photo or video.
- Don't #usedumbhashtags.
- Don't use more than one hashtag per tweet unless you have to.
- Measure everything (use trends.google.com, Bit.ly, twittercounter.com).
- Find out what's already viral and see what you can apply to your content (use Topsy.com, Reddit.com, favstar.fm, socialbakers.com)
- Tweet the same tweet three times, eight hours apart. In general, people only read the last 15-60 minutes of their feeds. We've found you can get nearly the same number of clicks on the third one as the first. You're also catching people at different times of day and living in different time zones.

- Make your tweet look out of the norm. For example, use --> before a link. By pointing to the link, the brain wants to know what that arrow does. This works for all non-standard characters (such as an occasional exclamation point!).
- Ask people to "Please Retweet" (it works better than "RT" or "please RT").
- People retweet more content after business hours (they need to look like they're working at work) and so don't ask them to "Please Retweet" during working hours.
- Use CAPS on occasion. CAPS one word in a tweet or post (NEVER ALL CAPS EVERY WORD IN A TWEET. That's just obnoxious).
- Separate paragraphs into smaller bite-sized chunks.
- Use periods. Not commas. It will make your writing more readable.
- Less is more. Imagine if someone would pay you $1,000 for every word you remove.
- Give people incentives to share.
- There is a honeymoon period to sharing. You need to push people to share as soon as possible (remember *cycle time*). Immediacy of action is the goal.
- Be real. Customers don't *want* you to be a business. They want you to be a *person*. They want you to be real. They want you to have a voice. Businesses that try to control their *social voice* do so very badly.
- One marketing channel will be your *money channel* (e.g., FB ads, setting up partnerships, etc.) You need to be hell-bent on finding *the one* user acquisition channel that works for your business. Commit to it.
- Inside Facebook's PageData is where you go to see what is working on FB.

- XYO.net is great for seeing mobile app data.
- BuiltWith is great for showing you what technology they are using.
- Usertesting.com is great for (wait for it) user testing.
- To test copy for anything, use Facebook. Set up different ad campaigns, e.g., create five campaigns with different headlines, shoot for 30 clicks/headline and you'll know what is the best headline. It may cost you ~$30 and be worth it.
- Write a GREAT headline. 99% of people will only see the headline. It's your entire sales pitch for your article or message.
- Put everything you can in list form! Odd numbered lists perform better than even numbered lists (Top 5, Top 7, Top 29, etc.).

Of all of these tips, according to Spartz, the headline you choose is the most important thing you can invest your time in creating. Says Spartz, "We've found the difference between a good headline and a great headline to have huge difference in virality. Think about that. We can sometimes get over twenty times as many people to engage with the same content simply based upon a better headline! You may spend three hours writing something that you could get twice as many people to read if you spent an additional hour testing headlines and finding the most-effective one. If you don't get them to read it, it doesn't matter what you say.

As both Walt Disney and Emerson Spartz have learned, people relate to people (even when people are in the form of a cute little mouse). Much of what makes content go viral has to do with this simple and timeless truth. When creating marketing messaging and content, don't forget that you are talking to human beings. Technology changes fast. People don't.

UNLUCKY 13

THERE IS NO Chapter 13 in this book because entrepreneurs need all the luck they can get.

ARE YOU A VENTURE BUSINESS?

"Never doubt that a small group of thoughtful,
committed citizens can change the world. Indeed,
it is the only thing that ever has."
Margaret Mead

I WORK IN THE BUSINESS OF INNOVATION. As a result, I get pitched a lot—good ideas and bad ideas. When it's a bad idea, I'll explain why I think it's a bad idea. They're disappointed, but once they see the Achilles heel in their logic, they're sometimes thankful. Other times, they'll ignore me, go forward and make it work (or fail). I'm not always right and I'm not always wrong. No one is. Accidents are known to happen in our field (as is luck). As head of investments at Betaworks, Matt Hartman explains: "Pavlov was studying biology not psychology." Some founders are able to start in one business and end up in an entirely different business. Mobile shopping app Tote became Pinterest. Podcast directory Odeo became Twitter. Camera operating system Android became mobile handset Android. The Point became Groupon. And so on. The list of entrepreneurs who've stumbled upon success is long. But the list of entrepreneurs who've stumbled upon nothing is even longer.

Then, there are the good ideas. Here's how *those* conversations go. The aspiring entrepreneur pitches the idea, holds their breath and waits for my reaction. When it's a good idea, I'll say, 'That's a good idea for a business!' They'll smile. More often than not however, I'll go on to say '…but it's not a venture business.' Their smile melts away. They're thrilled and disappointed all at once, but mostly they're confused. Here's why.

My intention is not to rain on their inspiration parade, rather it's to save them time and frustration. In my experience, I've found that many aspiring entrepreneurs simply don't know what a venture business looks like. Generally, there is a belief among would-be entrepreneurs that if people think it's a good idea, I should pitch it to a venture capitalist. After all, isn't that what venture capital is for? Isn't innovation about ideas? And isn't venture capital about funding ideas? This is true (sort of). Venture capital isn't for all ideas. Venture capital is for venture ideas. There's a difference. Founders are not the only ones to make this mistake. Venture investors do too. When a VC invests in a business they think has the potential to deliver venture returns and it doesn't, sometimes it's because they've invested in a non-venture friendly business themselves. In fairness, in the business of innovation, no one really knows what will work and what won't. It's why venture is a portfolio game: place many bets in the hope that one percent will knock it out of the park. That said: As a founder, it's helpful to know whether you have a venture business or not.

The intention of this chapter is to help you understand the differences between a small business and a venture business so that you can seek the right financing, leverage the right skills, plug into the right mentor networks, and save yourself frustration in the process. Before you pursue venture capital, you need to figure out if it is even worth your time.

In this chapter, we'll talk about:

- Whether your business model is an attractive model for venture investors
- Your odds of making it into the Unicorn Club
- Making sure you're raising venture capital for the right reasons
- Differences between small businesses and venture businesses
- Whether or not you should raise outside capital at all (VC or other)
- Determining the right financing options and mentor networks for your business

[Caveat: Any business could be attractive to any investor for any number of reasons. What we suggest in this chapter will not apply to every deal. These are rules of thumb to help you evaluate the viability of your business in attracting VC funding. Every rule has exceptions].

What Is a Venture Business?

According to the National Venture Capital Association, for every $1 of venture capital invested (1970 to 2010) $6.27 of revenue was generated in 2010. In aggregate, while annual venture investment equals less than 0.2% of U.S. GDP, VC-backed companies have generated revenue equal to 21% of U.S. GDP and employ 11% of the total U.S. private sector workforce. We know that venture businesses are vital to the economy, but what exactly is a venture business?

Venture-friendly businesses are high-growth, highly scal-able, and high impact. Small businesses *need not* be any of these things and they can still be fantastic businesses. One is not better than the other. But if you think you have one type of business and you really have the other, you risk unnecessary frustration, and aspiring entrepreneurs already have enough reasons to get frustrated.

A common source of frustration comes from getting rejected following a pitch to a venture investor. This can happen for all sorts of reasons: the business is not a fit for the fund, the firm has a competitive investment, the firm funded a similar business before and it didn't work, it all sounds good on paper but the entrepreneur has no data to show that the idea works or that customers will care, they like the idea but not the founder, they like the founder but not the idea, and so on. Among the reasons entrepreneurs are denied venture funding is when the entrepreneur thinks they have a venture business on their hands and they don't. This manifests itself as: *Those idiots don't know a good idea when they see one!* But that's not why the entrepreneur may have been rejected. They may have a good business—it's just not a venture business.

Here's what often happens. An entrepreneur will have defined the opportunity area correctly (i.e., Internet of Things is huge!). But their solution will be too small, too silly, or simply not scalable (e.g., *We have a team of professional installers that drive around in trucks to families' homes and retrofit individual Lego bricks—piece by piece—with GPS-enabled chips such that kids never lose a piece again.*). They have a venture problem but not a venture business. It's not high-growth. It's not high-impact. It's not scalable. In this example, they don't even have a viable business (much less a small one!). Okay, so GPS retrofitting of Lego bricks is a ridiculous example, but let's look at it a different way.

Think about how you could transform Uber from a *venture-friendly* business to a *non-venture-friendly* business. Step one: Buy a fleet of cars. Step two: Hire thousands of drivers. Step three: Put those drivers on your payroll. *That* is a non-venture friendly business. It's still a business. It's just not a venture business. Why? It's not scalable. Well, sure, you could scale it, but it will cost you a fortune, making the economics unattractive to a venture investor. Similarly, imagine how you could make Airbnb venture-unfriendly. You'd do it the same way you'd make Uber venture-unfriendly but with housing inventory. In both of these examples, you could create a black car service and a hoteling service, neither of which would be venture-friendly business models. Both however could be nice businesses. Generally, venture-friendly businesses are high-growth, highly scalable, and high-impact.

By highly scalable, we mean a few things:

1. the business meets a universal need
2. the business has attractive customer economics
3. the technology can support rapid growth
4. the business model has a built-in growth proposition

1. Universal Need

Great businesses can be built within a niche, but great businesses can also be built that touch the lives of hundreds of millions of people. Is the need big enough? Another way to look at universal needs is to find pain points or bottlenecks within a category that nearly 100% of people in that category struggle with managing. For example, human resources administration is something all businesses must do (e.g., payroll, benefits administration, employee onboarding, compliance issues, workers' compensation, etc.). This is a great example of a universal need within a category. The human resources software company Zenefits has tapped into this need and its growth trajectory proves it has discovered a pain point worth solving. Before you start building, consider sizing your market. Is it big enough? Do enough people within the category struggle with the problem? If you can find something that affects a large group of people, keep moving in that direction.

2. Attractive Customer Economics

Scalability often shows up in the economics of a business. If and when you can prove that customer acquisition costs (CAC) are significantly less than the lifetime value of customers (LTV), you're likely on to something interesting. For example, if it costs you $50 (CAC) to acquire a customer worth $150 (LTV), that's good. But if it costs you $50 (CAC) to make $5,000 (LTV), that's even better. The wider this gap, the better.

3. Technological Scalability

Beyond having a universal need and favorable customer economics, the technology must also be scalable (i.e., able to support rapid growth). If the need is big and the economics work, build for scale or at least have a plan to scale your technology quickly.

4. Built-in Growth Proposition

Scalable business models are typically designed not only with a value proposition that benefits customers, but also with a built-in growth proposition that benefits the company. The best example of this is the two-sided network. Think of companies like Airbnb, Craigslist, DoStuff Media, eBay, Kickstarter, OKCupid, OpenTable, SpotHero, and Uber. As an innovator, you really have two options to innovate. You can either *sell better stuff* or *sell stuff better*. If you can do both, which is rare, even better! Two-sided networks *sell stuff better*. They don't make products. They make markets. As attractive as these ventures are, market making is one of the most difficult business innovation challenges. Why? All market makers start with the same problem—an empty room. What's the empty room problem?

Imagine if you were the first potential customer to visit a new online dating site when it launched. You'd be the *only* person looking for a date in a room with no one in it. How would that make you feel? Right. You'd feel even lonelier than before you came to the site! That is the empty room problem. And so, how do you get people to show up? You need other people there. It's a classic Catch-22 situation, not unlike the high school party conversation—*Are you going to the party? Maybe. Who else is going?* OKCupid, the fastest growing online dating site, understood the problem of the empty room before they launched. To manage around the problem, co-founders Chris Coyne, Max Krohn, Christian Rudder, and Sam Yagan (all Harvard math majors) created a large database of single people before they launched their dating site. They created a room full of potential matches first and *then* they launched OKCupid.

Whether you're selling dates, parking spots, dinner reservations, or black car rides, you can't launch a two-sided network without liquidity. You need people on both sides of the market to make it work: buyers and sellers, holders of inventory and those looking for it. That is really, *really* hard to do. Why are there so many failed attempts at trying to replace Craigslist? Who cares how pretty your site is (and how clunky Craigslist's user interface is), Craig has the crowd. Everyone is at his house. He has scale and competing against scale is as difficult as creating it.

If you have a business that meets a universal need, has attractive customer economics, can scale technically, and has the potential to grow among users, you're likely on to something big. But scalability alone is not enough. Venture investors are also looking for high-growth potential, meaning the potential to deliver exponential returns to investors. Yes, there are funds looking for base hits and doubles as well, but there are others looking for multiple World Series wins. And so, before you take time out of your busy life to pitch a venture investor, take the time to understand whether or not your business is highly scalable and high-growth. If so, your business will likely have high impact with customers. Now the question is: What are the odds it's a billion-dollar idea?

The Unicorn Club

The odds of creating the next billion-dollar company are really, *really* low. I'm not suggesting that you need to create a billion dollar exit or even have the *potential* to create a billion dollar exit to be considered attractive by venture investors, but you do need to manage your expectations. There are seven billion people on the planet. There is one Mark Zuckerburg. That's not to say you are not the next Zuck. I hope you are, and I hope that this book helps you get there. But before you pull up a chair in Vegas, it's always good to know the odds.

According to research by Cowboy Ventures, "Thirty-nine companies belong to what we call the 'Unicorn Club' (by our definition, U.S.-based software companies started since 2003 are valued at over \$1 billion by public or private market investors). That's 0.07% of venture-backed consumer and enterprise software startups or 1 out of every 1,538 companies. It's really hard, and highly unlikely, to build or invest in a billion dollar company. The tech news may make it seem like there's a winner being born every minute, but the odds are somewhere between catching a foul ball at an MLB game and being struck by lightning in one's lifetime. Or, more than 100x harder than getting into Stanford." Managing expectations matters. Unicorns are rare making finding them even harder. Paul Lee, partner at Chicago-based venture capital firm Lightbank, puts it best: "A good venture capitalist fails

80% of the time. A great one fails 70% of the time." VCs want more Unicorns too, but there aren't that many out there.

Beyond chasing unicorns, keep in mind the economics of venture as this shapes a VC's worldview. It dictates the kinds of expected returns they need to see for an investment to make sense for the fund. Lon Chow, partner at Apex Ventures, suggests you put yourself in a VC's shoes to understand the economics driving the decision-making of some VCs. "Let's say you manage a $500 million venture fund," says Chow. "In order to get 3x returns, you'd have to create at least $1.5 billion in exits. Let's say the fund has 30 investments and owns 20% of each company. Of those 30 companies, one-third will likely fail and one-third may earn their money back, leaving 10 companies to generate the desired returns to satisfy shareholders and pay fees. It's hard. As a *large* fund, you need to swing for the fences. What this means for entrepreneurs is that you need to be aware of the fact that the larger the fund the bigger the bets but also the bigger the expected wins. I see so many entrepreneurs who simply do not do the homework to understand how big their market is. They just don't realize that the problem they are solving is too small or their solution to the problem is not scalable. Or even if it is scalable, it will never be big enough to matter. I've seen great businesses—$5 million, $10 million, $20 million businesses—that are fantastic. They throw off a lot of cash but they are not venture deals."

Take the time to do the homework on the potential size of the opportunity. If the category is big enough, then you need to make sure you are solving the right problem within the category. Be honest with yourself. Is it a problem? Is it a growing problem or a fad? Is it a problem that affects a lot of people? If you were to solve it, would you get credit for solving it (i.e., someone would pay you for the solution)? Can you scale the solution? Get granular on the problem you are really solving. A lot of new ventures fail simply because they didn't take the time to explore whether the problem was worth solving in the first place!

Are You Raising Venture Capital for the Right Reasons?

Before you start practicing your venture pitch, take some time to think about why you are really seeking venture capital. Says Chow, "I have found that a lot of entrepreneurs raise money for the wrong reasons. For a lot of people, it's validation of their businesses. They reason that if a VC likes their business, that must mean they're right. And if they don't like it, that must mean they don't have a good idea. Look, you may be right (or wrong) regardless of a VC wanting to invest in your business. You may have a $30 million business that is fantastic but will never draw the interest of a VC. And that's fine." Don't fall in love with the headlines and press releases about companies closing funding rounds. Raising money is not the goal. Making money is. Sure it feels great to close a round, just don't seek venture capital for self-validation.

"The second mistake I see entrepreneurs make," says Chow, "is that they rush out to raise capital too soon." The best form of capital is customer capital (revenues). "Look," says Chow, "if you execute on the business, are growing it, have worked your way through product/market fit, see that customers want your products badly, have figured out your sales model, customer acquisition process, how to make money and now all you need to do is turn that dial to grow, then by all means go raise venture capital. Go talk to a big fund, get a big check, and get back to work. On the other hand, trying to swing for the fences on day one not knowing if you have a business—that's tough to get interest from a VC. Now there are exceptions. If you are a serial entrepreneur and have exited multiple times successfully, you will get a deal. If you are that, then go ahead, raise a ton of money because you can. If your business goes sideways, you have a lot of leverage because of who you are. Sometimes when you throw enough money at a problem it will solve it, but the odds of that approach working are slim and it's still a risky move for a VC."

Small Business versus Venture Business: Key Differences

Beyond scalability, growth, and impact, there are additional differences between venture businesses and small businesses that you should consider before you set out to build either. Like venture-backed businesses, so too are small businesses instrumental to the U.S. economy. They employ 50% of all private-sector workers and are responsible for creating over 60% of new jobs. By knowing whether you have a small business idea or a venture idea will help you acquire the right skills, financing, and mentors. There are several things you will want to consider:

- Personal motivation
- Size of the prize
- Skills required
- Financing vehicles
- Mentor networks

1. Motivational Differences
Both small business ownership and venture are noble pursuits. The key is to know what you want. Start by asking yourself what you want your business to do—what are your goals? You need to figure this out before you even think about seeking funding of any kind. Otherwise you're not only wasting your time, but you won't make progress on your bigger goal to

build a business.

Small business owners often have very different goals than venture-backed business founders. Small business owners are often motivated to create businesses to employ themselves and to provide income for their families. According to the U.S. Census, 75% of U.S. businesses have no payroll (sole proprietorships and partnerships). In the Kauffman Foundation's research, nearly 60% have no employees and 82% have two or fewer employees. These typically are self-employed small business owners who, by definition, are not "employers" (other than employers of themselves). They generally work in services occupations, retail, and trades whereby they apply their own skills, knowledge, and assets in order to generate cash to pay for their respective lifestyles.

On the other hand, venture-backed entrepreneurs—though they may *start* small—have no intention of staying small. Daniel Isenberg of Babson College puts it best, "Small is not beautiful for entrepreneurs: small is a stigma! Small connotes self-employment and stagnation, which is not only different from entrepreneurship, it is fundamentally opposite." There is nothing wrong with wanting to be a small business owner (I am one myself). We need those too. But don't confuse a small business with a venture business if for no other reason than to save yourself time pitching VCs. One caveat here as well: high-growth, highly scalable businesses are not always financed by venture dollars by the way (although often they are). Franchising is certainly another model. But the bigger point is: motivational differences can be as important as financing methods.

For example, Ray Kroc, the visionary entrepreneur who grew McDonald's restaurants and its global supplier and franchise system, built one of the world's most admired companies. The McDonald brothers, on the other hand, who started the business that Ray discovered, were self-employed small business owners. Though Kroc grew through franchising, the fundamental difference between the Kroc and the McDonald brothers were their goals. Neither was right. They were simply different. As an entrepreneur, ask yourself what you want out of creating a business. You'll hear from Troy Henikoff later in the book about the value of knowing your "number." That is, the amount of money you'd need to achieve your goals, whatever they are. But beyond your number, also know what you want the business to do for you, for others, and for the world. You don't need to create a venture business to create wealth. Wealth accumulation may not even be your goal.

2. Size of the Prize

A second common difference between small business owners and venture-backed founders is that venture-backed founders generally tend to focus on innovating within large, lumbering categories (though there are small businesses in all categories). The difference is that venture businesses tend to work on big problems with the promise of big payouts. Chow suggests that you do the homework to determine if you are operating in a big enough category to be considered a venture-friendly pursuit. This doesn't require that the category be massive, but it certainly doesn't hurt. To quote venture capitalist Mark Suster when speaking in response to the glut of Groupon clones: "The auto industry is $1.6 trillion and you want to fuck with bars...?" This is not to suggest you should only enter multi-trillion dollar categories. It's *your* business. You can do whatever you want. But if you want to get a venture capitalist's attention (which, by the way, shouldn't be your end goal, but that's another issue), it might be worthwhile to make sure the problem you are solving is big enough for them to care.

Of course, sometimes you simply will not know if it will

be big or not. With innovation, often no one knows. To paraphrase another bit of hard-won advice from Suster: "If you're not sure there's a big market, raise less money. What I like about raising less money is that it allows you to move slower, and with a new company, you don't really know what the demand for your startup will be. If you realize *holy crap, we're on to something here*, then you can always raise more money. When you raise a lot of money early, you're on the express train. It's either a big outcome or nothing if you assume investors are expecting 4x their money. When you raise less money, you're on the local train. I'd rather be on the local train. It takes longer, but you have more chances to get off."

3. Applying Your Skills vs. Leveraging the Talents of Others
Small business owners tend to focus on leveraging their expertise whereas venture-backed founders typically focus on solving a problem or taking advantage of an opportunity whether it exploits their expertise or not. Steve Jobs likely knew as much about the music industry as Elon Musk knew about the automotive industry before they both chose to change these respective industries. You don't need to be an expert to be an innovator—often quite the contrary. If you are building a business around your skills, the question then becomes whether or not you can scale *yourself*. If so, go for it. If not, that's okay too, just be aware of what you are building.

4. Financing Vehicles
Once you determine whether or not you want to start a small business or a venture business, then you can think about how to finance it. The average cost to start a new business varies widely depending upon the type business. But more importantly, the forms of financing differ dramatically. Self-employed small business owners rely on retail and commercial

banking products, lines of credit, and micro-loans (less than $100,000) in order to procure equipment and other assets and to fund working capital. Most notably, 92% of small business loans in the United States are micro-loans, most of which came in the form of business credit cards. Why?

First, they are easier to get than bank loans and government grants (e.g., they do not require business plans to get approved). Second, they are accepted ubiquitously. Third, credit cards are anonymous funding sources (i.e., unlike friends and family, you need never have Thanksgiving dinner with your credit card company). The problem with credit cards, of course, is that they are very expensive forms of financing (between 15-30%). Small businesses carry between $3,500-$11,000 balances. Credit card debt reduces the likelihood that a new business will survive more than three years. Every $1,000 increase in credit card debt increases the probability a firm will close by 2.2%. That said: "due to the ease of acquisition and anonymity, credit cards are the most popular form of small business financing." Crowdfunding via AngelList, Indiegogo, Kickstarter, and other platforms are a movement in the right direction. Companies such as SecondMarket also provide alternative liquidity options for businesses unable or unwilling to go public and/or be acquired. While crowdfunding provides more cost-effective alternatives to credit card financing, startups need to be mindful of the number and types of investors they accept. You may not want three hundred people on your cap table.

A related difference regarding financing is that small business owners typically seek working capital, whereas venture-backed entrepreneurs are implicitly focused on growth and thus require financing in the form of risk capital at varying stages of development (e.g., angel/seed capital, bridge financing, venture capital, private equity, public markets). The fundamental difference between these financing vehicles is in the underlying collateral required. Whereas the self-employed trade on their assets by personally guaranteeing loans, venture-backed entrepreneurs trade on the growth potential of their idea (i.e., a capital gain for investors). Venture-backed entrepreneurs therefore are *unlikely* to find value in bank loans (much less to qualify) given the structure and requirements of those financing vehicles. Also, venture-backed entrepreneurs often seek "smart money" (i.e., investors who also provide industry connections and category expertise in a given area along with the capital infusion). So-called smart money is value-added to a venture-backed founder insofar as their venture investors may be able to connect the business to potential customers, suppliers, future investors, and employees that can help grow their businesses.

In the end, if after considering your motivation and business model, you determine that your goal is to start a small business, you're probably wasting your time trying to raise venture capital. Likewise, if you're a venture business, you're probably wasting your time trying to get a bank loan. Know which one you are. Save yourself the time.

5. Mentor Networks

One last difference between venture and small businesses are the respective mentor networks. Small businesses are often active in their local business associations while venture founders are often involved in incubator and accelerator programs. For small businesses, mentor networks such as SCORE (Service Corps of Retired Executives), the U.S. Small Business Administration, and local Chambers of Commerce are fantastic organizations. These institutions are also great sources of advice and networking for venture-backed founders as well, but there are other organizations better suited for the task, among them: Alpha Lab, AngelPad, The Brandery, Capital Innovators, Mucker Lab, Surge Accelerator, Techstars, Tech Wildcatters, YCombinator, and others.

Startup incubators and accelerators are popping up around the globe. And that's a very good thing. Accelerators are instrumental in supporting venture-backed founders by providing access to talent, education, media exposure, mentoring, seed capital, and very targeted networking opportunities with potential customers. The best of these programs reflect the same principles that have emerged naturally in technology epicenters around the globe. Here's what typically happens. A company succeeds in building a business. In turn, it generates liquidity in the form of an IPO or acquisition. This event generates cash for the company and its founders. Its founders then, in turn, typically spin up other high-growth businesses that create new wealth, infrastructure, and a cultural acceptance of innovation, thereby repeating the cycle. Such was the case of Fairchild Semiconductor (the company that gave birth to the Silicon Valley), as well as Dell (Austin), Medtronic (Minneapolis), Hybritech (San Diego), Groupon (Chicago), and Microsoft (Seattle). Similar movements are underway in New York City, Jerusalem, Los Angeles, Hong Kong, London, São Paulo, Shanghai, Sweden, and others. These natural ecosystems are as important to a founder's success as venture capital. The formal accelerator programs we have today—including Techstars—operate by the same principles that make these organic systems work. When great ideas come together with experienced mentors, smart money, and world-class entrepreneurial talent, magic happens.

The great value of mentor networks is that they likely already know the people you need to know, want to know, and should know in order to grow your business. In life, relationships matter. In venture, they matter even more. When creating anything new, trust is a necessary asset. Mentors trade in trust and social capital. If a venture mentor believes in you, members of their respective networks will be more likely to give you an audience than if that audience has never heard of you before. Social capital is a very real thing in our world. Don't abuse it, but do use it.

Given these fundamental differences in aspirations, skills, financing requirements, and mentor networks, before you set out to raise capital, figure out your personal goals for your business, determine if the problem you are solving is big enough and whether or not your business model is the high-growth, highly scalable, and high-impact variety attractive to venture investors. As Lon Chow suggests, "do the homework." Then, if you determine that you do in fact have a venture-attractive business on your hands, *Godspeed!* The following chapters will be priceless guides in helping you navigate the world of risk capital.

---

*Chapter Fourteen: Are You a Venture Business? draws heavily from the written testimony of Andrew J. Razeghi before the Committee on Small Business of the United States House of Representatives. Titled, "A Job Creation Roadmap: How America's Entrepreneurs Can Lead Our Economic Recovery," March 21, 2012. This testimony, in its entirety, can be found online.

CHAPTER FIFTEEN

ANGEL INVESTORS VS. VENTURE CAPITALISTS

"If you aren't willing to own a stock for ten years, don't even think about owning it for ten minutes."
Warren Buffett

"PEOPLE OFTEN THINK THAT ANGEL, venture, and private equity is the same thing just in the form of different sized checks," says Adam Koopersmith, a partner in Chicago-based Pritzker Group Venture Capital. "But there are vast differences. Founders must understand these differences and know how to navigate them."

In this chapter, we'll talk about:

- Motivational differences between angel investors and venture capitalists
- Structural and operating difference between angels and VCs
- Qualifying an investor
- Working with angels and VCs
- Getting your deal done

Every investor and investor group is different, but generally the most significant differences can be found in their motivations, organization structures, networks, expertise, and speed at which they fund deals. And, let's be honest, the depth of their pockets matters. As a founder, when it comes to angels versus VCs, you need to consider how to balance those who can write fast checks with those who can write large checks (and continue to write those checks, even in down rounds).

For these and other reasons, before you set out to raise money, you owe it to yourself to understand how venture investors work. The definitive book on the subject is Brad Feld and Jason Mendelson's *Venture Deals: Be Smarter Than Your Lawyer and Venture Capitalist* (required reading for all those looking to raise venture dollars). For our purposes here however, we'll cover some of the fundamental motivational and operating differences between angels and VCs as well as how to get your deal done.

Karin O'Connor, who has served as managing director of Hyde Park Angels, one of the Midwest's largest angel networks, has commented on these differences, among them, the motivational differences between angels and venture capitalists. "Making money is only one motivation for an angel investor," she suggests. "Angels want a return, of course, but they also want to learn. They want to work with entrepreneurs. They want to be a part of ideas that they think are cool. They want to be part of a great adventure. They are generally already pretty wealthy, which is in part why they are angel investors. So, their motivation is broader than simply getting a return. For some, it's even a hobby."

While this is a sentiment not necessarily shared by all angel investors, it is certainly more frequently the case with angels than it is with professional venture capitalists. But don't blame VCs. They have a job to do. They are paid to make money. Certainly they seek out entrepreneurs they want to work with and entrepreneurs with big ideas, but they also work for their investors. Angels have no investors other than themselves.

A simple mechanical distinction between angels and VCs is that angels invest their own personal money whereas venture capitalists invest *other* people's money with guidelines and expectations for desired returns. Koopersmith explains it simply: "The labels we use don't do VCs any favors. On one hand you have *angels* coming down from heaven giving you money, while on the other hand you have *capitalists* as a funding source. But a VC's job is to make successful investments and deliver profits back to their investors. If VCs don't make money for their investors, it's very likely they won't be able to raise another fund to invest (i.e., they lose their jobs). As a result, VCs will typically be a bit more analytical than angels. Companies seeking money from VCs should be prepared for a more detailed diligence process."

Organizational Structure & Operating Differences

Beyond motivation, angel groups and VCs also differ in how they are organized. "Many angel groups, like Hyde Park Angels, are run by member volunteers and are structured as opt-in networks rather than committed funds," O'Connor explains, "Typically, one member will 'take the lead' in investigating an opportunity, completing due diligence, and getting to know the team at the company. He or she will then send out a memo to the whole group, and then each individual member can opt to participate (or not) in the deal. A typical Hyde Park Angels' investment includes a pool of anywhere between 10 and 30 of our members, which allows us to be able to commit higher amounts than a typical individual angel would be able to commit. We set up an LLC for each deal and make it a clean, one entity investment in each company (as opposed to having 25 different investors on the cap table). We charge the investors a small percentage (3%). A key component in this structure is that each member angel gets to decide whether to participate in each deal. In a venture capital fund, investors do not."

Angel investors form groups in part so that they see an increased volume of deal flow. Any investor will tell you that investing only makes sense (with time and money) if they have a chance to see a lot of quality companies to invest in. There are people who do angel investments on their own, but groups get more deal flow as opposed to individuals. Unless a particular angel is well known as a prolific investor and thus gets good deal flow, it is most advantageous for an angel investor to join a group. According to O'Connor, "The challenge with this structure, though, is that we never know exactly how much money our members will want to commit to a particular investment until the end (because it fluctuates). Therefore, we typically only commit to a particular allocation of the raise and then oversubscribe to that round. And, that process can be a bit of a race for our angels."

"Venture capital firms on the other hand," explains Koopersmith, "have investment committees made up of key members of the team. The investment committee determines whether or not to make an investment. Once approved, the VC calls capital from its investors and makes the investment. As a company seeking money from a VC, it's important to keep the *investment committee* concept in mind. Typically the investment committee is made up of the partners of a fund, so having a partner arguing for your deal is better than having a more junior member of the team. If you've only dealt with an associate or a VP, it may be a sign that the fund is not that serious about investing yet. As a founder, you should work to see if you can get a partner engaged in conversations early in the process."

Speed to Funding

In addition to motivational and operating differences is speed at which you can get investment dollars in the bank. One of the goals of an entrepreneur looking for funding should be to get funded by the right investor(s) as quickly as possible. So, how do you speed up the process? Koopersmith suggests, "As VCs, our job is to find investments, figure out which ones are good fits for the fund, and then close the deal. When investors know the team and the market, it can speed up the process of closing a round (four to five weeks). It's also good to keep in mind that when we spend time on a deal, it is because we are interested and trying to resolve the deal killers."

When investors don't know the team and the market, it takes time to get to know the team, to get educated on the product and market, so deals can take longer to close (three to six months). So, when looking for investors, it would be in founders' best interest to find investors who they know are already interested in the industry that they are in and that have personal connection to the founders.

These differences in motivation, structure, operating models and speed are significant variables to consider when you go out to raise money. There is no right or wrong answer or magic formula for whose money you should take. It depends on many factors (i.e., how much you need, how fast you need it, whose expertise and networks you would like access to, and—on a very personal level—you need to ask yourself who you will get along with). Koopersmith suggests, "How a VC handles him or herself in the term sheet negotiation process is often indicative of how they will act in the future? So, pay close attention."

Keep in mind that your investors are not only going to be investing in your company. Some of them are going to be on your board. Sure it's about getting the deal closed, but the real work starts *after* the deal closes. Who's going to help? Who's going to share their network? How active do you want the investors to be? How often do you want them involved? Of course, it's your company but once someone invests, they will have opinions and, legally, a vote. Keep in mind that many venture deals outlive many marriages. Date first.

Qualifying an Investor

It has become cool to call yourself an investor these days. Koopersmith suggests, "If you go to LinkedIn and look around for long enough, you'll see that *everyone* is an angel investor. You'll see a banker (and angel investor), a lawyer (and angel investor), an athlete (and angel investor), a baker (and angel investor)." O'Connor adds, "The only thing that matters to me when determining whether an individual is an actual, real life angel investor is if he or she is able to write a check *right now*. An individual could have written a lot of checks recently, but can't really invest anymore at the moment because they are tapped out."

O'Connor adds, "Angel groups like Hyde Park track how much each member is investing and how often. We typically expect them to invest a minimum $250,000 over five years. We don't intend to be a purely social group, which would be a waste of the entrepreneurs' time. Ours is a serious group that is actively investing, and we expect our members to participate in that. Angels also need to get used to losing money because it happens often, but it can be worth it when one or two investments really hit. If an investor doesn't have the risk appetite to withstand a loss, they aren't a good fit for angel groups."

In terms of qualifying investors, think of it this way. The investor is going to be doing due diligence on you, so you might as well do some due diligence on them. Ask around your network to see if they have a good reputation. See if they are active as an angel, and talk to some of their portfolio companies. Koopersmith suggests, "If you get the opportunity (which you should), ask an angel: *Walk me through your portfolio. How do we fit? What background do you have? Why is this exciting to you?* What do you know about this market? As an angel, they need to understand that it's not a one-time arrangement. We strongly encourage angels not to think of it as a one-time investment because the company will likely need more capital down the road, especially if they are doing well.

Working with Angels and VCs

Mentorship support is formal in the venture firm. They will have an active role. So, do your due diligence. Ask them about themselves and make sure it is a great chemistry fit. Basically, do you like each other?

Koopersmith advises, "When you're raising money, it is more important to build a relationship with your partner (assigned to your company) than to build a relationship with the fund. They, at the end, are on the hook with the venture firm. So, when looking at the partner assigned to your deal, make sure they are going to be at the fund long term (continuity is important), they care about your company, and you have good chemistry—because you'll be working with them actively and you are going to need an advocate. Make sure there is senior level involvement in your deal because then you will have better buy-in from the fund in general."

The reason that the relationship matters is because it's not just their money they are investing in your company and in you. It's also their network's. Investors (good ones) know people. And hopefully know the right people. It's a big part of their jobs as VCs. Venture investors are great for connections.

Angels can be too. In Koopersmith's experience, "If they are actively investing in companies, they should know what's happening in the industry. For example, if a portfolio company needs a VP of Product, that's a great time to talk to your venture partner. It's highly likely that they know someone, or can help diligence candidates in your pipeline."

Beyond tapping their networks, you also want to figure out how venture partners operate as individuals. Sure their fund may be the world's most-recognized fund in your category, but you will be working with a partner within that fund, not the brand of the fund. And so, ask around. Koopersmith suggests, "Talk to other entrepreneurs that have experience working with that specific partner. Ask others: What's it like working with [insert venture partner name here]? How do they resolve disagreements? How have they helped you solve problems? By getting feedback from other founders who have worked with that specific venture partner, you can learn a lot about the capabilities of the folks you may be working with.

O'Connor adds her perspective by saying, "Mentorship support in the angel setting is usually relatively informal, and our group works hard to be a resource for our companies. We're good for connections and advice. Investors with domain expertise typically take the lead on both diligence and mentorship. For example, we recently made an investment in a company that makes gluten-free baking mixes. We have a member who worked in frozen foods for 40 years and he was able to help the entrepreneur with co-packing, distribution strategy, etc."

Getting Your Deal Done

Angel groups use a variety of structuring techniques. "At Hyde Park Angels," says O'Connor, "we prefer institutional-type term sheets. It streamlines the process and also puts the company in a favorable position to raise more money from institutional (VC) investors later on. When those different investors come on board, we don't want them to be hung up by weird terms set up by angels."

"In fact, just avoid weird terms altogether," Koopersmith advises. "Don't do weird investor deals early. It can wreck later stage investment. Also, if you give liquidation preference and/or dividends to early investors, you can expect to give those same preferences/dividends to every other investor later on. Your terms should be plain vanilla if you plan to raise money more than once. Often times, valuation is the sticking point. So, investors and founders try to spice up with deal with other characteristics. Bad decision. Raising money is hard. If you complicate things, it makes it harder."

O'Connor agrees, "If you have strange deal terms with existing investors and are halfway complete with a raise, those terms in the deal could become a deal breaker. The odds are already against you to secure funding, why make it harder? Keep it simple."

Some VCs get a bad rap for trying to take advantage of founders, but those VCs will have very short careers as VCs. Reputation is everything in the venture community. And more importantly, it's just bad business. As Koopersmith explains, "We always want to make sure that founders have a meaningful stake. If they don't have significant upside in their company, how can I expect them to work hard for the company? They need to have significant upside, or the whole thing starts to break down. Valuation is always a hard conversation. Because if a founder starts too high, then the investors might disengage because they feel the founder is asking too much. But, if they ask too low, then the founder is leaving money on the table."

As with all pricing decisions, the market will determine the fair price. You can ask for it but you may not get it. Manage your expectations. The most important thing is that everyone in the deal remains motivated after the deal closes. That includes you as the founder as well as investors. Otherwise, misaligned incentives will hinder the potential success of the business over time.

When raising money, it's not a question of should you work with angels or should you work with VCs? Every founder is different. Every company is different. Every deal is different. Do what works for you. But also keep in mind that in early stage investments, angels and VCs typically work closely together. As the adage goes: angels invest in points, VCs invest in lines (preferably up and to the right). An angel is more likely to invest in a founder and her idea before she's proven that she can acquire and serve customers profitably (a single point in time), whereas a VC is more likely to invest once there is data showing the economics of the business are working or are very close to working. Of course, this is a generalization and to quote Mark Twain, "all generalizations are false, including this one."

Don't get too caught up in angel versus VC. In order to "get them to sign on the line that is dotted," you must pique their interest. Raise interest and you'll have better chances of raising money. Of course, since we're all human, operating with similar reptilian brains, this works in reverse as well. Raise money and I can virtually guarantee that you will also raise interest! It's called herd mentality. Use it to your advantage in fundraising.

Lastly, when investors say 'no' (as many of them will), remember this advice from Koopersmith, "Just because your company isn't a good fit for an investor doesn't mean it's not a good company. It just means you need to knock on lots of doors."

CHAPTER SIXTEEN

RAISING CAPITAL

*"Magnetism, as you may recall from physics class, is a powerful force
that causes certain items to be attracted to refrigerators."*

Dave Barry, humorist

"VENTURE IS SOCIAL SPORT," says Techstars founder & managing partner David Cohen. "A big part of raising capital is momentum. Everyone wants to be part of something big. No one wants to get left out. As a hot startup, you are a cute little puppy in the pet store window that everybody wants. Use that to your advantage." But, as Cohen explains, "Interest in your company is not enough. You have to close on that interest."

Having been engaged in over 600 venture deals from $150,000 fundraising rounds to $1.2B rounds, Cohen knows what most seasoned investors know: *it's not about the money and it's all about money.* In this chapter we'll cover three topics related to both the financial side of venture deals and the human side, namely:

- Venture financing instruments defined (debt and equity)
- Behavioral differences between debt and equity
- How to get your deal closed

Before you read further, it's worth noting again that the definitive book on venture financing is Feld and Mendelson's *Venture Deals*. Buy it. Read it. It will save you time, money, and drama. Also a great resource—to save you both time and money—is techstars.com/docs. And, while you're at it, swing by the National Venture Capital Association for good measure. For our purposes here, we'll cover the rules of thumb on financing instruments, how to get your deal closed, and some fantastic storytelling by David Cohen on how to play the game and, as Cohen puts it, "sell the puppy in the window."

Equity v. Debt: Definitions

Debt and equity are the two most common financial instruments for getting a startup financing done.

Convertible debt is a loan that will convert into equity at some future date based on a pre-determined agreement between an investor and a founder. Convertible debt notes include a cap (i.e., a maximum valuation limit at which note holders' debt will convert into equity). They also include a pricing discount on what it will cost the note holders to acquire equity (i.e., typically between 15-20%), and an interest rate and time horizon during which the interest will accrue and be paid.

"As a founder," Cohen advises, "it's important to keep in mind that *a cap is not your valuation*. It is simply a mechanism to protect early stage investors (those taking the greatest risk) from getting washed out.

"For example, if, as a startup, you raise $1 million using convertible debt with a $4 million cap, how much of your company are you selling? You don't know the answer. It's a trick question. The $4 million cap is not the valuation of your company. It is the maximum value at which your convertible note holders' debt will convert into equity. Your valuation is determined in the subsequent fundraising round in which the company issues equity. A cap is included in the terms of the convertible note as an added incentive to early investors. It protects them by providing a maximum value at which their debt will convert into equity.

"Contrast this with *equity*. If you raise $1 million at a $4 million pre-money valuation, you will have sold 20% of your company (i.e., your post-money valuation would be $5M, of which investors own $1 million in equity or 20%).

"It is worth noting that there has been debate about *uncapped notes*. The argument against an uncapped convertible note is that they create misaligned incentives between founders and investors. Theoretically, your note holders (those who invested in your convertible debt with no cap) would have little motivation to increase the value of your company in advance of the conversion of their debt into equity. In fact, it could be argued (and it has been) that their motivation would be just the opposite—to depress the valuation of your company.

"For example, if an investor invested $1 million in your convertible note without a cap, the investor's motivation would be for your company to be worth $1 million upon conversion of the debt into equity, in which case they'd own 100% of your company. In practice, this would likely never happen. Why? *Reputation*. As an investor, if you intentionally worked to depress a valuation of a company, you would be blackballed from the venture community and likely never be invited to invest in another startup again. Just as momentum matters for founders, reputation is everything for investors.

"The primary thing to keep in mind with caps on convertible debt is to be careful that you are *in market*. Keep in mind you are competing for venture dollars along with thousands of other startups. You want to be within the same ballpark as other companies in your category when it comes to terms such as caps, discounts, and interest rates."

Behavioral differences between debt and equity

In addition to the mechanical differences between debt and equity, so too are there behavioral differences. "Equity is simple and aligning," says Cohen. "As a founder you know exactly what you're selling. As an investor, you know exactly what you're buying. Everyone has the same goal in mind—to increase valuation.

Debt, on the other hand, is more complicated and the longer you let it sit around, the greater the chance of losing alignment between founders and investors. Of course, once your valuation goes above the cap, you are completely aligned. At this point, everyone wants the company to be worth as much as possible. But in situations where things are not perfectly rosy, this misalignment can potentially create real problems."

Whichever you choose—debt or equity—the primary goal is to get aligned with your investors.

What Really Matters

"The two things that matter the most in your venture financing," says Cohen, "are price and control." Let's discuss both.

Pricing

In convertible debt, the valuation cap, discount, interest rate, and other terms control pricing. In equity financing, you will see things such as liquidation preference as well. For example, a 1x liquidation preference is another vehicle to protect an early stage investor. Let's say a company is raising $1 million on a $9 million pre-money valuation. Post-money valuation therefore is $10 million. After closing the round, let's say the very next day, the founder determines that the business sucks. He liquidates the company, winds it up, and moves to Hawaii. Let's say the company has $1 million in assets. How much does the investor with a 1x liquidation preference get? He gets the $1 million he invested. If the investor hadn't included the liquidation preference, he'd get only 10% of the remaining assets or $100,000. Essentially, the 1x liquidation preference allows the investor to get his money back if this situation (or others like it) were to occur. Although it is very rare, you may see 2x, 3x, 5x liquidation preferences. Stay away from them. They're non-standard and also signal lack of alignment in an equity deal.

Control

Control manifests itself in a number of ways including voting rights, protective provisions, Board positions, and so on. Agreements may include voting rights given to investors that require founders to include them when making critical decisions. Protective provisions may include things such as not allowing the company to sell without investor approval or not allowing the company to go into debt over a pre-determined amount without approval and so on. What is important to note here is that ownership percentage does not equate to control.

For example, an investor may only own 10% of your company but could have protective provisions that allow the investor to exercise control over the business. Don't confuse percentage of equity owned with control over the company. Let's say an investor with 10% ownership doesn't think an exit is good enough but has terms that allow that investor to exercise control over a sale. They could block the deal.

"However," explains Cohen, "here is why none of this shit matters. What is important is to have good investors. You want investors who are aligned with you on your vision and are going to stand behind you. Generally, you do not have to worry about institutional investors. On the other hand, if you work with an *inexperienced* angel who has only done a deal or two, check his or her reputation. You want them working *for* you and not derailing your progress by blocking an exit or anything else."

How To Get Your Deal Closed (aka "how to sell the puppy in the window")

Before you can close a deal, you need to open it. Getting the first investor is the hardest. In Cohen's experience, "Collectively the first third of your ask is the most difficult money to raise. This is why you need to work to create momentum. Companies that go through Techstars have an unfair advantage because we help create that momentum leading up to and at Demo Day. We have had companies that have not raised any money leading up to Demo Day and go on to fill their rounds and do just fine, but the momentum of the program is helpful." Interest and momentum help deals get done. So how do you create interest and momentum?

Cohen paints the picture well. "Imagine that I am a super cute puppy in the pet store window. The people walking by the window are investors. One day, an investor walks by the store and stops to admire the puppy. *That's one cute puppy*, the investor thinks. He then goes about his business thinking about the cute puppy. That's how you look to investors right now. You are a super cute puppy.

The next day, another investor walks by the store and sees the cute puppy. Then the other guy comes back, the investor that first saw the puppy. Suddenly, the cute puppy is even *cuter* than he was the day before. This is the feeling of momentum. If either investor goes away, there is no market dynamic.

There is no momentum. The more people you have hanging around the window the better. If you want to raise money, your job is to create that feeling."

Once you've created interest and early momentum, it's time to ask for the money. But first you need to figure out how much you should ask for. Don't miss the opportunity to keep the momentum moving. How much you ask for can help you or hurt you. General rule of thumb according to Cohen is to *ask for less and let the market take you up.*

"If you ask for too much and can't get it done, you're in trouble," says Cohen." "From our data at Techstars on over 380 companies that have gone through the program [at the time of writing of this book], only 5-6% of startups raise *exactly* what they set out to raise, but 60% raise more than what they ask for. Why? Expectations and momentum. For example, if you told me you were raising $1 million but have only $500k committed that is not as effective as you telling me you are raising $500k and have $1 million in *interest*. Raise interest first and the money will follow. The mode over the past four years has been to ask for $500k (and they end up raising $1.2 million)." In other words, if you want $1.2 million, don't ask for $1.2 million. Ask for $500k and let the market take you up. But there are other ways to create momentum as well, one of which is AngelList.

"The problem with AngelList," says Cohen, "is that most people don't know how to use AngelList. They screw it up by creating a lot of noise, but don't raise any money. With no social proof, a company that is blasted around the world with no momentum is essentially advertising that it sucks. The mistake companies make is that they create their profile and then advertise to the world that they are ready to take investors, and nothing happens. Why? No momentum."

"Instead," suggests Cohen, "get some commitments from

investors before you publish on AngelList such that you can illustrate how much of your round is already committed. This signals to potential investors that you are worth looking into further. And then, create as many *follows* as you can but ask your followers not to share yet. Once you have a following, ask all of your followers to share on the same day. All at once, *put that puppy on sale!* Create the crowd and then sell the puppy. It's much better than asking everyone that walks by your store if they want to buy a puppy."

The Art of the Soft Circle

Matt McCall, partner at Pritzker Group Venture Capital, often advises entrepreneurs: "The first time you meet an investor you shouldn't be asking them to write a check." In the venture world there is a term used in fundraising called the soft commitment. Cohen defines a *soft commitment* as an *informal agreement with specific, well-understood conditions.* "This is not the same as a commitment," says Cohen. "Nor is it the same as mere interest in investing in your company. The operative words are *specific and well-understood conditions.* If these specific conditions are met, the investor will invest. In order to ensure you have a soft commitment and not mere interest you need to do two things:

"First, be specific about what the investor needs to see in order to invest. For example, conditions may include things such as: signing of a specific customer contract, passing 100,000 active users, obtaining soft circle commitments for the balance of the round, getting a specific investor on board, making a key hire, and so on.

"Second, clearly communicate these conditions. Don't assume you and your soft committer are on the same page. Play it back to them to make sure you correctly heard what they said and they are still comfortable with what they said.

"How you manage building your soft circle is as much art as science. You need to be very careful what you say and how you say it. Don't make commitments you can't keep. Don't discuss a valuation that isn't real. Don't screw it up."

Make It Safe for an Investor to Say Yes

A soft circle conversation allows you to move a potential investor from interest to investment. But how you navigate this conversation is vital. You need to make it super easy for your first investor to make a decision to invest. The early investors are challenging to get and manage because you need to keep them alive the longest (i.e., a lot of time passes between when you start the conversation and when the deal closes).

Cohen offers the following conversation to illustrate his point. This is the arc of how you should approach a conversation with a potential investor. Cohen points out where many entrepreneurs make mistakes and how to avoid them. Imagine the following conversation between a founder and a potential investor.

Founder: Now that you've heard our pitch, how much would you like to invest?

VC: I'd like to invest $100,000 in your company.

Founder: Are you willing to commit today?

VC: I have some questions about valuation and the size of the raise.

Founder: We are raising $500k at $1M valuation.

Mistake #1: The founder said 'here's the valuation.' She just pegged herself and created an expectation in the investor's brain. Avoid this. Remember, you're looking for a soft commitment, an agreement with well-understood conditions.

The investor did not say that he would invest *only if* the valuation was $1 million. He simply asked about your valuation. That does not mean you need to give them a valuation (particularly if you haven't really figured out what your valuation should be at this point). So, what's a better question to ask the investor? Let's continue.

> **Founder**: Can you give me insights into what you need to see in order to firmly commit to the $100,000? [Memorize this line: *What do you need to see in order to firmly commit to the round?* This will allow you to identify their conditions].
>
> **VC**: You need a lot more money than my $100,000. You need $500,000. And I need to know more about your valuation.

Here is where you need to learn a technique is called *reflective listening*. Listen, playback, clarify, and ask for more.

> **Founder** (reflectively listening): Okay, so let me make sure I understand what I heard. We need to have an additional $400,000 committed in order for you to invest $100,000 and we need to get you more details on our valuation? Is that right?
>
> **VC**: Yes.

As the founder, you've listened, played back, and clarified.

However, there is one more step that people often forget: *ask for more.*

Founder: Is there anything else?

VC: Well, actually, yeah there is. I really care about who is on the board.

Founder: Is there any specific person or types of people?

VC: Yeah, someone who knows the industry well and who is known as a great board member.

Founder: Okay, so let me make sure I heard you properly. If we can get the additional $400,000, get back to you on the valuation, and identify the right board members, you'll invest the $100,000?

VC: Depending on where you come in on the valuation, yes.

That is a soft commitment. You've made it safe for the potential investor to say yes. They've not signed anything. They've not written any checks. But they've offered a soft commitment of $100,000 for the $500,000 you are raising. That is a successful conversation and one that will allow you then to go to other investors.

Now, let's explore what happens once you come back to the investor with the valuation figures.

Founder: We've pegged our valuation in the $2-$5 million range.

VC: That's too broad for me. I need to know what it is. Is it $2 million or $5 million?

Founder: [silent]

Mistake #2: Valuations are not ranges. You need to put a stake in the ground. Look around at comparable companies, talk to your mentors and advisors, and don't have this conversation until you're ready to commit to a valuation figure.

Raising money is sort of like dating. You don't want to be an aggressive jerk. You don't want to get defensive. And you don't want to be a wallflower. You have to be interesting. Small talk. Build a relationship. Have some compassion for the investor. You don't want the investor thinking, *is this a crazy person?*

Here is a way to manage the early valuation question:

VC: I will not commit without the valuation figure.

Founder: I absolutely understand. And we'll figure that out. Definitely. For now, I'm just excited that you have interest and are willing to consider investing once we have the right board member identified and the additional $400,000. I would never hold you to the commitment without knowing what the valuation will ultimately be. I'm not sure what is going to be yet. But assuming it's reasonable and in-line with other companies like us, you would be interested, right?

VC: Yes.

Where fundraising conversations go wrong is when a founder makes it *unsafe* for the investor. This typically happens when you start talking about numbers on day one. Don't do that. Understand their conditions first. Remember, fundraising is about raising *interest* not just money.

Now the next step is where you go after the conversation with the investor who is interested in investing the $100,000. You now have something useful. You have a soft commitment. Use it.

> **Founder**: Would you be comfortable if I let others know that you're interested in investing in our round (given the conditions you've shared with us)?
>
> **VC**: No problem.

Ninety percent of people will say yes, although there are some who don't want their names thrown around and so make sure you ask. You don't want to advertise a soft commitment with an investor who has not given you permission to use his or her name.

As you build momentum, what you'll find is that it is not uncommon for conditions to melt away. Now that you have other investors' soft commitments, the initial concerns that the $100,000 investor had about a board member for example may no longer be an issue. It will often melt away. Again, remember, venture is a team sport. People feel more comfortable knowing they are not alone in their assessment of your company and in their assessment of you as the founder.

Many venture investors know each other and talk with each and for good reason. They are investing in an inherently risky asset class. Manage your messaging and these conversations very carefully. Make it safe and easy for investors to say yes.

Managing Relationships & Getting Around the Networks

Now that we've discussed the art of the soft circle, the question is how do you actually find investors to have these conversations with? *Networking.* Like the soft circle, networking is also an art. There is a reason why fundraising is often called *friendraising.* Be careful how you approach people when asking for introductions.

"I can't tell you how many times I've been asked: *If you know of anyone who may be interested in my company, would you please introduce me,*" recalls Cohen. "Essentially, they are asking that process my giant contacts matrix in my head as if I knew what they all wanted, map it to you as the founder, and then tell you who's a good fit. Don't do that. You need to decide whom you want to target and then ask me to forward them something.

"As a person in the position to make connections for you, think of the position you are putting me in when making introductions for you. When you ask me to introduce you, you are asking me to burn my social capital for you. But if you sent me an email and told me why the person you want to meet makes sense for your business, I can forward it to them. It creates a good dynamic. You are flattering the target and you are setting me up such that it is *your* ask not *my* ask. It always needs to be *your* idea. *You* need to do the work. Then you control the email. It's an ask from you not me.

"Here is a good tool you can use. Create a Google spreadsheet. On the left-hand side, put all targets that you'd like to meet (their name, firm, etc.). Across the top put every mentor, friend, and advisor that you have who has agreed to help you. Your goal is to have your mentors working for you, helping make introductions. Send that spreadsheet to everyone. Let it live in public. This is called *social engineering.* Leverage that dynamic. As your network helps make connections for you, fill in the blanks and publish that. Recognize your mentors, friends, advisors, and others who have helped you make an introduction. Tell everyone how great that mentor is and was for helping you." Venture is social sport.

Recognition is Reward. Venture is a Team Sport.

As Cohen suggests, by publicly publishing how your network is working for you, you also avoid the deadly double intro. "I get six emails from six people introducing me to the same entrepreneur," says Cohen. "This is clearly a coordinated attack and doesn't work. Be more thoughtful and deliberate about how you manage your network."

In summary, keep these things in mind in regard to venture fundraising:

- Ask for less and let the market take you up.
- When you create momentum, you'll get a higher price.
- Stay away from committed valuation in the conversation.
- Manage your commitments.
- Create and maintain really clear communication.
- When things go wrong it's because the communication is not clear.
- Generally when you're telling people about commitments, they are soft.
- Every commitment is soft until you have the check in the bank.
- Be aware that you are asking people to burn social capital by making intros.
- Venture is a team sport. Build and maintain your network.

- Reward and recognize your network for helping you win.

CHAPTER SEVENTEEN

INTRODUCTION TO TERM SHEETS

"You must never try to make all the money that's in a deal.
Let the other fellow make some money too, because if you have a reputa-
tion for always making all the money, you
won't have many deals."

J. Paul Getty

EVERYONE IS FAMILIAR WITH A STORY of a founder who lost control of his or her company. This can happen for a variety of reasons—typically when things turn south—but it doesn't happen accidentally. It's spelled out in the terms and conditions of the agreement between a founder and investors. Before you raise outside capital, you need to understand the language investors speak, if for no other reason than to protect yourself. Welcome to the term sheet.

This chapter will help you understand the elements of a term sheet, how best to navigate them and how to avoid common mistakes. In this chapter, we'll talk about:

- Definition of the term sheet
- Why valuation is often a distraction (read the other fine print)
- Common terms you need to know (and the mechanics of how they work)
- A VC's mandate and types of returns

- Giving up equity and knowing your number

A Non-Binding Way Of Getting On the Same Page

The term sheet is the first written document that both sides of a negotiation, founder and investor, agree to. The term sheet is a non-binding agreement that outlines the fundamental terms and conditions of the deal but has none of the detail that the actual legal documents will have. Like a soft circle discussion with prospective investors, as a founder, you must first seek agreement on the fundamentals of your deal. The term sheet allows both parties to discuss the major points of the deal quickly and without incurring legal costs associated with drawing up binding agreements and contracts. Put simply, it helps founders and investors get on the same page both figuratively and literally.

The Great Distraction: Valuation

In Troy Henikoff's experience as an entrepreneur and venture capitalist, he's found that many entrepreneurs get far too caught up in negotiating their pre-money valuation and miss the fact that valuation is only one part of the deal. "Valuation," explains Henikoff, "is one of *many* terms, each of which can have a financial impact, control impact, or both. You cannot evaluate a deal without looking at *all* the terms. There are examples where you would want a lower valuation with better terms on liquidation preference for example. A $5 million pre-money valuation with the wrong terms can be much worse than a $3 million pre-money valuation with the right terms." Don't make the mistake of focusing exclusively on valuation. Certainly it is important, but so too are many other terms of your agreement with investors. Here's why.

Pre-money valuation is a number that is used to calculate

the percentage of a company that the investors will own for a given investment amount. It is *not* the actual value of your company. Henikoff recalls, "I have seen many cases where a company has multiple term sheets with different pre-money valuations, and the highest is not always the best!"

For example, let's consider the fundraising efforts of a fictitious company we will call Gigglesnort.com. Let's say they set their pre-money valuation at \$4 million and are in-market to raise \$2 million in venture funding. Based simply on the dollars taken in, how much would outside investors now own in Gigglesnort.com?

Mathematically, it's simple:

$$\$4MM \text{ pre-money valuation} + \$2MM \text{ in new money}$$
$$= \$6MM \text{ post-money valuation}$$

The new investors would now own 33% of the Gigglesnort. com: pre-money valuation + new investment = post-money valuation. But this is only the beginning of the story. Absent an understanding of the other terms, the valuation alone means nothing. It doesn't really tell you much at all. Don't make the mistake of focusing only on valuation. You must consider all the other terms on the term sheet including:

- Liquidation Preference
- Convertible Preferred Stock
- Participating Preferred Stock
- Interest Rates
- Vesting Schedule
- Option Pool
- Full Ratchet (an anti-dilution mechanism)
- Weighted Average Anti-dilution
- Board Composition

• Protective Provisions

Liquidation Preference

Investors invest for one reason: to get more money out than they put in. How the money gets distributed upon a liquidation event (selling of the company or company assets) is a critical part of the deal for both the investors and the entrepreneurs. While in the example above, it appears that the investors own 33% of the company, what should happen if the company were sold for $3 million the day after the investment? If there were no liquidation preference, then the investors would get 33% or $1 million (losing $1 million on their investment) and the entrepreneurs would get $2 million (not a bad payout for a day's work). This does not seem fair to the investor and would lead to far fewer investors investing. So, typically, the investors have a class of stock called *preferred stock* and with preferred stock, they get at least a 1x liquidation preference.

This means that with a 1x liquidation preference, the investors will get all of their money back before anyone who owns common stock gets paid. So, if Gigglesnort.com were sold for $3 million the day after the investment was made and the investors had the typical 1x liquidation preference, the investors would get their $2 million back and the entrepreneurs would get the remaining $1 million. The company was sold for 50% of the post-money valuation, but the investors had the downside protection in the form of a preferential return and were *made whole*. Seems fair.

Investors sometimes feel like they are taking a large risk and want *more* than 1x Liquidation Preference to compensate them for that risk. It is less common, but we do sometimes see 1.5x or 2x preferential returns. If there were a 1.5x Liquidation Preference on the Gigglesnort.com deal and they

sell for $3 million, then the investors get 1.5x of their invest-
ment ($3 million) and the entrepreneurs get zero.

Convertible Preferred Stock

In most cases, the preferred stock is *convertible preferred*,
which means that if the investor would get more money by
converting to common stock upon a liquidation event then
that automatically happens. "For example," offers Henikoff,
"if the sale of Gigglesnort.com were for $30 million then the
investor would rather get 33% ($10 million) than getting just
the preferential return. In that case, the preferred stock would
convert to common stock representing 33% of the total and
the investors would receive 33% of the proceeds.

Participating Preferred Stock

There is also participating preferred stock, which works a little differently than convertible preferred. With participating
preferred stock, the investors gets their preferential return but
they also get to convert to common and get their portion of
the common stock. "It is sort of like double dipping," says
Henikoff. "In the case of the $3 million exit for Gigglesnort.
com with a 1x liquidation preference and participating preferred, the investors would get their $2 million and then con-
vert to common stock and receive 33% of the remaining. In
this case they would get $2.33 million and the entrepreneurs
would get $667,000.

"Participating preferred is just another fancy mechanism
for adjusting the risk and return. In general, unless you are
getting a significantly higher pre-money valuation (or other
consideration) in exchange for accepting participating preferred stock, it seems *out of market* and weighted heavily
towards the investors benefit.

"One more consideration to keep in mind: whatever

investor-favorable terms are in the early rounds of financing will most likely appear in the later rounds. The new investors want to get at least what the previous investors got. So if you have participating preferred or a 2x liquidation preference in your first equity round, it is likely that all subsequent rounds will have it too. This is yet another reason you need to be careful with out of market terms in early stages."

Interest Rates

Most term sheets will have a coupon or dividend. It's typical to see 4–8% in an interest rate these days. Typically it is not paid until an exit. "You'll need to pay attention to whether or not it's a straight interest rate or compounding," advises Henikoff, "as compounding interest can add up over the many years it takes a company to get from startup to exit."

Vesting Schedule

You earn your equity over time (typically 4 years). "VCs will insist on it," explains Henikoff. "It keeps the founder engaged and keeps things fair if founders leave early (they only get the portion of equity they earned within the 4-year vesting schedule). When a company gets sold (before a founder is 100% vested), triggers are important. A founder's stock vesting can accelerate in two different ways.

"One way is *single trigger acceleration*. Single trigger means that if the company is sold, the stock vesting will accelerate and the employee will instantly be totally vested (whether you have restricted shares of common stock or stock options). But if the founders' stock is all vested upon a sale, what is to keep them at the new company? Acquirers will be far more interested in buying the company if they have leverage to keep the original founders engaged. As a result, most vesting schedules include a *double trigger* for founders and key employees.

"A double trigger means that if the company is acquired and they do not want to keep you on board with a substantially similar position, then and only then does your vesting accelerate. Otherwise your stock or options will just continue to vest on their original schedule and the acquiring company has some comfort that you have a reason to stay."

Option Pool

Option pools are really important for early stage companies. Option pools represent the percentage of stock to be given to employees who join the company in the future. Having an option pool is critical to attracting top executives when you need them. The option pool always comes out of common stock (the equity percentage of the founders).

Says Henikoff, "Anything above 15% is too much; anything below 5% is not enough. Typically a good range is 10% to 12%, which typically is calculated on the post-money valuation. The size of the option pool has a very big effect on how much you (the founder) take home at the end of the day—much larger than people realize. You need to build a cap table spreadsheet and run scenarios to see the impact on your particular situation."

Full Ratchet (anti-dilution mechanism)

A full ratchet requires that you give investors shares in order to keep their price per share equal to the lowest price per share sold. "For example," says Henikoff, "assume you have 6 million shares of the example above, Gigglesnort.com. Investors bought their shares at $1/share. Now, if you, as a founder, want to sell stock to your uncle for $0.50/share, you have to issue your investors another 2 million shares so that they get the same price as your uncle: $0.50/share. Full ratchets are rarely seen anymore."

Weighted Average Anti-Dilution

More common today is a weighted average anti-dilution. In a weighted average, investors get the same price as the average of the other investors. "Now," explains Henikoff, "selling a single share of stock to your uncle at $0.50 will have a tiny impact on the weighted average. While you may need to issue your investors a share or two, it would be nothing like the 2 million shares that result from having a full rachet!

Board Composition

The composition of the Board of Directors can be critical for founders. Having a board that works well together can be almost magical in how much it can help a company and conversely having a dysfunctional board can be a disaster! Control of the board is something that the founders should be aware of. If the investors have two board seats and the founders only one, then the investors control the board. If things are going well, it is usually not an issue, but when companies fail to meet expectations, who controls the board can greatly affect the outcome. In a seed or Series A round, it is common for the founders to control the board (have a majority of the seats) or at least have equal seats to the investors with one external board member to be agreed upon by both sides. In later rounds, the new investors will want seats too and the founders will likely have to give up control.

Protective Provisions

While the new investors likely own less than half of the company, they still want to protect themselves from downside. There is usually a section titled "Protective provisions" that outlines what actions require the majority of the investors to approve. Typically these will include: selling the company, hiring or firing of C-level executives, issuing more stock, taking on debt greater than a set amount, and approving the annual budget. That means that the investors can block any of these things from happening. You need to understand what the protective provisions are and if you are comfortable with them all.

A VC's Mandate & Types of Returns

In addition to classes of stock, and the terms and issues outlined above, also keep in mind what a VC is looking for in terms of a return. Says Henikoff, "If a VC invests $1 million in each of 10 companies, odds are that four will fail, three will tread water, two will do okay and one will pay back the entire fund. They *need* to have that one pay back 10x to break-even and 20x to 'make the fund.' Therefore, they are looking at your company and determining whether or not they can get 20x out of your company. Is it a 20x return opportunity? *That* is their baseline. Angels don't have this constraint because they don't have a fund to return, which makes their decision process different."

VCs also look at returns through two different lenses.

There are two types of return: Internal rate of return (IRR) and cash-on-cash. IRR is calculated by figuring out what rate of compounded interest over the time of the investment would have returned the amount of cash that was ultimately returned. When interest rates are low, people care less about IRR and are looking to measure cash-on-cash returned or the *multiple* they return. But, when interest rates are high and stock market is growing there is a higher opportunity cost for the money invested in venture and so they are looking at IRR (and comparing it to other investment options on a *per year* basis).

Giving Up Equity & Knowing Your Number

Much of the term sheet is a mathematical equation, but there is also a great deal of psychology and decision-making that is highly subjective and highly personal. One question you will continually find yourself asking is: *How much am I willing to give up in my company in order to grow?* A couple notes to help you think this through.

First, this phrase—*giving up equity*—you hear a lot in the venture world. It is not a healthy way to view what is actually happening. Keep in mind, you, as a founder, are also asking your investors to *give up* their money! Equity has value, but so too does cash. Recognize that they are parting with capital and you are parting with equity. No one is giving up *anything*! They are investing in you and you are investing their capital in your business. It's a deal, not a shakedown.

Second, know your 'number.' What is your number? "There are three types of money that matter," explains Henikoff:

1. Not enough to eat.
2. Enough to eat.
3. Enough to never have to work again.

This is the expectations management part of negotiating ownership in your company. How much is enough? To quote Chuck Templeton, founder of OpenTable, "I viewed fundraising as a way to get as many people vested in my success as possible." While Chuck had to "give up" a significant amount of equity to build OpenTable, it was ultimately the right decision and became a huge win for Chuck and all those involved once the company went public. Hopefully, you, like Chuck, will create a great company and be able to exit for a lot of money. It is important to think about how much you can realistically sell the company for. When exiting, there is a big difference between *having enough to eat* and *never having to work again.* "For example," explains Henikoff, "the difference between $2 million and $10 million can be life changing for most people. It is right between enough to eat and never have to work again. But, the difference between $44 million and $52 million (still $8 million) is far less impactful. Everyone has his/her own *never have to work again* number. It is important to keep that in mind when taking on venture investment and determining equity percentages and terms of your deal."

Valuation means nothing absent an understanding of all the terms on your term sheet. Know them. Study them. Work with mentors who have negotiated term sheets not once but dozens of times. You've worked too hard to get to where you are and you'll work even harder to get to where you want to go. Don't make the mistake of inadvertently agreeing to terms that will ultimately undermine your motivation to work hard. Seek help.

CHAPTER EIGHTEEN

FOUNDER AND TEAM COMPENSATION

"All companies that go out of business do so for the same reason—they run out of money."

Don Valentine, Founding Partner, Sequoia

TANDEM COMPUTERS, founded in 1974 by Jimmy Treybig, was an early computing pioneer. The company dominated fault-tolerant systems for things like ATM networks, stock exchanges, and commercial transaction processing. One of the peculiarities of Tandem was the fact that they would not tell people their salaries before they hired them. After several rounds of interviews, if things went well, attractive candidates would be told that the company thought they'd be a good fit. If, during the interview process, candidates asked about salary, they would be told it would be competitive. If people insisted on knowing salary, they would not be offered the position. Treybig believed, "if people come for the money, they will leave for the money."

Treybig understood a fundamental fact of business. Money is a commodity. If the only thing you use to attract talent is money, you have no competitive advantage in hiring. Sure you may attract a lot of people with higher salaries, but you'll also attract people for whom money is everything. This isn't always the case, but it leaves the door open for them to leave easily when offered better packages elsewhere. What would make them stick around? Treybig believed that if people joined because they were attracted to the industry, the people, the culture, and the values of the organization they would be better employees and would also be more likely to stay longer.

It's the same reason Zappos pays new hires to leave. Zappos calls their program *The Offer*. The Offer is made to all employees. What started as a $100 incentive to quit graduated through $500, then $1000, and now stands at one month's salary. The Offer is made to each employee during the company's training program. Jeff Bezos has adopted a similar program at Amazon called *Pay to Quit* for its fulfillment center employees. The first year it's $2000. It then increases by $1000 per year up to a maximum of $5000.

Sounds crazy, right? Don't most companies pay bonuses for people who stay, not to those who quit? While these programs may not work for all companies, for Amazon and Zappos, Pay to Quit and The Offer are brilliant ideas. You can think of these programs as an opportunity to deepen employee engagement. Here's why.

Don't think about the people who take the packages. Think about the people who don't. If every year, as an employee, you are given a chance to ask yourself what the company means to you and then you are given a choice that actually tests that meaning (a dollar figure), think about how much the company and the job must mean to those who stay. They are clearly not in it only as a transactional relationship. Recall the 13% of employees who are engaged at work and the 900 million people globally who are not. It's about more than money.

In this chapter, we'll talk about:

- Where to find data on non-founder startup employee salaries
- Rules of thumb on average founder salaries (tied to monthly revenue)
- Ballpark salary, bonus and equity for non-founder team members

Startups, of course, often can't compete by dangling large cash packages around. And so they also use equity. However, be careful. As a founder, it is good to have a sense of what you will eventually need to pay people in order to attract talent at market rates. Otherwise, you could risk either giving away too much equity, paying too much, or—equally challenging—not being taken seriously for not offering enough. While there are an endless number of websites that provide salary data for established companies, for startups it has been much less transparent. This too will change over time. One emerging source is a tool offered by AngelList, an online community of startups and investors. AngelList has a feature that gives greater transparency to non-founder startup salaries. Using data from the companies on the site, the tool allows you to filter by *role, location, skill,* and *market.* For example, you could filter for Data Scientist (role), San Francisco (location), Python (skill), and Enterprise Software (market). Or you could search for Marketing, Chicago, Social Media, Health Care.

Every market is different. Every company is different. Every situation is different. That said, there are a few data points on founder cash compensation for you to consider. Compass collected salary data from 11,160 startups globally. What their data shows is that 75% of startup founders make less than $75,000 per year and 66% of startup founders make less than $50,000 per year. Average salaries globally range from $30,208 in India to $72,363 in Australia.

The primary predictor of startup founder salaries, according to their data, is current monthly revenue. Until the company makes $10,000 per month in revenue, the average founder salary does not break the $50,000 mark. Not until the company books over $1 million in monthly revenue do founders' salaries break the $100,000 mark. Of note, their data shows that age is also a predictor. Older founders (age 41+) pay themselves 71% more than younger founders (under 40). It is worth noting however that the highest salary age range still barely breaks $60,000 per year—it's all relative. The most important thing to keep in mind as a founder is that, whatever you choose to pay yourself, you are setting a precedent and a signal. If you take a low salary, you will send a much better message to others who you ask to take a lower salary than if you take a big salary and ask them to work for Ramen noodles and a bag of chips.

In addition to cash compensation, of course, is founder equity. It's difficult to know how much equity a founder will retain simply because—at the very early stages—you do not know how the business will perform over time or how many funding rounds you may need to go through to grow the business. It's also a personal decision. Some founders are willing to "give up" more equity to fund growth whereas others aren't. "Generally," says Techstars' Troy Henikoff, "after their seed round, founders' remaining equity should still be 60% plus (i.e., 20-30% for investors and 10-15% for options). In the next round, they will likely be around 40-45%, but it really, *really* depends on a lot of factors, i.e., the financial shape of the company, growth trajectory of the business, negotiating skills of the founders and investors, and so on. Every situation is different."

Some startup founders will do the seed round themselves and get to a working prototype. In these situations, the question is: How should the money invested be treated? Matt McCall, partner at Pritzker Group Venture Capital advises: "I would first divide up the equity pre-money. Once that is set, determine a value for the company (most likely between $2 million to $5 million) and let the money buy an ownership stake. A simpler approach so as to avoid the potentially contentious pricing of the firm by founders is to have the money come in as a convertible note that converts at the same terms as the first professional money. This works if a venture or angel round is likely in the next year. Else, price it yourselves."

Beyond founder compensation and equity, as a founder it would behoove you to have some sense of what you should plan to pay those you'll need to hire. And so we've included some rules of thumb below offered by McCall. It is important to note that his general guidance is focused more on early/expansion stages of a company's life cycle more than the very early startup stage (or later stage). You may be in a situation where you don't have enough money in the bank to pay salaries at all, whether that's money in the form of revenue or venture capital. Once you do, however, this should be useful. Also keep in mind that this is data from the time of the writing of this book. Wages change over time, but this will give you a general ballpark.

"In addition," says McCall, "There are several caveats you need to keep in mind with the following data. First, these are non-founder salaries and equity. Founders will make much less cash and much more equity. Second, you need to be prepared to make cuts to these numbers depending on the cash flow of the company at any point in time. It is not uncommon to reduce cash and increase equity grants in order to manage burn rate. And third, every situation is different. These are general guidelines only. Beyond cash, a founder should think about carving out 10-15% in an equity or option pool for the first wave of hires. These shares can be either stock grants with reverse vesting or options that vest over four years. The core founders can divide the remaining portion equally or based upon perceived value being brought to the game. Equal division for the core allocation creates the most egalitarian approach, though it might not be the fairest one."

1. **CEO** (non-founder): $180k-$200k salary, $50k+ bonus, 5-7% equity
2. **CMO**: $150k-$175k salary, $50k-$75k bonus, 2% equity
3. **COO/CFO**: $150k-$175k salary, $50k bonus, 1-1.5% equity
4. **VP Sales**: $150k salary, $50k-$75k (bonus tied to sales), 1-2% equity
5. **Other VPs**: $140k-$150k salary, $25k-50k bonus, 0.75-1% equity
6. **Director** (and below): The market will dictate these. Directors are typically in the $110k-130k range, key programmers in the $90k-$120k range, controller in the $50k-$80k range depending on experience.

"Again," reminds McCall, "these are very rough cuts. For example, a rock star CEO could easily end up at $225k-$250k in salary with a $75k-100k bonus. The thing you have to remember most is to have enough runway (target at least 18–24 months, 12 months minimum). This is your key life-line. If or when you get in a tight situation, you need to sit your team down and discuss an across the board pay cut (with equity bonus tied to goals). You need to do this now so that the company has a number of months to stretch out the run-way. Firms almost always wait too long, hoping that things will turn, and start efforts like pay cuts with only a couple of months to go. This does little to impact the runway as you have too few pay periods of savings. I have never (yes, never) heard a CEO bemoaning the fact that he/she reduced his/her burn too soon. I have frequently heard them comment that they wish they had done so 6-8 months earlier."

One last thing to know because it's a question sometimes raised by founders: Can a founder take money off the table in subsequent funding rounds? First off, don't worry about this now if you are early-stage. You've got much bigger problems to worry about than when you will be able to get liquid. That said, in McCall's experience, "If and when that may happen, the company is usually cash flow positive and the only way for the VCs to get enough money to work in the deal is to buy founders' shares. There are two things to note:

"First, this stock is usually common and the new money coming in is preferred. If preferred is priced at $1.00, then common will be priced at a discount to this (often 20-50%) depending on the size of the preference stack (preferred money in). The more preference in, the greater the discount. Also, remember to keep this pricing of common consistent with how you are pricing your options. This common sale is a third-party pricing of the common. You have to issue your options at that price as well.

"Second, VCs generally don't like to see founders take money off the table. It can lead to founders losing drive and motivation if they already have their nest egg and the rest is house money. Some founders remain equally motivated, but it's hard."

General rule of thumb on founder and team compensation: it's hard to compete on cash and equity alone. Remember, cash and equity are commodities and other companies have the same commodities. Generally, you should be in market and competitive. However, don't forget, your real source of competitive advantage for attracting the best talent will often be derived from things other than cash and stock—they are only two of the motivators at your disposal as a founder. Do not underestimate the importance of culture, values, category, and other perks that have nothing to do with finance. Money isn't everything.

CHAPTER NINETEEN

BOARD OF DIRECTORS

*"The only thing to do with good advice is to pass it on.
It is never of any use for oneself."*
Oscar Wilde

DON VALENTINE IS A LEGEND in the venture community. He was a founder of National Semiconductor and a sales and marketing executive for Fairchild Semiconductor (the company that gave birth to the Silicon Valley—look it up!). Think: Gordon Moore, Eugene Kleiner, C. Sheldon Roberts, Robert Noyce, Victor Grinich, Julius Blank, Jean Hoerni, Jay Last. Legends all.

Valentine founded Sequoia Capital in 1972. They were the original investors in Apple, Atari, LSI Logic, Oracle, Cisco, Electronic Arts, Google, YouTube, and many others. He is known not to mince words. Says Valentine: "I am 100% behind my CEOs right up till the day I fire them." His reasoning could be explained by another Valentine maxim: "The trouble with the first time entrepreneur is that he doesn't know what he doesn't know."

As a founder, know this: When you raise venture capital, you get two things in return—money and an opinion. In this chapter, we'll talk about:

- The board's job
- Mechanics of creating and managing a board
- How to run board meetings

The Board's Job

"Your board is a big deal," says Techstars' David Cohen. "The group that controls the board controls you and runs the company." Let's be clear: Cohen is not suggesting that the board's role is to *operate* the company. That's management's job. The board, however, has significant influence due to their fiduciary responsibility to shareholders. Boards work for the company not for the founder or the CEO. The board's primary job, as Cohen points out (as does Valentine), "is to hire and fire the CEO." Among other things, they are responsible for making sure the right team is in place to run the company. "Of course," says Cohen, "you want to have board members who are active and who want to be there every meeting and hopefully in between when asked. It's not a bad thing. You just need to have balance on your board." Meddling board members do exist. Contrary to popular opinion, board members are human just like the rest of us. You want to be mindful and deliberate when selecting and electing board members. Stuart Larkins, a well-regarded venture capitalist and partner at Chicago Ventures, advises founders to do their homework on investors. "The investor is likely going to sit on your board," says Larkins. "You're going to be working with them. Talk to other CEOs who've had that person on their board, both successful companies and ones that have folded. When things go wrong, that's when the true colors come out. You want to know how potential board members may react in different situations."

There are libraries full of books on boards (and one big

Internet). The most definitive source on startup boards is Brad Feld and Mahendra Ramsinghani's book, aptly titled *Startup Boards*. If you want to go deep on the subject, buy it. Even if you don't want to go deep, buy it anyway. You won't regret it. Also, Fred Wilson, co-founder of Union Square Ventures and Mark Suster, partner at Upfront Ventures, have written some fantastic blog posts on the subject. Where relevant, I've cited their posts heavily in this chapter.

For our purposes in this book, we've outlined the primary issues you should be thinking about as a founder, namely:

- The Board's fiduciary duty
- Board structure
- The startup board's unique character (it changes)
- Directors vs. observers
- Board chair
- Board committees
- Board composition
- Board meetings

As is our agenda throughout this book, one of our goals is to help you avoid common mistakes. One such lesson is this: It is a lot easier to test and learn with an MVP than with a BOD. Be deliberate. Be careful. Be informed. Boards of Directors are composed of people not product features. You can't just turn them off on a whim—quite the contrary.

The Board's Fiduciary Role

First, make no mistake, the board has a legal and ethical responsibility to do what is in the best interest of the company. The board works for the company. At times, this can even mean acting against board members' interests as shareholders. For example, to paraphrase Fred Wilson, co-founder of

Union Square Ventures: "Let's say an accounting irregularity is discovered that will adversely affect the underlying value of the stock. The board has a duty to disclose and investigate this situation. Is this in the best interest of shareholders (invariably the stock price will likely drop on this news)? (That's a trick question.) It's not just a *responsibility* to shareholders. The operative words are *legal* and *ethical* responsibility to shareholders." The board must act in good faith, always.

Board Structure
In terms of structure, what size board is the right size and what should you expect as a founder when taking outside capital? It depends. "Is it reasonable for a founder to give up board control for a $1 million seed investment?" asks David Cohen. "Likely not. Should the board be equal? (i.e., one founder, one investor, one mutually agreed upon outsider). Probably. You want it to be balanced. It's good to have outside perspective. The thing you want to be careful about are those who want to come in and control the board at a seed stage. That is scary, although it will likely never happen." Reputation is at work. That is out of market and word will spread quickly. The result: that particular investor will not see a lot of deals in their future. "Generally," says Cohen, "if you're raising $3-6 million you should expect balance on the board. If you're raising $10 million, it will likely tilt in the direction of investors. At some point, it's really not your company anymore. It's everyone's company. And that is not necessarily a bad thing. That hopefully means you are succeeding in a big way." The key is to make sure your board is manageable both behaviorally and functionally. Size helps (don't get too big).

The Startup Board's Unique Character (it changes)
Boards are not only sources of advice, they are invaluable

sources of networking, expertise, and, of course, access to capital. You need a board for no other reason than, as a startup, you need help, and a lot of it! That said: It is important to note that startup boards are significantly different than the boards of mature companies. Namely, startup boards change over time based on the needs of the business. A business without customers (or a handful of early adopters) will likely need to be governed differently than one operating at scale. As Feld points out: "The role of board members changes at different stages of the startup's growth: early stage (customer discovery, product development), revenue (strategy, sales) and growth (finance, HR, strategy)." Unlike many mature company boards, startup boards play more than an oversight role. In the very earliest of stages, some members of startup boards are as deep into the operations as the founders. Keep this in mind when you start operating with a board. Their role will change (and you will want it to change over time).

Board Chair

Just as the Board makes sure management is doing its job, the Board Chair makes sure the Board is doing its job. This includes orchestrating board meetings, ensuring participation of each board member, and communicating with the CEO. The Board Chair also plays an important arbiter role in debates (a frequent and desired occurrence). You don't want fights, but you do want debate. Dissent is not a bad thing.

Fred Wilson puts it best: "When there are debates and disagreements, the Board Chair should make sure all opposing points of view are heard and then the Board Chair should push for some resolution." Wilson goes on to suggest: "The Board Chair should be on the nominating committee and should probably run that committee. I do not believe the Board Chair needs to be on the audit and compensation committees, but if they have specific experience that would add value to those committees, it is fine to have them on them. Either way, the Board Chair needs to be on top of the issues that are being dealt with in the committees and making sure they are operating well."

Wilson goes on to suggest that small boards (three or less) generally do not really need Board Chairs. "In many cases," says Wilson, "the founding CEO will also carry the Chairman title, but in a small board, it is meaningless. Once the board size reaches five, the Board Chair role starts to take on some value. At seven and beyond, I believe it is critical to have a Board Chair."

On the issue of a founder/CEO also playing the Board Chair role, Wilson has an informed opinion on this too. "I am not a fan of this," say says. "I think the Chair should be an independent director who takes on the role of helping the CEO manage the board. The CEO runs the business, but it is not ideal for the CEO to also have to run the board. A Chair who can work closely with the CEO and help them stay in sync with the board and get value out of a board is really valuable and CEOs should be eager to have a strong person in that role."

Board Directors vs. Board Observers

As stated earlier, when you raise venture capital you'll get money and an opinion in return. So, from a board perspective, whose opinions will you be getting exactly? There are two: board *directors* and board *observers*. They are different and you should know these differences.

Directors have two fiduciary duties: *the duty of care* and *the duty of loyalty*. Basically, they are expected and required to exercise sound judgment in good faith. Directors also vote on important decisions such as approving strategy, executive compensation, and so on.

So what's a board observer? In a startup not every investor will have a seat on the board. That would be a hot mess. When the number of investors exceeds the number of board seats, venture capitalists often ask for (and get) observer rights. Observer rights allow them to attend board meetings and be privy to the same information as directors. They do not however vote or have access to attorney-client privileged information. Sometimes VCs view the observer role as an opportunity to "train" their associates (give them exposure to what goes on in board meetings). Other times, observer roles are granted to investors who come in on later rounds. The primary difference and one that you should seriously consider is that, unlike directors, observers have no fiduciary duty to the company.

Whereas directors can be held liable for participation, observers (generally) cannot. For this reason and others, some investors do not like to have observers on the board unless observers are associates or partners of a VC firm. Generally, unless you end up in a situation where you do not have control (or you choose not to accept a given investors capital who is requesting an observer role), the decision to allow board observers is yours. Before you get too worried about observers, keep the golden rule of venture investing in mind: *reputation is everything*. An observer who acts with malice or, frankly, is simply a pain in the ass will likely not be invited into many deals. This isn't always the case, but do know that most people act in good faith. But also know that you can control the range of possible outcomes by spending the time to define observers' rights upfront. Make it explicit. Everything in life is negotiable. In venture, even more things are negotiable! Put it in writing.

Board Committees

Board committees vary by company, but generally you will have committees responsible for audit, compensation, nominating, and governance. The *audit* committee is responsible for oversight of financial reporting. The *compensation* committee is responsible for approving executive compensation. The *nominating* committee nominates members for election to the board as well as CEO succession, and the *governance* committee provides procedural guidance to the board and evaluates the board. The primary goal is to have someone take the lead on each of these important areas and have specific responsibility for them.

Board Composition

There are a several factors you need to consider when putting your board together. A few of the most important factors we'll discuss here are the following: *board selection, election, evolution, control, independent directors,* and *term limits*.

Selection & Election: When selecting board members, you want to take into account several factors including their personalities. Remember, you are going to be working with these people very closely. Feld suggests: "In terms of personality, the director can be the cheerleader, truth teller, or domain expert, and is chosen for his or her experience, skills, and networks." A balanced board should reflect a good measure of each of these attributes. Remember, not only will you be working with the board, the board must also work together. They are people not machines. You want debate, but you don't want dysfunction. You're a startup. It's hard enough already. Be mindful. In terms of the election process, the nominating committee puts directors up for election by shareholders who, in turn, elect the Board of Directors. In situations where the founder controls the company, the founder is the nominating "committee."

Evolution & Control: As Feld suggested earlier, a startup board's role evolves over time. At the very early stages, the founder often retains control. Eventually, as you go out to raise venture capital, investors (institutional investors, not angels, usually) will negotiate for board seats. Says Wilson, "The way investors negotiate for a board seat is usually via something called a *Shareholders Agreement*. This is an agreement between all the shareholders of the company. It contains a bunch of provisions, but one of the provisions can be an agreement that all shareholders of the company will vote for a representative of a certain investor in the election of the Board of Directors. The representative can even be named specifically." It is important to note that this does not mean the founder will lose control of the board. "For example," explains Wilson, "it can remain a three person board with one investor and two founder directors. Or the board can expand to five and the investor can take one or two seats and the founder can control the rest."

In the same way that a startup board's role will evolve over time, a company's center of power will often shift from founders to investors. This is not a bad thing. To Cohen's point, it likely means you are succeeding.

During the evolution of your company from founder control to investor control you may want to consider the role of an independent director. Suggest Wilson: "An independent director is a director who does not represent either the founder or the investors. Boards that are full of vested interests are not good boards. The more independent minded the board becomes, the better it usually is."

Term Limits: As your company grows, so too will the skills, experiences, and networks you will require. This also holds for board members. The board members you have in the very early days are not necessarily the same types of folks you will need later on. Therefore, it is common practice to maintain term limits for board members (four years) and to recruit board members regularly. This also provides a healthy dynamic to bring in new voices and opinions that can look at the business through a new lens. Of course, with venture investments, it is not uncommon to have members on your board that may be on your board for a decade. Eventually, should your company go public, your Shareholder Agreement will terminate, at which point you'll have an entirely new set of issues to deal with. We'll save that for another book!

Board Meetings

Boards operate by virtue of meetings. Meetings are a human invention prone to both inspiration and soul sucking (depending on how they're run).

In the very early stages of your company, your board may meet monthly. Over time you will likely want to dial it back to twice quarterly. Generally, it's good form to have one board meeting at the beginning of the quarter and one at the end. You can meet in person or via phone (though in-person board meetings are very, *very* highly recommended). You should also build in updates between meetings. We'll cover a few great ways to do this later in a concept coined by Mark Suster called the *agile board*.

General rules of thumb for board meetings: Have structure. Promote open discussion. Don't force your way through an agenda when the conversation hits a critical issue. *That* critical issue may not even be on the agenda but it could be the issue that makes or breaks your company. Stop. Listen. Good boards are always on the lookout for the Achilles heel. *Manage the downside; let the upside take care of itself.* If this means you run out of time before you get to the other items on your agenda, that's okay. Come back to it later, in a subsequent board meeting (or update).

Brad Feld has been to literally thousands of board meetings. Given his abundance of experience (and the fact that he is an entrepreneur himself), he has spent a lot of time trying to figure out how to make board meetings better. Two principles that Feld has found helpful: "To be effective, board meetings need to be (a) in-person and (b) there is immense value in a board dinner the night before a board meeting (maybe not every meeting, but at least once a quarter)." Feld's point about board dinners reminds me of the ancient Persian tradition governing decision-making. *Make all decisions twice: once while drunk, once while sober.* If you come to the same conclusion, move forward. If not, continue deliberation. Of course, Feld is not suggesting you add alcohol. Rather, what Feld knows from experience is that how humans interact over a good meal is far different than how they act across a boardroom table.

Feld also suggests that you be very careful when designing the board agenda. Information generally comes in three forms: what *happened*, what *is* happening, and what *needs* to happen. Feld suggests a bias on the latter. "I have found," says Feld, "that board meetings should be forward-looking. Ironically (and frustratingly), the general culture of many VC-based boards—especially large ones—is to be backward-looking. What I mean by this is that most board meetings are 80% status updates, 10% strategy and issues, and 10% administration. I'm fine with the 10% administration, but the 80% and 10% split on status vs. strategy should be reversed. There are plenty of different ways to organize the 'strategy.' I'm using strategy as shorthand for 'forward looking discussion' and strategy includes a blend of short-, medium-, and long-term issues, as well as plenty of 'tactical stuff.'"

Here is what Feld advises to make your board meetings

most effective:

Send Pre-reads: All board material goes out 48 hours in advance, including a detailed financial package and operating review of the business. This material includes any administrative stuff (draft 409a report, options grants, compensation stuff, audit stuff, prior board meeting minutes.) Everyone reads this in advance—if the materials go out 48 hours in advance there's no excuse to have not read it.

Break Bread: There is a dinner the night before that is at least the board and the CEO. Sometimes it includes non-CEO founders; other times it includes various members of the leadership team. This is a casual dinner (e.g., not expensive or full of pomp and circumstance). It's a chance for everyone to catch up with each other. If the board meeting is an afternoon meeting, sometimes you can pull off a lunch prior to the meeting that acts as a proxy for the dinner, or a dinner after, although I find the dinner after to be much less helpful.

Admin First: The first 30 minutes of the meeting are administrative. Everyone settles down, you go through any formal board business, discuss it, and get it done. Often it takes five minutes (which gives you an extra 25 minutes for the strategy stuff); sometimes it takes the full 30 minutes. I can't think of a case where it has ever needed to take longer.

Show the Money Slide: The CEO then puts up *one* slide summarizing prior period financial performance and asks if anyone has any questions about the board package. This discussion takes however long it takes.

Show the Issues Slide: The CEO then puts up *one* slide with the issues he or she would like to discuss. These are bullet points that are crisp yet detailed enough to know what the issue is. This is then the bulk of the meeting.

"In my experience," says Feld, "some CEOs are capable of running a two-hour plus discussion off of one slide (I *love* these guys!). Others need slides to prompt them through the setup for each topic (which is fine). Either way, the setup for each topic should be brief (five minutes at most) and the bulk of the activity should be a discussion. The CEO and management team is looking for board feedback, input, advice, and guidance. Ultimately, the CEO has to synthesize this and decide what he or she wants to do, but by engaging the board in an active discussion, the team will generally get useful input as well as discover where there might be additional domain expertise around the table on the particular issue.

"I've found that the more time that is spent on #5 (the issues slide), the more impactful the meeting is. Obviously, it's difficult for people on the phone to engage as effectively, which draws them into physically attending the meeting, or not participating."

Fred Wilson seconds Brad's thoughts and also offers a few tips of his own:

CEO 'Keeping Me Up at Night' List: To paraphrase Wilson: "A technique I like a lot is when the CEO puts up a list of the three or four things that are 'keeping me up at night' at the start of each meeting. This can be a way of teeing up the discussion items for the meeting. Or it can just be a way for the Board to get into the mind of the CEO quickly. The best way I've seen this done is when the CEO has a slide that shows the items that were on the 'keeping me up at night' slide from the prior meeting and the items that are on the current list. Show what things have been 'resolved,' 'not resolved,' and 'new things that have popped up' in the time since the last meeting."

Executive Session: Wilson continues, "Possibly the most important technique I've observed over the years is the executive session at the end of the meeting. This is when the Board meets *without* the CEO and team in the room and has a discussion of the meeting and what the key takeaways are. The executive session can be five minutes or it can be a half hour. Sometimes there is very little to discuss in executive session. Sometimes there is a lot. After the executive session ends, the CEO should either be invited back to have a debrief on the executive session or the Chairman of the Board should meet with the CEO to debrief on the executive session. This is an opportunity for the Board to provide feedback to the CEO on the business, the team, and performance, and the strategy. Boards should not miss this opportunity to provide feedback and CEOs should demand it of them."

Whatever You Do, Do Not Do This: Do not use this time as a CEO as simply an operational reporting session. Nor should you have a one-way dialogue or spend the entire time educating the board on industry happenings. The board meeting is not to 'update the board.' The board meeting is to help the CEO and his or her management team. If you're wrestling with decisions that need to be made or changes in direction you are considering or major shifts in strategy, these are the sorts of items you want to get board input on.

Agile Boards

Like Feld and Wilson, Mark Suster has suggested a spin on trying to make board meeting more productive in what he calls the *agile board*.

Suster's focus with agile boards is not what happens *at* board meetings as much as it is about what happens *in between* them. "Doing nothing between board meetings," suggests Suster, "is like running the waterfall software development process. We all know that modern software companies run on the 'agile' development process by having short release cycles and frequent communication. Boards will thrive on this, too."

Suster suggests a few tips on running an agile board:

Make the Business of Making Introductions Easy &

Transparent: Create a 'need to meet' spreadsheet and publish it to your board. Suster suggests you map it over time (i.e., who you need to meet now, in the next 3 months, 6 months, and so on). Make this public to all board members and thank them when they make the connections. David Cohen suggests a similar technique. What both Suster and Cohen understand is the social nature of venture investing. People want to help. And people want to be recognized for helping. It's human nature. And it's a good thing. Use it to your advantage.

Don't Assume They Remembered Everything That Is Happening: Never assume that board members will remember every single item discussed at the last board meeting. Take time to—very quickly—remind them of what's changed, what competitors have done since then, and how you're responding. Be careful. This is not an operational update. It's more strategic in nature. To paraphrase Suster: your board can't keep up with the constant changes as much as you can. Don't assume they know what you know.

Save Surprises for Birthday Parties Not Board Meetings: Keep in mind that VCs that sit on your board also have partners. The last thing any VC wants to do is to surprise their partnership with bad news. But they also want to be able to share the positive stuff that is happening. They, like you, have an office to return to and people they work with. What will their partners ask them about you when they get back to the office? Suster suggests three things: What's working? What's not working? And when will you run out of cash? Says Suster, "When you think you'll run out of cash is the single biggest thing your board and investors should *not* be surprised about. Even if it's 15 months away they need to know when you think you'll need to be fundraising."

Board Sprint Process: One last suggesting from Suster—in the spirit of agility—is to send out a single page of bullet point notes via email every two weeks. Here's what he suggests:

- Don't do it as an attachment (put it in the body of the email itself).
- Use bullets.
- Keep it short.
- Send it every two weeks (if appropriate).
- Break it into major wins, plans, help I need (on a running two-week cycle).
- Make it clear that they do not need to dig in to every one (it's more about cadence).
- Keep it high-level or it will feel like overkill.

Boards are important. And how you manage them is critical. Starting and building a company is hard enough, don't make it more difficult by inadvertently ending up with a dysfunctional board. Take the time to identify the right board members, establish operating procedures and rigor early in your development as a company. Remember, VCs want to help. Sure they have opinions, but they also have experience. Don't forget Don Valentine's maxim about first time entrepreneurs not knowing what they don't know. Great venture investors and great board members *know* what you do not know. As the adage goes: it costs $150 million to train a venture capitalist. They've already made the mistakes. At least give them the benefit of the doubt.

CHAPTER TWENTY

INVESTOR COMMUNCATION

*"The single biggest problem in communication is
the illusion that it has taken place."*
George Bernard Shaw

AS AN INVESTOR, the only thing worse than getting bad news from a founder is getting no news from a founder. Personally, I love to get updates from the founders I've backed. Great news, good news, not-so-good news, news that makes me wonder why I ever wrote the check to begin with—I love it all. Okay, that's a lie. Bad news sucks. But I'd rather know about it than not. It's all part of the innovation process. It's a mess at times, but a fun mess.

In this chapter, we'll talk about:

- Why you need to open communication after you close your round
- Benefits of deliberate and consistent investor communication
- A hypothetical example of a founder email update to investors

Your Round Is Closed, Now Open Communication

Communication between founders and investors is vital for early stage companies. Just because your deal has closed, the relationship has not. Now that you have your investors' money, they are going to be quite interested in talking with you or, at the very least, hearing from you now and then. They'll want to know how you're doing, how the team is doing, what customers are saying about the product, the challenges you are having, and so on. Money has a way of focusing one's attention. *Don't make the mistake of closing communication after you've closed your round.* If anything, err on the side of overcommunicating at first. You can ramp down once you've established a rhythm with your investor team.

As director of the Chicago-based Techstars program, Steve Farsht has seen many companies go through the program. Says Farsht, "I often think about the dozens of early stage companies that I have worked with over the last several years. I think about their teams, I think about their business models, and I think about the success I hope to see them achieve. But I also think about what went wrong. In my opinion, one of the greatest factors contributing to a company's demise has been the lack of a communications strategy by the CEO, specifically as it relates to nurturing long-term relationships with their investors and potential investors. While communication during the fundraising process is critical, it's even *more* important in the post-fundraising stage of a company's early life. Identifying goals and metrics and communicating updates about them on a regular basis creates a cadence that will undoubtedly help you when you start to run out of money."

As Farsht points out, the odds are very likely that you will run out of money and it will likely sooner than you plan to.

Entrepreneurs often overestimate revenue and underestimate costs. It's the *only* thing that is actually predictable in venture! You will likely need an investors' next check as much as the one they just wrote. If you want them to keep the checkbook open, keep communication open. According to Farsht, "As a start, I strongly encourage founders to be disciplined in communicating with their investors on a monthly basis. For companies that have an established business model and are beginning to scale, this could include financial statements against budget (income statement and balance sheet), updates on human resources, product development, number of months of cash in the bank at the current burn, and where your investors can help if needed. For companies that are still working on product/market fit, all of these items listed above can be included in addition to the tests that are being conducted and the results of such tests. This approach will give your investors confidence that you have your shit together as well as a better idea of how you're allocating the capital you've raised. This transparency should pay huge dividends when you look to raise more capital down the road.

"It is critical to solicit feedback from your investors (and board members) on whether you are communicating in an effective way. In my experience, one of my most frustrating experiences was pulling together comprehensive monthly updates, emailing them off to investors/board members and assuming that they were being read. I believed that I was doing such a great job of keeping our stakeholders in the loop. It took me a few bad board meetings to realize that even if I sent them information, that didn't mean that I was communicating effectively. And this takes humility to understand. You can take their lack of attention to your emails as disrespect (i.e., the high-powered VC is too important to read your emails). Or you can look at it through a different lens: that people consume information in different ways and that it is your responsibility to figure out the way that best resonates with your investors (and board members). It still bothers me that they didn't read my updates. I also believe it was their loss. But I take responsibility nonetheless for the breakdown in communications."

Benefits of Great Investor Communication

There are a number of reasons why you should develop a habit of communicating with your investors regularly, among them: it's a great way to leverage your investor team's knowledge and network, to hold yourself accountable, and to improve internal communication.

1. *Leverages your investor team*: Lean on your investors. Keep them close. In a startup, there is no need to hide. Pushing bad news under the rug or not admitting to mistakes will ruin you, or at the very least it will cause suspicion. All venture investors are used to tough news. Also, remember that your investors have relevant experience, deep networks, and a very strong desire to see you win. At the same time, they are busy people. They have jobs to do as well. You are not their only investment. And so you want to make sure you get the most out of your investor team. You need to stay on their radar. They won't forget about you, but they will worry about you.

2. *Holds founders accountable*: Farsht adds, "This [reporting] approach also holds founders accountable to themselves. In early stages, most founders don't have boards to hold them accountable. They're working their tails off, hours becoming days, days become weeks, then weeks become months, and suddenly

you've lost complete track of time and can't believe how much has happened. By taking a few hours a month to pull together these communications, you're able to take a step back from the business and assess it from a different perspective. In the end, you may find yourself looking at the business in a completely different way."

3. *Improves internal communication*: This process will also help you communicate more effectively with your co-founders and employees. Farsht suggests, "You will be able to reuse much of what you pull together to provide better insight to your employees on the company's progress. They will see more of the bigger picture, which should give them more confidence in you and more attachment to the company. If executed well, you will have documented the progress you've made over a 12–18 month period of time, and this information will be very helpful when raising your Series A (or Seed Extension). If you aren't doing this now, it's not too late, but it will be too late if you start when you're running out of cash. I've seen the latter too many times."

To give you an idea of what types of information you may want to consider sharing with your investors on a monthly basis, here is an example of an investor communication from the CEO of fictitious company we'll call YoyosAndPoodles. com. For our purposes here, we're keeping it simple, but you can also imagine the detail that you could provide behind each of these update headlines (e.g., Financial Update, Product Update, Team Update, High Fives, Growing Pains, What We Need From You). One note: You should always have an "ask" in your updates. Contrary to folklore, entrepreneurship is not a solo endeavor. It's a team sport. You never know who may have the answer or know someone you need to meet: a key hire, a potential customer, a follow-on investor, and so on. Ask.

Hello YoyosAndPoodles.com Investors,

Things are going well in the Yo-yos & Poodles biz. I'm writing to give you an update on Q1:

- Financial Update (financial statements also attached to this email)
- Product Update
- Team Update
- High Fives
- Low Fives (aka "Growing Pains")
- What We Need From You

Financial Update
- Revenue is up ($2M revenue run rate)
- Burn is down (Q1 = $15K average monthly burn vs. $18K in Q4 of last year)
- Runway is $750K

Product Update
- Our MVP v1.0 failed to hit our goals. We take solace in Reid Hoffman's observation, "If you're not embarrassed by the first version of the product, you've launched too late.") Version 2.0 hit the mark (see: customer comments).

- We have successfully moved tech development in-house with a new hire (and thus have cut our testing cycle time in half; the guy doesn't sleep).
- We are launching on iOS next week! (wOOt).

Team Update
- Our intern quit (He fell in love and is moving to Sri Lanka, see photos here).
- We received 168 applications to fill his role (two of them are rock stars).
- Morale is at an all-time high (the great media coverage helped! see below).

High Fives
- The media loves us (see: stories by *The New York Times*, *TechCrunch* here).
- Acquired a major distribution deal (announcement here).
- Received these great customer love letters (see: Dave, Barb, and Steve here).
- Our part-time CTO accepted our offer to join full-time! (She rocks!).

Growing Pains (aka "Low Fives")
- Our servers couldn't handle the awesome press. We were dark for 3 hrs last week.
- Our biggest enterprise customer threatened to move to our competitor over price.
- Our biggest competitor just closed a $10M Series A round.
- Our SEO strategy has stalled (we hired Brent Payne and we're working on it).

What We Need From You

- We are hiring a full-time salesperson/who do you know? (see: job specs).
- We've outgrown our co-working space and need a larger office/know any companies that are looking to sub-let space in the southern Main Street area?
- Once we launch on iOS, we could use everyone's help in promoting. Please post the following to Facebook, Twitter, and LinkedIn (see: canned post and tweet language that each investor can simply cut and paste to their followers about the iOS launch).

In summary, team morale is high due to the great media coverage, but the media coverage crashed our servers. Our biggest competitor raised a big round to test our creativity. But, the good news is our burn rate is down and our run rate is up. Based on the most recent version of our financial model (shout out to Board member Troy Henikoff), we are cautiously optimistic that our launch on iOS will significantly impact our results. Thanks again for all your help! Please do not hesitate to reach out to Doug or I if you have questions.

Your YoYosAndPoodles.com co-founders,
Brenda & Doug

As with most all things in venture, you need to be proactive. Don't wait for your investors to ask you for status. Don't wait for them to reach out. Establish open lines of communication with them early, be honest, transparent, and—most of all—remember that a closed round means it's time to open communication. Don't assume they know what's working and what's not. You have to tell them. And even after you've told them, don't assume they've heard you. Email updates are easy, but it's okay to jump on an old-fashioned phone now and then as well. Keep talking. And keep listening.

CHAPTER TWENTY-ONE

GETTING DISTRIBUTION

"He made his own breaks."

Branch Rickey, inventor of baseball's minor league farm system on
Ty Cobb, the first-ever inductee into the baseball Hall of Fame

"NO ONE EVER WENT OUT OF BUSINESS because they had too
many customers," quips venture capitalist Mark Achler, a
partner at MATH Venture Partners. "Everyday I meet with
enthusiastic entrepreneurs who are pitching me to invest in
them. I've been an entrepreneur five different times and have
been mentoring and investing in entrepreneurs for almost 30
years. The very hard truth and reality is that over 50% of all
entrepreneurs are no longer in business five years after they
started. It's a tough world out there."

There are endless reasons why businesses fail, but among
them is the simple fact that those businesses are unable to
attract customers. Or, worse yet, they attract scores of customers none of whom have plans on paying them anytime
soon. Part of this has to do with founder bias and focus on
the product. Says Achler, "When I meet with the vast majority
of entrepreneurs they invariably focus on the product and all
of the features of the product. The problem is that a product
without customers is not a business. It's a product." As an

entrepreneur, you have to make your own breaks. You have to get distribution or you won't have a business. You will only have a product.

It's easy to fall in love with your product. You should fall in love with it. After all, if you don't love it, why would you assume anyone else would? Products are the shiny objects of innovation. But it's not only the product you should fall in love with. Fall in love with your customers because, to quote Jeff Bezos, "Those are the ones who have the money." And so, how do you attract customers? First, have a great product. Second, sell it. Sales matters. A lot. Get comfortable doing it. But make sure you're selling the right thing. Make sure you're telling the right story. It's not that founders don't have sales stories to tell. They often don't know how to tell them. And so, Achler offers several lessons from his career as an entrepreneur and as an investor on how to think about your role as Chief Sales Officer.

In this chapter, we'll talk about:

1. Learning to talk from your customer's perspective (it's not about you)
2. Creative ways to get distribution
3. Developing trust and empathy in strategic partnerships
4. The right time to hire a head of sales
5. Reducing friction and delivering value
6. Who the most important sales person is at your company

Principle #1: Talk From The Customer's Point of View

Don't tell me about the features of your product. Talk from the point of view of the customer. Describe what problems your customers are having (right now) and how you can solve them. Talk from their point of view not yours. As an investor, I may be familiar with the general problem, but it's your job to make it crystal clear for me. You want me to feel the pain your customers are experiencing. Help me understand them.

Principle #2: It's Always About Sales

The vast majority of tech entrepreneurs are wicked smart. They often have great domain expertise. They can identify a significant pain point and usually build a product to solve it. And most of them believe that *If we build it, they will come.* I can't tell you how many times entrepreneurs look at me with that blank look when I ask them about how are they going to acquire customers. It goes something like this, *Great idea. What is your distribution strategy?"* [Insert cricket sounds here]. According to Achler, there are several questions you need to answer when thinking about how you are going to get distribution, and the answers to those questions will help guide you in the right direction.

Piggyback on someone else's customer base.

Every business is unique so it's hard to create a generic one stop fits all solution. Building a distribution strategy is based on trust and access. If yours is a brand that the customer does not yet know can you "borrow" the brand and the pre-existing relationship of someone or entity that already has a privileged, trusted relationship with the customer? Who do they already know and do business with?" An example of a founder who has built a very successful business around the question that Achler raises is Larry Levy, founder of Levy Restaurants. Levy is a leading provider of food and beverage services at arenas, convention centers, racetracks, stadiums, and other venues. Unlike restaurants, which Levy also owns and operates, where you must figure out a way to convince customers to come to your restaurants, sports stadiums and other entertainment venues already have customers. The venues have done the work of getting the customers there. Levy does the work of feeding them. That is piggybacking on someone else's brand or customer base. It's a brilliant distribution strategy. And it's a win-win. Venues get high-quality food and service and Levy gets access to customers. He gets distribution. He gets sales.

Join a conversation already happening.

In his previous role as Chief Marketing & Innovation Officer at Redbox, Achler offers his experience in figuring out a distribution strategy. "Redbox is a great example of a focused distribution company aided by a key strategic partner. We had decided to focus on larger retail stores, primarily grocery stores to begin with. The company didn't go from store-to-store. We focused on the corporate office of the entire chain. In some cases we went after the master brand that controlled many sub-brands, so they could sign one contract and sign up thousands of stores at once. In the early days it wasn't always easy to get in the door. The company partnered with Coinstar, whose green coin-counting machines were already in most grocery stores. The Coinstar sales team were able to open the doors and smooth the way for Redbox to get easily introduced with much less friction."

Develop trust and empathy for those who can help you get distribution.

Says Achler, "The biggest hurdle to customer acquisition is often attention. You are asking the customer to stop, listen and pay attention—to *you*! Customers are bombarded with an unending cacophony of noise all trying to garner their limited attention and focus. It's hard to break through the noise. The great companies are one that are more aspirational and speak with true empathy from the customers' point of view." It's not about you selling the distributor or those who already own the customer relationship. It's about you illustrating to them why working with you or carrying your product or promoting your service will somehow benefit *them*. It's about *them*, not you. By working with you, will it help them increase their revenues or decrease their costs? Will it make their customers more sticky? Will it help give them access to a new and growing category that they don't serve today? Help them win and they'll help you. The last thing they need is just another product to sell or another startup founder looking for time on their calendar to pitch their idea. Know the problem they are also trying to solve. If your product or service is a fit to help them solve their problems, great! If not, don't waste their time. And, more importantly, don't waste your time. Time is a competitive advantage in early stage companies.

Getting customers is good, but keeping customers is better.
"Customer retention is by far the most important goal you should have," says Achler. "It is far easier to keep a current customer happy than to convince a new customer to change their behavior. That said, from an investor point of view, it takes scale first. Getting to the large customer base of course is vital, but don't do that at the expense of keeping current customers happy. Want to raise money? Want to get a VC's attention. Tell investors how you are going to acquire customers."

VCs, like Achler, see a lot of deals. It is very likely that you are not the only genius. There are 7 billion humans walking around this giant ball of mud. Once a VC is convinced that a given category or trend is worth investing in, at that point they are not necessarily asking themselves who has the better product (certainly that matters, a lot). But they are also asking who has the better acquisition strategy. Who can win the most customers the fastest and the most profitably? The history of innovation is littered with superior products that lost to those that may have had slightly inferior products but infinitely better distribution strategies. You need to assume that in the lobby of the VC's office are a dozen founders with products just like yours. What will differentiate you? How you acquire customers. Don't let creativity be wasted on product alone. Get creative in how you get customers. And get even more creative in how you plan on keeping them around.

Principle #3: Don't Wait Until the Product Is Built to Hire a Head of Sales.

"Most entrepreneurial teams I meet," observes Achler, "consist of a domain expert, a tech lead and maybe a business or finance person. Most times they say 'we will wait to hire their customer acquisition leader until after the product is in the market.' I can't emphasize enough how important it is to have customer acquisition sensitivity baked into the core founding team and the DNA of the company." In part, suggests Achler, it creates a mindset early in the company that is focused on the customer. Jeff Bezos has taken this to the point of having an empty chair at meetings to represent the customer's point of view. The customer must have a seat at the table of decision-making. One way to do that is to have someone responsible for customer acquisition, marketing, or sales early.

"A sales mindset is really a metaphor for thinking from the point of view of the customer," says Achler. "Especially in tech companies, many developers guess what customers really want. They are not really sure and often overcompensate by overbuilding the product and layering in too many features. My strong recommendation is to keep it simple, do one thing extraordinarily well and don't try to boil the ocean and throw in a lot of tertiary features that don't really matter." By having a head of sales in early, this should help.

Principle #4: Scale trust fast.

Achler's 30 years as an entrepreneur have taught him the value of trust. Says Achler, "Customer acquisition is really hard. I mean really, *really* hard. Trust is everything." As an early stage company, of course, the challenge of trust is that you can't rush trust. It takes time to build trust. The question is how can you accelerate the speed at which you build trust with customers? After all, your customers are likely human and most humans need time to warm up to new people and to new things. Although difficult, Achler suggests that it is possible to scale trust quickly by partnering with those who already have relationships with your desired customers (the example offered early about Levy). Not only does this give you access to customers, it gives you access more quickly. You can trade on the their trust, just be careful not to lose it. If you are asking a distributor or sales channel to partner with you in order to access their customers, you are asking for a lot! You are asking to be inserted to a conversation between their sales force and their customers about your products and services. It's possible, but be mindful of what's at stake. Now, it's not only your reputation, it's theirs. Don't screw it up.

So how do you find the right strategic partner? "It starts with shared values and consistent long-term goals that are aligned," suggests Achler. "Remember it's not only about you. You have to find a company that really values your product or service and has the brand and customers to help sell them into."

Principle #5: Get comfortable being uncomfortable selling.

Says Achler, "We gravitate to what we are good at and what

we are comfortable doing. It's just the simple truth. Most people avoid going out of their comfort zone. Let's face it, sales is hard. Most technical founders tend to avoid it like the plague. I can't tell you often I hear, *We will just hire the sales guy after we build the product and let him/her deal with it.* There is a direct correlation between the success of the company and the willingness of the founding team to directly roll up their sleeves and get involved in the selling process. It is essential for the CEO to be involved with sales and listening to what the customer truly wants and needs. Yes, it is important to have a lead salesperson but the CEO must always be selling and always be listening.

Principle #6: Get out of the office.
You can't build products in a vacuum without iteratively talking to and engaging with your customers. And it's really hard to sell from a phone. Get out. Go forth and conquer!

Principle #7: Less is more (no, seriously, it is).
William Faulkner once advised, "In writing, you must kill your darlings." It's a theme you have heard throughout this book: less is more. "No seriously," says Achler, "you don't have to put in every feature and bell and whistle. It doesn't have to be perfect. Pick the one or two key pain points and solve that and that alone. You can always add features later. That said, as a CEO and product manager I invariably tell my developers no when adding new features (unless our customers are howling for it). And I mean howling."

Principle #8: Reduce friction.
Friction is the aggregate of all the stuff your customers have to go through simply to do business with you. It sucks. Get rid of it. Look no further than the process you must go through

to renew your driver's license, to open one of those terrible plastic clamshell product casings, or to reach a live human being at the end of an automated call center. It's maddening. Friction creates frustration, and frustration creates the anti-customer.

As Achler suggests, "Every single extra step reduces sales. Every word, every feature, and every step in the purchasing process means someone will drop out. Get down to the essence. The faster you can get your customer to purchase the better. Reimagine and rebuild the sales process from the point of view of the customer—not yours."

Principle #9: Everyone believes they are getting fleeced. Deliver value.

"At Redbox," recalls Achler, "we provided a night's entertainment for just a buck. In a world where customers feel ripped off with every interaction with the entertainment world, Redbox was the one place where we were on the side of the customer and our customers loved the service and the brand for it. Literally one-third of all U.S. households use Redbox on a monthly basis." Look for opportunities to deliver value.

Principle# 10: Raising venture capital is a sales job.

"The secret to raising venture capital is sales," says Achler. "No kidding. The better you can credibly articulate your sales strategy and, better yet, have some proof points in place, the better you will be able to raise capital. We speak the language of finance. As a VC, talking sales and distribution strategy is like whispering sweet nothings in my ear. We are looking for an unfair advantage in customer acquisition. What's yours?"

Entrepreneurs who spend more time listening and talking with customers and thinking about how to most effectively sell them are the ones who will both survive and thrive. Remember, no one ever went out of business because they had too many customers.

CHAPTER TWENTY-TWO

ENTREPRENEURIAL SELLING

"Desire is greater than talent. Knock on one more door."
Christopher Eastwood, Co-founder, OrangeRuler.com

"I SOLD AS400S TO MANUFACTURERS," recalls Craig Wortmann, founder & CEO of Sales Engine, Inc. "I was a coin-operated sales guy. Put in the coin, wind me, and I could close. I did well in some areas, and not so well in others, but in the end I now realize that I was really learning how to be a professional and how to connect with people. I can thank IBM for that. Fast-forward a bunch of years. Fifteen years ago I became an entrepreneur with a software company called WisdomTools. After eight years in that business, I sold it. And, it was not a fun sale. In fact, it was more of a fire sale. Bottom line is that I was way too overconfident. I thought I knew a lot about professional sales, which I did, but I did not know about *entrepreneurial* selling. There is a big difference between professional selling and entrepreneurial selling.

"After selling WisdomTools, I took over a struggling digital marketing agency, turned it around, and ended up selling that company successfully ten months later. It was a dead sprint, really hard, but an awesome experience. Now, I run a consulting company I started six years ago called Sales Engine. We help companies build and tune their sales engine."

In this chapter, we'll talk about:

- The difference between marketing and selling
- Definition of selling
- How to know if/when you should hire a professional salesperson
- Wortmann's Sales Model Process
- Handling objections
- How to work a crowded room

The Selling Entrepreneur

"What do you see in your mind when you imagine a salesperson?" asks Wortmann. "Most people may say things like outgoing, pushy, bold, manipulative, or liar. Let's just say salespeople get a bad rap. But, I'm going to pick on two of those words. Is aggressive a good word or a bad word? I think it's a good word. There is a line between aggressive and annoying. I have crossed that line before, and it's not good. But, you have to be pushy to get things done. You have to push your ass off to get what you want. Occasionally, you will cross the line, and it's not good. But, if you don't push, you're going to hurt and it's going to be worse.

"Now, what do you see in your mind when you imagine an entrepreneur? Most people say things like visionary, innovator, risk-taker, optimist, passionate, or leader. Entrepreneurs have a good reputation. Why is that? There is a dichotomy. There is a dark side of the word 'salesman' that sometimes gets justified by bad behavior from sales professionals. But, that doesn't mean there are no wonderful sales people that have win/win in mind and do it with grace. It also doesn't mean that there are no sleazeball entrepreneurs that lie and manipulate to get their way. Both salespeople and entrepreneurs get shit done."

As a founder, you need to learn how to sell yourself, your product, your company, and the dream. Whether you are an engineer or a designer or an artist, it doesn't matter. If you can't sell, you will not succeed.

"One of my favorite thing to do when I'm here at Techstars," says Wortmann, "is to ask founders how their sales are coming along? They say, *Oh, pretty good. We created a big database and we are starting to send emails out. We are getting x% conversion rate and it seems to be going pretty well.* That's great I tell them. But, emails are marketing not sales. I ask, *Who are you talking to?* And they say, *Just the email blast. That's how we talk to our customers.*

"I stop them right there. Then I tell them to get their phone and computer because we're going to make some calls. We hop in one of these little rooms and we make *fifty* phone calls together to prospect customers. They make one. I make one. They make one. I make one. We do it *right* then. It's great! And, I don't have a *clue* what I'm talking about, but I learn. I learn because I'm *practicing.* I am trying things that work and things that don't, and refining my approach every single time."

Wortmann talks about selling and learning to refine a pitch not unlike launching an MVP and learning what features customers like and which they don't. The same goes for your sales story. Customers will respond to some things. They won't care about others. There is only one way to learn that. You need to talk to a lot of prospects.

Wortmann quotes a friend of his, Professor Waverly Deutsch at the University of Chicago Booth School of Business, "Marketing is one to many. Selling is one to one." "I don't care what kind of business you are in," says Wortmann. "Whether you're raising money, trying to get a channel partner, or walking around the train station to get customers, you have to be selling."

Knowledge + Discipline + Skill = Selling

"Successful selling is a combination of knowledge, discipline, and skill," says Wortmann. "Typically, entrepreneurs have too much knowledge, and we punt on skill and discipline. Knowledge gets in the way of developing skill and discipline. I'm not saying don't gain knowledge. I'm just saying to build skills and discipline. They are essential to success.

For startup founders, I always ask them, What are you doing every week to sell? Notice I'm not saying every hour or every day. I know that as a startup founder there are other things that you need to do: build your product, lead your team, manage cash flow, talk with your board, etc. I am saying that you need to institute practices so that you are spending time every week selling. And, you can't outsource the sales engine in the early days of a startup even if it is an extremely high performing salesperson. It's too important. No one will be able to answer questions, cast the vision, or resolve issues like the founder. While it is a temptation (especially if a founder is afraid of selling) to quickly hire a sales team to do the dirty work, it won't work. Trust me, I've experienced that from personal experience.

How to Know If You're Ready to Hire a Professional Salesperson

"When a founder says they are ready to hire a salesperson, I ask them these questions to determine if they are ready:

1. What's your sales process?
2. How long is your sales cycle?
3. What are the five main objections that you hear from

prospects?
4. What are the filters you assign to your target market?
5. What are five success stories?
6. What are five failure stories?

If you can answer *all* these questions and more, then you are ready to hire a salesperson. If you can't answer them quickly, then you are not ready. Sorry. There is only one person who can discover the answers as your product is taking shape, and that's you."

As Wortmann suggests, really great salespeople will want to know the answers to these questions. They will interview you as you are interviewing them. If you do not know the answers to these questions, you will not attract the best salespeople. Great salespeople interview for their jobs each and every day. Every time they meet with a customer is a chance for them to keep their jobs. Sales is an art, but it is also a science. There is a process to it. As my colleague, Dr. Robert Wolcott, founder & executive director of the Kellogg Innovation Network, says, "Never leave serendipity to chance." Be deliberate about sales.

The Sales *Model* Process

According to Wortmann, "A sales process should be very straightforward. The thousands of books on Amazon about selling all say the same thing and are very relevant to *professional* sales. But, they are not especially relevant to *entrepreneurial* selling because entrepreneurs must stretch the sales process backward (targeting the right customer) and forward (managing the relationship going forward to retain that customer).

The biggest mistake I see startup founders make is bad targeting or put another way *broad* targeting. I made this mistake in a huge way with my failed company. I'll hear a founder say, *We target parents*. You might as well say, *We target people who breathe*. It's way too broad and will get your nowhere. You must decide why some people are more enticing to your sales process than others. If you don't, you'll be unsuccessful.

"Just as parents and those who breathe are not target markets, neither is the Fortune 500. The Fortune 500 is not a market! There are 490 different types of businesses in the Fortune 500! If you say, *Our target is the Vice President of Sales at a Fortune 500 company who have a large professional sales team*, that's a little better, but it can and should be more granular.

"As you continue to sell your product when it is at its earliest stages, you will learn how to tweak the characteristics of your target customer as you experience interaction with them. Therefore, in a startup, there is not just a *sales* cycle (i.e., how long it takes to close a deal). There is a sales *model* cycle. The sales model cycle is the constant iteration of targeting, identifying, presenting, closing, and then managing each customer and adjusting your targeting a little bit more each time to dial in exactly who is your best customer fit. If you can do that on a consistent basis, it gets easier."

Wortmann's advice is priceless. Use the sales process as you would use your MVP and customer development process. Think of selling the same way. Wortmann continues, "Here is an example from a former student of mine. He learned how to do this really well. He started a digital technology company. In the early days of the company, we were sitting down for coffee and I asked him, 'Who are you targeting?' He told me, 'We are targeting sales people.' And, as you can expect, I was ready to pounce on him and tell him he had to do better, but before I could say anything, he kept going.

"He said, 'But, not just that Craig. We have a small CRM system that works best for *small* companies. Therefore, we think we are going to target companies with one to two salespeople.' He then pauses. 'And, because our system has a lot of user experience in mind, we are going to target web designers and architects.' He pauses again. 'And, since I'm living in New York, we are going to target companies in New York.' I wanted to hug him because he was a freaking genius!

"Now that he has his target dialed in, here's what happens next. He will invariably get a call from a large Fortune 500 company saying that they are looking at companies large and small for CRM solutions. With confidence in the targeting that my student selected, he can now say to that company, *Go with large company X, I'm not your guy.* When you know your product well (and who it best works for), you'll be able to not waste the time talking to the wrong customer (who likely won't pick you any way).

"So, once you target your customer, you go out and try to sell. You will get rejected, and *that's okay.* It's just a no. Go to the next prospect. But you can also determine if you've even got a shot before you waste too much time on a prospect. For example, if you get a call from a very large customer and you get excited, I've learned to ask a very important question at the *beginning* of the conversation. I ask, *Do we have a chance to win? Because we are small. We have huge vision and are going to have an amazing product, but tell me, do we have a chance of winning this deal.* And, nine times out of ten, they will tell you if you do. Asking that question could save you months and dozens of meetings.

"In general, you always want to be asking more questions than you talk. *They* should be talking about 70% of the time in an initial conversation. This is hard. Because you are the founder, you are especially tempted to tell them everything about your product. That's a mistake. The more your prospect talks, the more you understand whether or not the prospect has a chance of turning into a sale."

The Hardest & Most Important Part of Sales: Handling Objections

There's an old adage: *selling begins when the customer says no.* Everything else is simply sharing information. "Any good sales process has objections," says Wortmann. "You know you're selling well when you have objections. *It's too expensive* is a classic objection. High-performing salespeople are prepared for objections. Don't treat an objection like a NO. Treat it as an opportunity to learn more.

Here is a general framework that I use to handle objections:

- *Encourage.* Demonstrate your willingness to listen. Say: 'Tell me more about that.'
- *Question.* Express curiosity in their situation. Ask: 'Has your budget been reduced? Is it gone? If you can share that?'
- *Confirm.* Show that you heard them. Repeat what they said back to them, and admit that there is a problem. It gives you massive credibility.
- *Provide.* Tell a story of how it can be solved. And the story has to be real.
- *Check.* Make sure that you resolve the issue, or are going to continue to discuss later by asking, 'Great, can we move on to the next thing?'

Don't skip the first three steps. 'Stay high' in the process. The longer you can stay there, the more credibility and trust you will build with your client/customer. Draw potential objections into the early part of the conversation. The objections are coming, whether you want them to or not. By addressing objections early, you demonstrate understanding and save yourself (and them) time by getting to Y's in the road quickly."

How to Work a Crowded Room

If there is one thing the venture community the world over does well, it's throw a good party. Startup breakfasts, tech cocktails, sponsored speaker events, panel discussions. Throw down some free pizza and someone is bound to show up. With increasing interest in the venture community by those not only in the startup world but also among large companies, government agencies, professional service firms, these events are often attended by people who could be potential customers or, at the very least, distribution partners. When in doubt, go. You never know whom you'll meet. The hard part of course is navigating these events. They can be fun but they can also be huge time sucks. Therefore, Wortmann has developed a very nuanced, creative, and ridiculously practical way for working a crowded room.

"Imagine there is a wine and cheese event tonight from 5:30pm to 7:00pm. They're expecting a hundred people. You *know* that there will be at least five people in that room that you can do business with, but you don't know *anyone*. Regardless, you go. You show up, and now what do you do? Well, if you're honest, this is what typically happens. You walk in and where do you immediately go? Right! The bar. Everybody goes to the bar. You grab a drink (that's your safety blanket). And then what do you do? You walk over to the first guy that makes eye contact with you. You make small talk and you get comfortable. You spend 20 minutes talking with him. Then, you see another person who makes eye contact and so you talk to her for 20 minutes. Then, you see someone you know and so you talk to them for another thirty minutes. All of the sudden, the event is over. *And you haven't done shit!* It's harsh, but it's true. And, we all do it unless we are applying skill and discipline to these types of events.

"So, what do you do?

"Here is where I start. Before you step a foot into the room on a night like this, you have to ask yourself a *very* important question: *Am I drinking? Or am I working?* If you're drinking, that's fine. Go have a couple drinks. But, if you're working, then WORK! It's really, really hard, but that's why it's work. You've got to work that room because you *need* to find those five prospects and do it in a graceful, productive way.

"Once you've established that you are working, here's what you do next. It is highly unlikely that you are going to find all five prospects in a room full of one hundred people without coming across as sleazy. But, I'm very confident that you could talk to fifty people. In order to do that, I've developed a conversation framework that begins with something I call the Sales Trailer. Just as a movie trailer exists to sell you the movie, a sales trailer exists to sell your story.

"Here's how it works. Walk up to any individual and introduce yourself. Do a little bit of small talk. And then, you will be asked the same question every single time: *What do you do?* This is the most pivotal question in the conversation. The answer can be very vague and unproductive, or the most powerful moment in the conversation. Saying, 'I'm a startup founder.' Okay, great. That does nothing for you. It doesn't move the conversation anywhere toward your goal. Instead, here's what I say, 'I run a company called Sales Engine. We help people build and tune their sales engine.' And then, *I shut up!* 95% of the time he or she will ask, *What does that mean?* And when they ask it, I say, 'We look at the sales process companies use, the tools used to manage the sales team, and then the skills, knowledge, and disciplines of the sales team itself.' And then, *I shut up!* I've memorized both of these statements to the word. Why? Because I need a sales tool to make this conversation productive.

"Now, what if this individual says that he is a beet farmer

from Iowa? *How do you get out of this conversation?* (Because he is not a prospect I want for my business). What do you do?

1. Lie? No, that's wrong.
2. Walk away? No, that's rude.
3. Explain why he is not a fit? No, that's a waste of your time.

"You avoid the situation in the first place! Here's what you do.

"When you first establish the conversation, you need to say something: *It's great to meet you. It's fun to be here. There is a whole bunch of people I need to see, and I'm sure you're the same way. Tell me about yourself.* By doing this, you've built an exit door for yourself if you discover that the individual is not in your five targets. When the guy says he is a beet farmer, you ask him *one more* question about himself and genuinely express interest in him. Then, no longer than 90 seconds later, you say, *That's great. Well, it's great to meet you, but as I said I have a lot of people I need to meet tonight, as I'm sure you do. All the best to you.* And, you move on to the next conversation.

"Let's say the conversation goes a different way. This guy isn't a beet farmer. He is a Vice President of Sales and he says he has 75 people on his sales team and has problems with his tools and process. Then, what do you do? You need to determine if he is a qualified prospect. Is he a decision maker? Does he have budget? What is his timeframe? Ask as many qualification questions as seem appropriate. If the individual seems qualified, then you exchange information, set up a follow-up conversation, and then use the same exit tactic stated above. You may be asking, *Why wouldn't I stay and build a relationship?* Because you have four more people to meet in the room, and time is running thin! You are working! So, WORK! And, you'll be surprised the impression that leaves. You say, *It's fantastic to meet you. I want to be respectful of your time, as I know you need to meet some other people tonight and I do too. But, we'll talk soon.* Scarcity and influence works in your favor."

Of course, before you get into a conversation you need to get into the conversation circle. You know what a conversation circle is. They are at all of these events. When was the last time you went to a party and everyone stood in one giant circle? Never, right? We stand in small circles, typically three to five people or so.

So, Wortmann asks, "How do you get into a conversation circle? Here's what you do. Walk up to the circle, find the widest gap, and stand just outside the perimeter of the circle. *Don't step into the circle.* It's common human respect. Eventually, someone will reach across the circle and invite you into the conversation. Then, you slow down. Quickly introduce yourself (saying your name very clearly), and let the conversation keep going without giving your sales trailer. At some point in the conversation, someone will inevitably ask you, *What do you do, Craig?* I follow the Sales Trailer format, but without the pauses. In a group setting, people rely on each other to talk, so you are less likely to get the follow up questions. So, I would say, 'Hi, I'm Craig. I run a company called Sales Engine. We help companies build and tune their sales engines. What that means is: we look at the sales tools an organization uses, etc.' I ask my own questions as I go through my sales trailer. And, believe me, *it works!*

"Now, I realize this whole 'working the room' thing may feel icky to you. But, consider this. The more people you meet, the more people you can *help*. If you meet more people and learn about what they do, maybe you can help *them* connect with the people *they* should be talking to. Maybe you'll run into someone looking for farmers. Wait! You already met the *beet* farmer! Go find him and introduce the two. If you only talk to four people, you can't do that."

Never leave serendipity to chance. Define your ideal customer. Create your sales trailer. Pick up the phone, get the meeting, and start learning which messages work and which ones don't. And, while you're at it, go to that tech mixer this week and work the room.

AFTERWORD

HOPEFULLY THIS BOOK HAS INSPIRED YOU and you've learned some things that will help you.

One last thing however before you go.

As much as we can teach you about how to make innovation work, there are two things that cannot be taught: *risk* and *motivation*. These things come from within you. Ironically they are perhaps the most important attributes of high-potential entrepreneurs.

On *risk*, Linda Darragh, executive director of the Kellogg Innovation & Entrepreneurship Initiative (KIEI) puts it best: "Risk is not teachable. It is different for each individual based on his or her individual history and perceptions of the future. Many entrepreneurs will say they are not worried about 'sinking the boat,' they are worried about 'missing the boat.' The final decision to jump into an entrepreneurial venture is highly personal." Though, to quote McDonald's Ray Kroc, "If you're not a risk taker, you should get the hell out of business."

Whatever your risk tolerance may be, don't let that stop

always been part of the fabric of Chicago. Sandburg recognized this as well. Later in his now-famous poem, Sandburg describes Chicago's entrepreneurial spirit:

> *Fierce as a dog with tongue lapping for action, cunning*
> *as a savage pitted against the wilderness,*
> > *Bareheaded,*
> > *Shoveling,*
> > *Planning,*
> > *Building, breaking, rebuilding...*

Sounds like some founders I know, including many in this book! That said, the mentors you have met in this book are only a *very* small handful of all those who make the magic happen at Techstars Chicago. We have hundreds of talented and scrappy people who contribute their time, networks, and capital to the program. As Kevin Willer—an early Google employee, Techstars mentor and now partner at Chicago Ventures—suggests, "There has never been a better time to start a tech company in Chicago. With the success of companies like Groupon, GrubHub, Braintree, Fieldglass, and TrunkClub to name a few, Chicago is proving that it can build world-class tech companies here more than ever before."

To all the mentors of Techstars Chicago, thank you for your commitment to entrepreneurship. Also thank you to David Cohen, Brad Feld, David Brown, and Jared Polis for introducing the concept of Techstars to the world. I'd also like to thank Casey Bankord, who has been my dedicated and creative writing partner in this effort. There is *no way* this book would have happened without his discipline. Thank you as well to my editorial and publishing partners at FG Press— Dane McDonald, Dave Heal, Kevin Kane, and Eugene Wan. Your agility, creativity, and collaborative spirit have made writing this book an inspired and meaningful pursuit. A debt of gratitude is owed as well to Troy Henikoff, for his bulldog determination in wrestling together the contributors to this book and for his leadership of Techstars Chicago. Even though the following list of mentors is long, it too is only representative of all those who touch our program in some way. Each of these mentors maintain vast personal and professional networks, people that represent potential customers, investors, and future employees for Techstars companies. Imagine, as a founder, having access to these mentors and all the mentors in the Techstars network globally. The good news is, you can. We hope to see you at Techstars.

Thank you: Mark Achler, Hank Adams, Charles Adler, Shradha Agarwal, Arjun Aggarwal, Michael Alter, Jeff Anderson, Melissa Anderson, RH Bailin, Cam Balzer, Greg Barnes, Bruce Barron, Esther Barron, Dennis Barsema, Stopher Bartol, Jeffrey Bennett, Mike Bilder, Ben Blair, Tony Bombacino, Joe Born, Andrew Boszhardt, Wayne Boulais, Gale Bowman, Ryan Broshar, David Brown, Paul Budak, Dick Burke, Michael Burke, Don Burton, Samantha Buyniski, William Campbell, Jeff Cantalupo, Ellen Carnahan, Jeff Carter, Carter Cast, Raman Chadha, Mus Chagal, Lewis Cheng, Leon Chism, Sean Chou, Lon Chow, Sal Cilella, David Cohen, Jacob Cohen, George Colis, Steven Collens, Chris Conn, Ron Conway, Brian Corrigan, Daniel Cummings, Jordan Curnes, Dave Dahl, Linda Darragh, Jan Davis, Dean DeBiase, Len Defranco, Matt Dennewitz, Rick Desai, Colum Donahue, Timothy Draper, Jim Dugan, Joe Dwyer, Mike Evans, Stephanie Farsht, Steven Farsht, Bob Fealy, Brad Feld, Jason Felger, Michael Fineberg, Brian Fitzpatrick, Jason Fried, Ryan Fukushima, Mike Gamson, Shruti Gandhi, David Gardner, Blair Garrou, Aziz Gilani,

Chris Gladwin, Rob Go, Moises Goldman, Harry Gottlieb,
Gabe Greenbaum, Joel Grossman, Michael Gruber, Sam
Guren, Brian Hand, Thomas Harman, Mark Hasebroock,
Jason Heltzer, Troy Henikoff, Jason Henrichs, Brent Hill,
Adam Hitchcock, Jordan Ho, Fred Hoch, Chris Hochschild,
Jeff Hoffman, Adrian Holovaty, David Hornik, Jason Huggins,
Joe Jablonski, Mike Jakob, Christopher Jensen, Bryan Johnson,
Larry Kaplan, Zach Kaplan, Timothy Keane, Brad Keywell,
Ross Kimbarovsky, Adam Koopersmith, Alex Kormushoff,
Kevin Kotowoski, Michael Krasny, Tim Krauskopf, Seth
Kravitz, Kristopher Kubicki, Logan LaHive, David Lambert,
Amanda Lannert, Stuart Larkins, Gregg Latterman, Mark
Leahy, Paul Lee, Larry Levy, Roger Liew, Will Little, Bart
Loethen, Tom Loverro, Brian Luerssen, Eric Lunt, Dan Lyne,
Jeff Lyons, Bob Mahon, Matt Maloney, Dan Malven, David
Mann, Jim Marzullo, Alan Matthew, Bret Maxwell, Chris
McAvoy, Matt McCall, Dave McClure, Jonathan McCulloch,
Liz Michaels, Bob Michelson, Steve Miller, Doug Monieson,
Matt Moog, Brad Morehead, Jeffrey Moss, Suzanne Muchin,
Alicia Mullen, Karin O'Connor, Eric Olson, Eric Paley, Andy
Palmer, Armando Pauker, Brent Payne, John Philosophos,
Thea Polancic, Michael Polsky, Jeff Pomeranz, J.B. Pritzker,
Dan Ratner, Uri Ratner, Harper Reed, Mig Reyes, Dylan
Richard, Shawn Riegsecker, John Roa, Nik Rokop, Nick Rosa,
Scott Roth, Jason Rubinstein, Greg Rudin, Pat Ryan, Michael
Sachaj, Orlando Saez, Aaron Salmon, Mike Sands, Steve
Sanger, Ed Scanlan, Wil Schobeiri, David Schonthal, Reese
Schroeder, Jon Seed, David Semmel, Ted Serbinski, Rishi
Shah, Jai Shekhawat, Luke Shepard, Uzi Shmilovici, Susan
Silver, Ryan Singer, Ravi Singh, Sarah Somers, Emerson Spartz,
Matt Spiegel, Jim Streibich, David Tahara, Jon Taiber, Peter
Tapling, Mark Tebbe, Chuck Templeton, Howard Tullman,
Guy Turner, Gary Vaynerchuk, Gabe Vehovsky, Jason Wadler,

Scott Wald, Kate Walker, Todd Warren, John Weinlader, David Weinstein, Ira Weiss, Sandor Weisz, Alex White, Pete Wilkins, Tony Wilkins, Kevin Willer, Donna Williamson, Walter Winshall, Robert Wislow, Kirk Wolfe, Craig Wortmann, Todd Wyder, Wenz Xing, Sam Yagan, Joel Yarmon

FEATURED MENTORS

THE FOLLOWING MENTORS are featured extensively in the book. The combined experience of this very special group of people is nothing short of remarkable.

Foreword: Sam Yagan, CEO, The Match Group
Chapter 1: Chuck Templeton, Founder, OpenTable & Chairman, Impact Engine
Chapter 2: Jeremy Smith, Co-founder & COO, SpotHero
Chapter 3: Amanda Lannert, CEO, The Jellyvision Lab
Chapter 4: Jason Fried, Co-founder & CEO, Basecamp
Chapter 5: Joe Dwyer, Partner, Digital Intent & Founder Equity
Chapter 6: John Kenny, EVP, Head of Planning, FCB Chicago
Chapter 7: Suzanne Muchin, Co-founder & Principal Mind + Matter Studio
Chapter 8: Troy Henikoff, Managing Director, Techstars Chicago & Partner, MATH Venture Partners

Chapter 9: Esther Barron, Director, Entrepreneurship Law Center Northwestern University School of Law
Chapter 10: Joel Grossman, SVP, Technology & Operations, Leapfrog Online
Chapter 11: Brent Payne, Founder & CEO, Loud Interactive
Chapter 12: Emerson Spartz, Founder & CEO, Spartz
Chapter 14: Lon Chow, Partner, Apex Venture Partners
Chapter 15: Karin O'Connor, President, Perimeter Advisors Adam Koopersmith, Partner, Pritzker Group Venture Capital
Chapter 16: David Cohen, Founder & Managing Partner, Techstars
Chapter 17: Troy Henikoff, managing director, Techstars Chicago & Partner, MATH Venture Partners
Chapter 18: Matt McCall, Partner, Pritzker Group Venture Capital
Chapter 19: Brad Feld, managing director, Foundry Group
Chapter 20: Steve Farsht, Director, Techstars Chicago
Chapter 21: Mark Achler, Partner, MATH Venture Partners
Chapter 22: Craig Wortmann, Founder & CEO, Sales Engine, Inc.

Mark Achler is the managing director of MATH Venture Partners - an early to mid-stage technology venture capital fund and a Lecturer of Entrepreneurship and Innovation at Northwestern University's Kellogg School of Management. Mark was recently the senior vice president of new business, strategy and innovation at Redbox, where he managed the Company's long-term planning and expansion into new business opportunities. Achler was featured as a mentor to a tech startup on Bloomberg TV's "The Mentor" and in *Inc. Magazine*'s Trep Life series. Achler started his career by co-founding one of the first personal computer retail stores in the country and participated in the launch of the IBM PC in Boca Raton in 1981. He then moved to Apple, where he was the worldwide introduction manager for the Apple //c. Upon leaving Apple, Achler co-founded and served as chief executive officer of the Whitewater Group, a company that specialized in development tools and programming languages and shipped the second application for Windows 1.0. After building and eventually selling the Whitewater Group, he co-founded the video game company, Kinesoft Development, where he served as president. Kinesoft was instrumental in developing the technology that allowed Sega and Nintendo scrolling action arcade games to be played on Windows 95. After leaving Kinesoft, Achler served as a founding general partner in Kettle Partners, an early stage venture capital fund. While at Kettle, Achler was the lead investor in local Chicago companies such as Surepayroll (sold to PAYX) and Novarra (sold to NOK). Fueled by a lifelong passion for building new businesses, Achler also has helped to co-found Emmi Solutions, a provider of patient education, where he first served as president and later became chief executive officer. Achler is a frequent speaker, resource and ardent champion for the entrepreneurial community where he is a mentor for Techstars and the Chicago High Tech Academy. He thinks he has had a fun and eclectic career and his wife thinks he can't hold a job—all a matter of perspective.

Esther Barron is the Harry B. Reese Teaching Professor of Law, the Director of the Entrepreneurship Law Center at Northwestern University School of Law and a Clinical Professor of Law. In addition to her clinical work with the ELC, her other courses include Entrepreneurship Law, Venture Capital, NuVentions Medical Innovations and Business Associations. She recently co-taught a massive open on line course on entrepreneurship law. She also oversees the Law School's Structuring Transactions program, which is a series of practical courses focused on specific areas of transactional law. Prior to joining Northwestern Law School's faculty, she practiced at Goldberg Kohn in Chicago in its commercial finance department. She represented lenders and other financial institutions in middle market debt transactions. In 2005, she also co-founded a startup handbag company, Elezar, LLC. She is the coauthor of the legal casebook Entrepreneurship Law. She is a mentor for TechStars Chicago, a leading startup accelerator and 1871, a nationally recognized technology shared workspace located in Chicago. She received a Dean's Teaching Award in 2010, the SBA Faculty Appreciation Award in 2012 and the Association of American Law Schools Teachers of the Year Award in 2013. She serves on the Board of Directors of the Coleman Foundation. Professor Barron graduated Cum Laude from Brandeis University and received her JD from Northwestern University School of Law.

Lon Chow is a Chicago-based venture and angel investor. Lon is a general partner with Apex Venture Partners, where he has been investing nationally in software and software-enabled businesses since 1997. Lon is also an active angel investor with investments in over forty companies, primarily in the Chicago area. Prior to Apex, Lon was a partner with Mercer Management Consulting (now Oliver Wyman), where he worked with clients in the telecom, media, and computing industries. Lon started his business career in the telecommunications industry. He joined Pacific Telesis' management program out of undergrad and learned the importance of execution, people, and leadership in various operating roles there. Lon received an MBA from the Wharton School and a BA from The University of California, Davis.

David Cohen is the Founder & Managing Partner of Techstars, a mentorship-driven seed stage investment program for Internet startups. Previously, David was a founder of several software and web technology companies. He was the founder and CTO of Pinpoint Technologies, which was acquired by ZOLL Medical Corporation (NASDAQ: ZOLL) in 1999. You can read about it in No Vision, All Drive [Amazon]. David was also the founder and CEO of earFeeder.com, a music service which was sold to SonicSwap.com in 2006. He also had what he likes to think of as a "graceful failure" in between. David is an active startup advocate, advisor, board member, and technology advisor who comments on these topics on his blog at DavidGCohen.com. He is also very active at the University of Colorado, serving as a member of the Board of Advisors of the Computer Science Department, the Entrepreneurial Advisory Board at Silicon Flatirons, and the Board of Advisors of the Deming Center Venture Fund. David is also a member of the selection committee for Venture Capital in the Rockies, and runs the Colorado chapter of the Open Angel Forum.

Joe Dwyer is an investor, technologist, and serial entrepreneur. He is a partner at Digital Intent, a firm that creates disruptive digital businesses for clients, and sister company Founder Equity, a fund that employs a novel approach to early stage investing. He also teaches innovation and entrepreneurship courses at Kellogg School of Management. Over the past twenty years as a serial entrepreneur and venture capitalist he has built, grown, invested in, and sold high-growth technology businesses. Joe is a mentor for Techstars, a Charter Member of TIE, and a mentor for Founder Institute, among other activities. Joe holds an MBA with Distinction from the Kellogg School of Management, and a law degree Cum Laude,

Order of the Coif, from the Northwestern University School of Law.

Steve Farsht cofounded Corazon Capital in January 2014 and co-managed Techstars Chicago in 2013 and 2014. Today, he serves as a Board Member of Techstars Chicago and as an Advisory Board Member of Hyde Park Venture Partners. Steve also spent 18 months as Chief Operating Officer of Tap. Me, leading its sale to MediaMath in 2012. Previously, Steve was a general partner with Norwest Equity Partners. Over his 9 years with the firm, Steve invested $280 million of equity in 13 management buyouts and growth capital investments across a variety of industries. His platform companies completed 9 add-on acquisitions. Steve served on 8 Boards of Directors and led the sale of several companies to strategic and financial buyers. Steve also ran one of the firm's portfolio companies where he conceptualized, developed and commercialized Probate Finder OnDemand, the first and only automated estate location and claim filing solution. He also developed and launched MyWayForward.com, the first online resource designed specifically for people who are dealing with the death of a loved one. Steve is a Lecturer of Entrepreneurship and Innovation at Northwestern's Kellogg School of Management where he also received his MBA. Steve has an undergraduate degree in accounting from the University of Wisconsin Madison.

Brad Feld has been an early stage investor and entrepreneur since 1987. Prior to cofounding Foundry Group, he co-founded Mobius Venture Capital and, prior to that, founded Intensity Ventures. Brad is also a co-founder of Techstars. In addition to his investing efforts, Brad has been active with several non-profit organizations and currently is chair of the National Center for Women & Information Technology, co-chair of Startup Colorado, and on the board of UP Global. Brad is a nationally recognized speaker on the topics of venture capital investing and entrepreneurship and writes the widely read blogs Feld Thoughts, Startup Revolution, and Ask the VC. Brad holds Bachelor of Science and Master of Science degrees in Management Science from the Massachusetts Institute of Technology. Brad is also an avid art collector and long-distance runner. He has completed 23 marathons as part of his mission to finish a marathon in each of the 50 states.

Jason Fried is Co-founder and CEO of Basecamp (formerly known as 37signals), a Chicago-based company that builds web-based productivity tools that, in their words, "do less than the competition—intentionally." 37signals' simple but powerful collaboration tools have included Basecamp, Highrise, Backpack, Campfire, Ta-da List, and Writeboard. 37signals also developed and open-sourced the Ruby on Rails programming framework. Fried is the co-author, with David Heinemeier Hansson, of the book *Rework*, about new ways to conceptualize working and creating.

Joel Grossman is Senior Vice President of Technology and Operations for Leapfrog Online. He has over fifteen years of experience designing interactive solutions in the CPG/Retail, Education, Government, Insurance, Media, Non-Profit, B2B Services and Publishing industries. Prior to the acquisition of its intellectual property by Leapfrog Online, Joel was Founder and Managing Principal of Pivotal Click, a user experience strategy and design firm. He built the Interactive Branding practice for Lipson Alport Glass & Associates, a nationally-recognized brand design & innovation agency. Joel has held senior positions with Playboy Enterprises and Encyclopedia Britannica, as well as heading up product development for Edventions, a Startup acquired by Edison Schools. Joel began his career as an independent information technology consultant, working on application development and networking projects in Chicago, Minneapolis and Tokyo, Japan. He is a member of ACM SIGCHI, proudly serves as Chicago's Local Ambassador for UXNet, a global organization for collaboration within the user experience community, and is a judge for the International Academy of Digital Arts & Sciences' Webby Awards.

Troy Henikoff is managing director of Techstars in Chicago. Troy was a co-founder of Excelerate Labs, which became Techstars Chicago in 2013. Additionally he helps manage the FireStarter Fund, teaches Entrepreneurship at Northwestern University's Kellogg School of Management, is on the board of the Chicagoland Entrepreneurial Center and recently cofounded MATH Venture Partners. Prior to Techstars Chicago, Troy was the CEO of OneWed.com, President of Amacai, and co-founder and CEO of SurePayroll.com. Troy built the technology for Jellyvision (creators of "You Don't Know Jack!"), was the President of Systemetrics, and his first company was Specialized Systems and Software. Troy has an undergraduate degree in Engineering from Brown University and a Masters Degree in Project Management from Northwestern.

John Kenny has headed up strategic planning at FCB Chicago since 2012. He brings to this role experience working in Europe, Asia and the U.S., on brand, digital, and retail assignments, in categories as diverse as CPGs, QSRs, healthcare, financial services, and alcohol beverages. Since joining

FCB Chicago in 2006, John has worked on brands such as Nokia, MillerCoors, Jack Daniels, Nestlé, GSK, Cox Cable, Discover Financial Services and KFC. Passionate about the intersection of technology, psychology and business, John co-founded the Institute of Decision Making in 2011, building bridges between FCB Chicago and leaders in the world of behavioral economics. Prior to joining FCB Chicago, John worked market research with clients such as Kraft, Visa and McDonald's and then in Diageo Europe on the Guinness and Smirnoff brands. A native of Ireland, John received a PhD in the Social Sciences from the University of Chicago.

Adam Koopersmith joined Pritzker Group Venture Capital in 2004 and primarily focuses on companies dedicated to bringing to market novel SaaS applications, interactive marketing solutions, or interactive health applications. Prior to joining Pritzker Group Venture Capital, Adam held various senior operating and business development roles at Sportvision (the world's leader in technology-based enhancements for live sports programming, and a Pritzker Group portfolio company), helping the company grow from the "business plan" stage to eight figures in annual revenue. Prior to Sportvision, Adam worked at Berkshire Partners, a leading private equity investment firm with $11.5 billion of capital under management. His experience at Berkshire included investment evaluations and closed transactions in several industries, including business services, retail and manufacturing, in addition to significant work helping portfolio companies achieve their strategic objectives. Before joining Berkshire, Adam worked as an investment banker for Alex Brown (now Deutsche Bank) and participated in a broad range of merger and acquisition and public equity transactions for mid-sized companies. Adam graduated with a B.S. in economics with concentrations in finance and international management from the Wharton School at the University of Pennsylvania and received his M.B.A. from Northwestern University's Kellogg School of Management with concentrations in organizational behavior and decision sciences.

Amanda Lannert is the Chief Executive Officer of The Jellyvision Lab and has been a key figure in driving the company's direction since its founding in 2001. Her focus at The Jellyvision Lab is on furthering the company's digital strategy, improving processes to better scale operations, and client acquisition to continue fueling the company's growth. Under Mrs. Lannert's leadership, The Jellyvision Lab has doubled its revenue three out of the last four years and has grown to serve hundreds of mostly Fortune 1000 clients with interactive communication solutions for desktop, mobile, and emerging platforms via the company's digital agency work and ALEX, the Jellyvision Benefits Counselor, the leading platform that helps employees make smarter decisions about their benefits. Prior to joining The Jellyvision Lab, Mrs. Lannert managed global brands for Kellogg's while at Leo Burnett, where she developed strategies and implemented campaigns for Pop-Tarts and Nutri-Grain bars, in addition to spending two years in a new business and new brand development think tank. Mrs. Lannert was recently listed in Crain's Tech 50 as one of Chicago's top technological leaders, CEO of the Year at Built In Chicago's Moxie Awards, and has been profiled in the Chicago Tribune. She is also active in Chicago's startup community, serving on the advisory board of 1871 and The Starter League, as well as mentoring at Techstars Chicago, where she was named 2013 Mentor of the Year, and Sandbox Industries.

Matthew McCall is a partner at Pritzker Group Venture Capital and was formerly a partner with DFJ Portage. McCall has been involved with investments in Analyte Health, AwesomenessTV (acquired by DreamWorks), Beachmint, BrightTag, Cognitive Concepts (acquired by Houghton Mifflin), Eved, EverDream (acquired by Dell), Feedburner (acquired by Google), FindTheBest, Imago Scientific (acquired by Ametek), Lefthand Networks (acquired by HP), Performics (acquired by Doubleclick/Google), Playdom (acquired by Disney), SMS-Assist, Siimpel (acquired by Tessera), SimpleTV and TicketsNow (acquired by Ticketmaster). McCall has been honored on Crain's annual "40 under 40" list of leading people under age 40 and their top Tech 25 list. He has been named as one of the Top 100 VCs in the U.S., a Media 100 and a Hollywood 100 Power Player. He has keynoted or been a panelist at over 100 conferences and events nationwide. He is the founder & trustee of the McCall Family Foundation, focused on encouraging social entrepreneurship and global human/girls' rights. He has served on numerous regional high technology advisory boards. He is the author of a popular venture blog, www.VCConfidential.com. Previous to 1995, McCall worked in the Boston Consulting Group's Chicago office, where he managed consulting and client teams on projects in the telecommunications, health-care and financial services industries. During and after college, McCall worked for Bankers Trust in Merchant Banking as well as at Merrill Lynch and U.S. Trust. McCall holds a B.A. in economics and history from Williams College and an M.B.A. with Honors from Northwestern University's Kellogg School of Management. He also holds a Master in Manufacturing Management from Northwestern University's McCormick School of Engineering.

Suzanne Muchin is a brand strategist and radio host of The Big Payoff. She lives, eats, and breathes the challenge of forging new markets for big ideas. Before launching Mind + Matter Studio with her long-time business partner Rachel Bellow, Suzanne was a founding partner and Lead Strategist of Frequency540, a strategic communications agency that acquired the company she founded, ROI Ventures (Return on Inspiration)—a strategy firm that packaged social impact for the marketplace. Suzanne began her career at Teach For America, where she served for three years as the Vice President of National Programs after having been a TFA Charter Corps Member in the South Bronx. She was the CEO of Civitas, a communication and marketing firm for the early childhood field that was founded by the former president of Harpo Entertainment. In 2012 Suzanne was inducted into the Chicago Entrepreneur Hall of Fame, and is a frequent public speaker and guest lecturer at Northwestern's Kellogg School of Management and the Booth School of Business at the University of Chicago.

Karin D. O'Connor recently served as managing director of Hyde Park Angels, a Chicago-based angel investment network. To date, she has invested in fourteen deals with the group, served as its representative on the board of portfolio company FeeFighters, which was acquired by Groupon, Inc. in 2012, and is currently a director at Moxie Jean. She is also the founder of Perimeter Advisors, an advisory firm that assists owners of promising mid-market companies with planning and execution of value enhancement strategies. Since beginning her career at Continental Bank over 20 years ago, Ms. O'Connor has invested in and advised entrepreneurs in a variety of industries that includes financial services, business services, technology distribution, health care, and manufacturing. She has invested at all levels of the capital structure—from senior debt to mezzanine, venture leasing, and equity—and in companies ranging from early stage to mature. Ms. O'Connor received her BA in Finance from the University of Illinois, where she graduated magna cum laude and was elected to Phi Beta Kappa. She earned her MBA from Northwestern University's Kellogg School of Management, where she was an F.C. Austin Scholar and was elected to Beta Gamma Sigma. She served on the Kellogg Alumni Council and enjoys guest lecturing and judging student business plan presentations for the school's Entrepreneurship Program. She has also received a CFA (Chartered Financial Analyst) charter.

Brent Payne is the founder and CEO of Loud Interactive, a boutique SEO optimization consultancy in Chicago. Brent started doing 'SEO' before it was even called 'SEO'. He's an Internet marketer with over a decade of experience and proven success. He cut his teeth in online marketing as a vendor for Amazon.com where he became Amazon's second largest electronics vendor by driving demand to Amazon from search engines. Brent is esteemed as one of the top SEOs in the world. He speaks around the world (just Google 'SEO presentations' to find them) at online conferences and has held online marketing roles at prestigious companies such as Tribune Company, where he grew Tribune's search engine traffic from 500,000 visits per day to 1,700,000 visits per day in just 3 years. He's been consulting since 2009. He did so part time at first as he drove success at Tribune. He began consulting full-time in 2011 with the advent of BaldSEO.com. He has helped several different companies in several different industries. In fact, his success necessitated the expansion of the consulting firm beyond himself, which eventually led to the creation of Loud Interactive. Brent is a powerful online sales and marketing asset to any organization especially in the areas of search engine marketing, viral marketing, and business relationship development.

Jeremy Smith, a hustler turned entrepreneur, graduated from the University of Illinois in 2008. After graduation, Smith worked at Motorola as a Financial Analyst and he eventually ended up becoming roommates with his now co-founder Mark Lawrence. During his short time in Chicago, he amassed thousands of dollars in parking tickets! That's when SpotHero was born. Jeremy realized there was a major parking problem that millions of people deal with every day and it needed to be fixed. Jeremy teamed up with his friend Mark and together they've changed the way people think about parking. When he's not out making life easier for the daily driver, Jeremy loves catching sporting events with friends, traveling the world (and his home city of Chicago), and frequenting fun dive restaurants all over the city.

Emerson Spartz was raised in La Porte, Ind. At the age of twelve, Spartz convinced his parents to allow him to drop out of school and homeschool himself. He developed his own curriculum, which his parents supplemented by requiring him to read four short biographies of successful people every day. Spartz founded the MuggleNet website in 1999. In 2007, Emerson co-authored a book—MuggleNet.com's What Will Happen in Harry Potter 7—Who Lives, Who Dies, Who Falls in Love, and How the Series Finally Ends. As of July 21, 2007, the book sold 335,000 copies and reached #2 on the New York Times Children's Bestseller List, where it spent six months. In 2009, Spartz launched Spartz Media. In January 2010, Spartz launched OMG Facts. OMG-Facts.com receives 30 million monthly page views, has 500,000 subscribers on

YouTube, and 5.5 million followers on Twitter. Spartz graduated in May of 2009 with a degree in management from the University of Notre Dame's Mendoza College of Business, while also devising his own self-teaching curriculum around initialisms, mnemonics, and flash cards in order to retain larger quantities of information. He is a voracious reader and aims to read at least one book of nonfiction per day.

Chuck Templeton is passionate about early stage and emerging companies, and is focused on using business principles to find solutions to the world's most pressing problems. He has had the pleasure of being involved with over two-dozen startups as an investor, board member, or advisor, but spends the majority of his time helping impact companies as the managing director of Impact Engine. He took his first big step as an entrepreneur in San Francisco when he founded OpenTable, which went public on the NASDAQ in May of 2009 (OPEN). He helped build an industry leading company that changed the way full-service restaurants manage their top-line growth and diners make their dinner reservations. While CEO, he recruited and hired the first management team, obtained and allocated company resources, led the business and product strategy, and carefully crafted a highly dedicated culture. OpenTable is the global leader in restaurant reservations with customers in all 50 states and more than a dozen countries. He used that experience to support the GrubHub team as an advisor and director. They grew to be a national leader in providing hungry diners with food delivery and take-out options, while also helping independent restaurants use technology to operate more profitably. Chuck serves as Chairman of the Board for GrubHub and is on the Board of Directors for Getable.com, TaskRabbit, and PVPower. He spent three years serving in the U.S. Army, becoming Ranger and Sniper qualified. Most importantly, he has an amazing wife and two awesome daughters.

Craig Wortmann is the founder and CEO of Sales Engine Inc. Craig and his team help firms build and tune their sales engine. Craig's firm works with teams all over the world to develop their knowledge, skill and discipline and to translate those key assets into higher performance. He spent his first year in sales being trained by IBM Corporation in the classical selling style and was the #2 performer in his yearlong sales school class. Post-IBM, Craig covered three-quarters of the country selling to large retailers. After earning his MBA from Kellogg, Craig joined a midsize consulting firm called the Forum Corporation and quickly became the firm's new product launch and client recovery specialist. In 2000, Craig was recruited to join a Startup company called WisdomTools as its CEO. Craig ran and grew WisdomTools and then successfully sold the company to a larger firm in 2008.

As a Clinical Professor of Entrepreneurship at the University of Chicago's Booth School of Business, Craig designed, developed and teaches the award-winning course called Entrepreneurial Selling, recently recognized by Inc. Magazine as one of the "Top Ten" courses in the country. He also teaches Building the New Venture and a course on leadership called Building Leadership Capital for the executive education program. He is the recipient of the 2012 Faculty Excellence Award for teaching. In his capacity with Booth, Craig travels the globe teaching and motivating leaders, business executives and alumni about how to create a more powerful impact. Craig has been a sales person and entrepreneur for more than 20 years.

Sam Yagan is the Chief Executive Officer of The Match Group, an operating segment of IAC/InterActive Corp (Nasdaq: IACI) and co-founder of OkCupid. In this role, Sam oversees the management of IAC's global online dating portfolio that comprises over forty brands around the world, including leading properties like Match, OkCupid, Tinder, OurTime, Meetic, Twoo, FriendScout, and ParPerfeito. These businesses generate revenues of over $800 million and profits of over $250 million. The Match Group also contains smaller businesses such as Tutor.com, Daily Burn, and The Princeton Review. Sam has been a leader in the dating industry since he co-founded OkCupid in 2003 and grew it into one of the most popular dating sites in America, amassing over four million active users. OkCupid has earned widespread media acclaim and has been described as "the Google of online dating" and where "dating meets Facebook." In 2011, Match, Inc. acquired OkCupid for $90 million. Sam's prior entrepreneurial ventures in the consumer internet sector include SparkNotes (founded in 1999), still the dominant brand of study guides and eDonkey (founded in 2002), once the largest P2P file-sharing network in the world. He sold SparkNotes to Barnes & Noble, Inc., where he served as Vice-President and Publisher and oversaw the expansion of the previously all-digital brand into an expansive multi-platform media business. Outside of work, Sam's primary passion is working with early-stage entrepreneurs. In 2009, he co-founded Excelerate Labs (now TechStars Chicago), a leading start-up accelerator, and served as its first CEO. In 2014, Sam founded Corazon Capital, a small angel fund; he sits on the board of several start-ups, including ShiftGig, SpotHero, Brilliant Scholars, Telnyx, StatHat, and OVM. He also advises several venture capital funds, including Hyde Park Venture Partners, Great Oaks Venture Capital, and the FireStarter Fund, which he co-founded. Sam has been named to *TIME Magazine*'s "100 Most Influential People in the World," *Fortune Magazine*'s "40 Under 40," *Crain's Chicago* "40 Under 40", *Billboard Magazine*'s "30 Under 30" in the entertainment industry, *Crain*'s "Tech 25," and *Silicon Alley Insider*'s SAI 100 and has received the Chicago Innovation Awards' "Visionary of the Year Award," IMSA's "Distinguished Leadership Award," and the DCIA's "Pioneer's Award." He has testified before the Senate Judiciary Committee and has spoken at the CATO Institute, Digital Hollywood, IRCE, the Federal Trade Commission, and numerous other industry events. Sam has a BA with honors in Applied Mathematics and Economics from Harvard College and an MBA from the Stanford Graduate School of Business, where he earned distinction as a Siebel Scholar, an Arjay Miller Scholar, and the Henry Ford Scholar, the award granted to each class's valedictorian.

ABOUT THE AUTHOR

Andrew Razeghi is an educator/author/speaker/consultant (and angel investor).

Professor Razeghi is on the faculty at the Kellogg School of Management at Northwestern University where he teaches coursework on innovation. He is also founder & managing director of StrategyLab, Inc., a growth strategy & innovation consulting group. His work spans industries from consumer-packaged goods to media; technology to financial services; and entertainment to professional sports. A few of consulting clients include Allstate, BNP Paribas, The New York Times, Novartis, Procter & Gamble, PepsiCo, Qualcomm, TricorBraun, and others.

In addition to advising the executive teams of Fortune 500 and private equity backed companies, Razeghi is a Limited Partner in Techstars. He is a direct investor in several startups including BespokePost, DoStuff Media, Giveforward, Koa Natural Olakino, NowSpots/Perfect Audience (acquired by Marin Software, NYSE:MRIN), Paradise4Paws, SpotHero, and Tap.Me (acquired by MediaMath, Inc.).

Andrew has served as Vice Chairman of the Wright Centers of Innovation at the National Academy of Sciences in Washington, DC and has provided testimony to the Congress of the United States on driving economic recovery through high-potential entrepreneurship and innovation. He has appeared in a number of media outlets including *BBC, BusinessWeek, China Daily, CNN, Fortune, Forbes, Investors Business Daily,* and *The New York Times* and has been listed by Inc. Magazine among the 100 best leadership speakers.

He is a contributor on innovation for a series of shows on The Travel Channel and is the author of several books including *The Future of Innovation, The Upside of Down: Innovation through Recessions,* and *The Riddle: Where Ideas Come From and How to Have Better Ones. The Riddle* was chosen by Fast Company as one of its "Smart Books." For speaking engagements, contact info@strategylab.com. You can reach Andrew by email at andrew@strategylab.com or follow him on twitter @andrewrazeghi.